「なぜ？」に答える！

Wonders of Japan
and the Japanese
in Simple English

英語対訳
でわかる
ニッポンと日本人の
不思議

牧野髙吉・著
William Chesser・英文監訳

辰巳出版

Preface

When we talk with foreigners visiting Japan, we are sometimes puzzled by their questions about Japan and the Japanese such as "Why do many Japanese always wear a surgical mask on their face?" or "Why do the Japanese eat eggs raw?"

These days, various world sports competitions and international conferences as well as the Tokyo Olympic/Paralympic Games are held in Japan, so a great number of foreigners are expected to visit Japan. On these occasions, Japan needs to offer information about Japan and the Japanese to the world. I hope this book will be of some help to put it into practice.

Also, some of the information about Japan and the Japanese introduced in this book are not hard facts, but only the views which are widely spread and are thought to be especially powerful. Therefore, I hope this book inspires you to find other points of view which this book cannot introduce.

The explanations and interpretations are written in simple English and presented with the side-by-side Japanese translation on the facing page. Moreover, some difficult words and phrases are underlined and have the Japanese translation attached, so that you can read this book without English-Japanese dictionaries.

Finally, I would like to give much thanks to Mr. Yuasa Katsuya of TATSUMI PUBLISHING CO., LTD., who planned out this project, Mr. Ogino Mamoru, Representative of Office ON, who gave me lots of editorial advice and Mr. William Chesser who read all of the English sentences in this book and made them flow as simply and naturally as possible.

January, 2020
Kushiro, Hokkaido

MAKINO Taka-Yoshi

はじめに

　訪日している外国人と話していると、「なぜ、いつも『マスク』をしている人がいるのか？」とか「なぜ、日本人は卵をナマで食べるのか？」など、日本や日本人について思いがけない質問に戸惑（まど）うことがあります。

　このところ、東京オリンピック・パラリンピックをはじめ、さまざまなスポーツの世界大会や国際会議があり、数多くの外国人の訪日が予想されます。日本は、世界に向けて、日本と日本人に関する情報を発信する必要があります。筆者は、本書がその一助になることを望んでいます。

　また、本書で紹介した日本と日本人に関する情報は、唯一無二のものではなく、諸説あるなか、一般的に広く伝わっている説や特に有力とされる説を紹介しました。したがって、ここに紹介できなかったほかの説もあることをご理解ください。

　本書の解説や説明は、英語と日本語で対訳になっています。英文はなるべく簡単な英語にしましたが、辞書なしでも読めるように、難しいと思われる単語やフレーズには下線を引き、日本語の意味を併記しました。

　最後に、本書の出版を企画してくださった辰巳出版の湯浅勝也氏、編集上、いろいろなアドヴァイスをしてくださったオフィスON代表の荻野守氏、さらにすべての英文を平易で、かつ自然な流れにしてくださったWilliam Chesser氏に、深く感謝を申し上げます。

2020年1月
釧路の寓居にて

牧野　髙吉

3

Wonders of Japan and Japanese in simple English 《CONTENTS》

● preface／はじめに 2

[第1章]	Wonders of Japan and the Japanese　Current Topics
	英語対訳でわかる　ニッポンと日本人の不思議　「今どき」のなぜ？

01. Why do some Japanese always wear a "surgical mask" on their face? 14
なぜ、いつも「マスク」をしている人がいるのか？

02. Why do the Japanese make a pose with the "peace sign" for a picture? 16
なぜ、写真を撮るとき、「ピース・サイン」のポーズをとるのか？

03. Why do the Japanese hold our "dishes" when having a meal? 18
なぜ、「食器」を手にもって食事をするのか？

04. Why do the Japanese slurp "noodles"? 20
なぜ、「麺類」をすすって食べるのか？

05. Why are many Japanese people glued to a cell phone on the train? 22
なぜ、多くの人が電車の中で携帯電話に夢中になっているのか？

06. Why do some Japanese women put on "makeup" on the train? 24
なぜ、電車の中で「メイク」(化粧)をする女性がいるのか？

07. Why do we take a public bath or soak in a hot spring "in the nude" in Japan? 26
なぜ、銭湯や温泉でタオルを持たず「すっ裸」になって入るのか？

08. Why do Japanese parents sleep "together with" their small children? 28
なぜ、親は幼い子どもと「一緒」に寝るのか？

09. Why do the Japanese put our "seal," not our own signature, on documents? 30
なぜ、書類等に自筆のサインではなく、「ハンコ」を押すのか？

《COLUMN 01》
Why do the Japanese have different concepts called "hon-ne" and "tatemae" depending on the situation? 32
なぜ、「本音」と「建て前」を使い分けるのか

[第2章]	Wonders of Japan and the Japanese　Customs
	英語対訳でわかる　ニッポンと日本人の不思議　「慣習」のなぜ？

10. Why do the Japanese say "Kampai!" when drinking alcoholic drinks? 34
なぜ、お酒を飲むとき、「乾杯！」というのか？

11. Why do the Japanese say "moshi, moshi" when making a phone call?　 ………36
なぜ、電話をかけるとき、「もしもし」というのか？

12. Why do the Japanese say "Sumimasen" to mean both "appreciation" and
"apology"?　 ………38
なぜ、お礼も謝罪も「すみません」というのか？

13. Why do the Japanese say "Tsumaranai-mono-desuga …" when giving
someone a present?　 ………40
なぜ、贈り物をするとき、「つまらないものですが……」というのか？

14. Why do the Japanese "bow" rather than shake hands when they greet?　 ………42
なぜ、挨拶するとき、握手よりも「おじぎ」をするのか？

15. Why do the Japanese say "arigatou" when expressing their thanks?　 ………44
なぜ、感謝の気持ちを述べるとき、「ありがとう」というのか？

16. Why do we stand in a "line" and wait with patience in Japan?　 ………46
なぜ、「行列」を作って、辛抱強く並ぶのか？

《COLUMN 02》
Why do the Japanese say "Itadakimasu" and "Gochisosama" when
having meals?　 ………48
なぜ、食事をするとき、「いただきます」「ごちそうさま」というのか？

[第3章]　Wonders of Japan and the Japanese　Conventions
英語対訳でわかる　ニッポンと日本人の不思議　「しきたり」のなぜ?

17. Why do the Japanese "bow two times, clap hands two times and bow
one more time" at a Shinto shrine?　 ………50
なぜ、神社では「二礼二拍一礼」をするのか？

18. Why do the Japanese put a "noshi" on a present?　 ………52
なぜ、贈答品に「熨斗」をつけるのか？

19. Why do the Japanese exchange "san-san-ku-do" cups at a wedding ceremony?　 ………54
なぜ、神式の結婚式では「三三九度」の盃を交わすのか？

20. Why do the Japanese strike wooden clappers for "Fire patrol"?　 ………56
なぜ、「火の用心」で拍子木を鳴らすのか？

21. Why do the Japanese close a banquet with "ippon-jime"?　 ………58
なぜ、宴会の最後に「一本締め」をするのか？

22. Why do the Japanese bind a "hachimaki" (headband) around their head
at festivals? 60
なぜ、お祭りのとき、「鉢巻き」をするのか？

《COLUMN 03》
Why do the Japanese celebrate "kanreki" wearing red chanchan-ko
when they become sixty years old? 62
なぜ、60歳になると、赤いちゃんちゃんこを着て「還暦」の祝いをするのか？

[第4章]　Wonders of Japan and the Japanese　Life in Society
英語対訳でわかる　ニッポンと日本人の不思議　「社会」のなぜ？

23. Why do we drive on the left side of the street in Japan? 64
なぜ、日本ではクルマは「左側通行」なのか？

24. Why are there so many "sotobiraki" (out-swinging doors) which we have to
pull in Japan? 66
なぜ、日本の家のドアは手前に引く「外開き」が多いのか？

25. Why is the Japanese currency "yen"? 68
なぜ、日本の通貨単位は「円」なのか？

26. Why do only Japanese 5 yen and 50 yen coins have a hole? 70
なぜ、日本の硬貨は5円と50円だけ穴があいているのか？

27. Why are there so many "ichou" (gingko) as roadside trees in Japan? 72
なぜ、日本の街路樹には「イチョウ」が多いのか？

28. Why are there so many "cedar" trees on the grounds of a shrine and "pine"
trees on the grounds of a castle in Japan? 74
なぜ、神社には「杉」の木、城には「松」の木が多いのか？

29. Why does "machiya" in Kyoto have a narrow frontage and a wide depth? 76
なぜ、京都の「町家」は間口（入り口）が狭く、奥行きが広いのか？

30. Why is "shachi-hoko" set on the top of a castle in Japan? 78
なぜ、お城のてっぺんには「しゃちほこ」が付いているのか？

31. Why do we call the small characters attached to kanji "rubi" in Japanese
printing terms? 80
なぜ、漢字に付ける小さな文字のことを印刷用語で「ルビ」というのか？

32. Why are there two paper sizes, size A and size B, only in Japan? 82
なぜ、日本だけA判・B判の2種類の用紙があるのか？

《COLUMN 04》
Why do the Japanese call the Kyoto and Osaka areas "Kinki"? 84
なぜ、京都や大阪などのことを「近畿」と呼ぶのか？

[第5章] Wonders of Japan and the Japanese　Traditions
英語対訳でわかる　ニッポンと日本人の不思議　「伝統」のなぜ？

33. Why is "Gengo" (the Japanese Imperial era name) used besides
the Christian era in Japan? 86
なぜ、西暦年号以外に「元号」があるのか？

34. Why do the Japanese respect the "Emperor" as the national symbol? 88
なぜ、「天皇」を国の象徴として敬愛するのか？

35. Why is the Japanese national flag "hinomaru"? 90
なぜ、日本の国旗は「日の丸」なのか？

36. Why do we celebrate children who are seven, five, and three years old
("shichi-go-san")in Japan? 92
なぜ、「七五三」でお祝いをするのか？

37. Why do we call an attractive guy an "otoko-mae"(handsome man) or
a "nimaime"(good-looking man)in Japanese? 94
なぜ、イケメンを「男前」とか「二枚目」というのか？

38. Why is a special skill called the "number eighteen"(jyu-hachi-ban)
instead of the number one in Japan? 96
なぜ、得意わざを一番ではなく、「十八番」というのか？

39. Why do we turn "chawan"(teacup)two times to drink tea in a tea party
in Japan? 98
なぜ、茶会で二回「茶碗」をまわしてから飲むのか？

40. Why do males play "female roles" too in Kabuki in Japan? 100
なぜ、歌舞伎では「女役」も男が演じるのか？

41. Why do many Shinto shrines have a red "tori-i gate" in Japan? 102
なぜ、神社には赤い「鳥居」が立っていることが多いのか？

42. Why do sumo wrestlers put on mawashi and tie a topknot in the "o-ozumo" (grand sumo wrestling) in Japan? 104
なぜ、「大相撲」では力士がまわしをつけて、髷を結うのか？

43. Why do the Japanese feel a sense of beauty in "wabi" and "sabi"? 106
なぜ、日本人は「わび」や「さび」に美意識を感じるのか？

44. Why does a "bride" wear white clothes (shiro-muku) in Japan? 108
なぜ、「花嫁」は白い衣装（白無垢）を着るのか？

45. Why is a "kaimyo" (a Buddhist name) given to the people after the death in Japan? 110
なぜ、亡くなると、「戒名」をつけてもらうのか？

46. Why are there so many sects in one Buddhism in Japan? 112
なぜ、1つの仏教にいろいろな宗派があるのか？

《Column 05》
Why in some places are a Shinto shrine and a temple erected on the same grounds in Japan? 114
なぜ、神社と寺が同じ境内にあるところがあるのか？

［第6章］　Wonders of Japan and the Japanese　Legends
英語対訳でわかる　ニッポンと日本人の不思議　「言い伝え」のなぜ？

47. Why is it considered a bad omen to "sleep with the head toward the north" in Japan? 116
なぜ、「北枕」は縁起が悪いとされるのか？

48. Why is it said that we had better not cut our "nails" at night in Japan? 118
なぜ、夜に「爪」を切ってはいけないといわれるのか？

49. Why is it said that it is a good omen when a "tea stem" floats upright in a teacup in Japan? 120
なぜ、「茶柱」が立つと縁起がよいといわれるのか？

50. Why is it said to be a good omen if a "swallow" makes a nest in a house in Japan? 122
なぜ、「ツバメ」が家に巣をつくると、縁起がよいといわれるのか？

51. Why is it not good to step on the "edge of a tatami mat" and a "threshold" in Japan? 124
なぜ、「畳のへり」や「敷居」を踏むのはよくないのか？

52. Why are the age 42 for men and 33 for women considered to be of "yaku-doshi" (unlucky ages) in Japan? 126
なぜ、男42歳、女33歳が「厄年」(大厄)とされるのか?

53. Why do the Japanese "ghosts" have no legs? 128
なぜ、日本の「幽霊」には足がないのか?

《Column 06》
Why is "eggplant" included in the objects considered good luck in Japan in the first dream of a year? 130
なぜ、初夢に見ると縁起がよいとされるもののなかに「なすび」が入っているのか?

[第7章] Wonders of Japan and the Japanese　Ways of Life
英語対訳でわかる　ニッポンと日本人の不思議　「暮らし」のなぜ?

54. Why do the Japanese place "piles of salt" on both sides of an entrance? 132
なぜ、玄関わきに「盛り塩」をするのか?

55. Why do the Japanese "pat" a child's head when praising the child? 134
なぜ、子どもをほめるとき、子どもの頭を「なでる」のか?

56. Why are there short-sleeved kimono and long-sleeved kimono for women in Japan? 136
なぜ、女性の着物には袖丈が短いものと長いものがあるのか?

57. Why are we apt to take off the "footwear" when entering a house in Japan? 138
なぜ、家に入るとき、「履き物」を脱ぐことが多いのか?

58. Why are there the Western-style age system and the "traditional Japanese age system" in Japan? 140
なぜ、満年齢と「数え年」があるのか?

59. Why are "taian," "butsu-metsu," "tomo-biki," and so on, printed in Japanese calendars? 142
なぜ、日本のカレンダーには「大安」「仏滅「友引」…などが記されているのか?

60. Why do the Japanese do "yubi-kiri" (linking one's pinky fingers) when making a promise? 144
なぜ、約束事をするとき、「指きり」をするのか?

61. Why do we say in Japanese "furu" (dump someone else's feelings) and "furareru" (be dumped by someone else) in love? 146
なぜ、恋愛で「振る」「振られる」というのか？

62. Why do many Japanese handle a "mikoshi" (portable shrine) so wildly in which a kami (Shinto God) rides during festivals? 148
なぜ、神さまの乗り物である「神輿」を乱暴に扱う祭りが多いのか？

63. Why is one of the eyes of "daruma doll" painted black with Chinese ink when a candidate wins an election etc. in Japan? 150
なぜ、選挙に当選したときなどに、「だるま」の片目に墨を入れるのか？

《Column 07》
Why do the Japanese call our wives "okusan" or "kamisan"? 152
なぜ、妻のことを「奥さん」とか「かみさん」と呼ぶのか？

[第8章] Wonders of Japan and the Japanese   Seasonal Events
英語対訳でわかる　ニッポンと日本人の不思議　「歳時記」のなぜ？

64. Why do the Japanese send "New Year's cards" at the beginning of a new year? 154
なぜ、新年の始めに「年賀状」を出すのか？

65. Why do the Japanese give "New Year's pocket money" to children in the New Year? 156
なぜ、新年（お正月）に子どもに「お年玉」をあげるのか？

66. Why do the Japanese scatter beans in "setsu-bun"? 158
なぜ、「節分」に豆をまくのか？

67. Why do Japanese enjoy "cherry blossom viewing" in spring? 160
なぜ、春になると、「桜」をめでて花見をするのか？

68. Why is there a five-colored "streamer" among carp streamers in Japan? 162
なぜ、鯉のぼりに5色の「吹き流し」があるのか？

69. Why do the Japanese shout "Kagiya!" or "Tamaya!" when watching fireworks? 164
なぜ、花火を見るとき、「かぎや〜」「たまや〜」というのか？

70. Why do the Japanese hold a memorial service for our ancestors during "o-bon"? 166
なぜ、「お盆」に先祖供養をするのか？

71. Why do we strike a bell 108 times at a temple on New Year's Eve (December 31st) in Japan? 168
なぜ、大晦日（12月31日）にお寺で鐘を108回打つのか？

《Column 08》
　Why do the Japanese write their wishes on strips of paper on "Tanabata"
　(the Star Festival)?　　　　　　　　　　　　　　　　　　　　　………170
　なぜ、「七夕」に願いごとを短冊に書くのか？

[第9章]　Wonders of Japan and the Japanese　Words
　　　　　英語対訳でわかる　ニッポンと日本人の不思議　「言葉」のなぜ？

72. Why is Japan named "Nihon" or "Nippon"?　　　　　　　　　………172
　　なぜ、日本は「日本」というのか？

73. Why do we call the area around Tokyo "Kanto" and the area near Osaka
　　"Kansai" in Japan?　　　　　　　　　　　　　　　　　　………174
　　なぜ、東京中心に「関東」と呼び、大阪近辺を「関西」というのか？

74. Why do we call five prefectures altogether including Tottori Prefecture,
　　"Chugoku-Chihou" in Japan?　　　　　　　　　　　　　　………176
　　なぜ、鳥取県をはじめとする5県をまとめて「中国地方」というのか？

75. Why is it called "Kyushu" (nine countries), even though there are only
　　seven prefectures in Kyushu?　　　　　　　　　　　　　　………178
　　なぜ、7県しかないのに「九州」と呼ぶのか？

76. Why do we call the sushi which are served in Tokyo "Edomae-zushi" in Japan?　………180
　　なぜ、東京で食べる寿司を「江戸前寿司」と呼ぶのか？

77. Why do we call a store which mainly sells vegetables "yaoya" in Japan?　………182
　　なぜ、野菜を主に売る店のことを「八百屋」と呼ぶのか？

78. Why do we refer to bad fortune and bad economic conditions as "hidari-mae"
　　in Japan?　　　　　　　　　　　　　　　　　　　　　　………184
　　なぜ、運が悪いことや経済状態がよくないことを「左前」というのか？

79. Why do we say "miginideru-monoga-inai," when we praise the best person
　　in Japan?　　　　　　　　　　　　　　　　　　　　　　………186
　　なぜ、一番すぐれている人をたたえるとき、「右に出る者がいない」というのか？

80. Why do we refer to flattering the other person as "goma-wo-suru" in Japan?　………188
　　なぜ、相手にへつらうことを「ゴマをする」というのか？

81. Why do we call having a good connection with another person "umaga-au"
　　in Japan?　　　　　　　　　　　　　　　　　　　　　　………190
　　なぜ、気が合うことを「馬が合う」というのか？

82. Why do we refer to the two people getting along well with each other as "aun-no-kokyu" in Japan? ·········192
なぜ、2人の息がぴったり合っていることを「あうんの呼吸」というのか?

《COLUMN 09》
Why is the Chinese character "do" used in the name of Hokkaido in Japan? ······194
なぜ、北海道には「道」という漢字が入っているのか?

[第10章] Wonders of Japan and the Japanese   Food Culture
英語対訳でわかる　ニッポンと日本人の不思議　「**食文化**」のなぜ?

83. Why do we refer to boiled and cooked food as "sukiyaki" in Japan? ·········196
なぜ、煮て調理するのに「すき焼き」というのか?

84. Why do we refer to sliced raw fish and shellfish as "o-sashimi" or "o-tsukuri" in Japan? ·········198
なぜ、生の魚介類の切り身を「お刺身」や「お造り」というのか?

85. Why do we eat "soba" on the New Year's eve, and "osechi-ryori" on New Year's days in Japan? ·········200
なぜ、大晦日に「そば」、お正月に「おせち料理」を食べるのか?

86. Why do we eat "sekihan" or "mochi" on happy occasions in Japan? ·········202
なぜ、おめでたいときに「赤飯」や「餅」を食べるのか?

87. Why do we call the dish which seems to have no relationship to stones "kaiseki-ryori" in Japan? ·········204
なぜ、石と関係がなさそうな料理を「懐石料理」というのか?

88. Why do the Japanese eat eggs raw? ·········206
なぜ、日本人は卵をナマで食べるのか?

◎ 装幀／杉本欣右　　　　　◎ 日本語解説協力／オフィスON
◎ イラスト／笹森 識　　　　◎ 編集協力／荻野 守（オフィスON）
◎ DTP作成／サッシイ・ファム　　◎ 企画編集担当／湯浅勝也

第1章

英語対訳でわかる
ニッポンと日本人の不思議

「今どき」のなぜ?

Wonders of Japan and the Japanese

Current Topics

01. Why do some Japanese always wear a "surgical mask" on their face?

① Many foreigners visiting Japan say that one of the wonders
多くの　　外国人(たち)　　〜を訪れている　日本　いう　　　　　　　不思議なこと
they have is that some Japanese lead a life wearing a "surgical
　　　　　　　　　　　　　　　日本人　　生活する　　身につけて(いる)　外科[手術]用の
mask" on their face. ② This is because they always wear a mask
マスク　　　　顔　　　　　　　…だからである　　いつも
when they walk on the street, when they are on the train and even
　　　　　歩く　　　通り　　　　　　　　　　　　電車　　…でさえ
when they talk with others. ③ Indeed, when they have meals, they
　　　　〜と話をする　他の人(々)　さすがに　　　　　　食事
take off their mask or move it a bit, but except when having meals,
はずす　　　　　　　　ずらす　少し　　〜を除いて
they always wear a mask. ④ It seems that they are used for various
　　　　　　　　　　　　　…のようである　　　　　　　　　　いろいろな
reasons such as preventing colds and pollen allergy, and protection
理由　　　〜のような　予防すること　風邪　　花粉　アレルギー　　　防止
against the cold in winter. ⑤ Sure enough, recently, many kinds of
〜に対する　寒さ　冬　　　確かに　　　　最近　　　　種類
pollen float in the air all year round. ⑥ So, a number of the Japanese
　　　ただよう空気中に　　一年中　　　　そのため　数多くの〜
develop pollen allergies, and many of them say that this is why a
発症する　　　　　　　　　　　　　　　　　　　　　　　　　〜の理由
mask is indispensable to them. ⑦ However, it seems that's not all.
　　　不可欠で(ある)　　　　　　しかし
⑧ Some Japanese women try to wear a mask, because they don't
いくらかの〜　　　女性たち
have time to wear make-up, so they hide their face with a mask,
　　　　　化粧をする　　　　　　隠す
and some others show only their eyes and want to be perceived as
　　　　　　　見せる　　　　　目　　　　　　　　気づかれる
beautiful by others. ⑨ Moreover, through covering up their face
美しい　　　　　さらに　　〜によって　おおうこと
with a mask, some hope to relieve their anxiety by avoiding being
　　　　　　　(〜することを)望む　和らげる　　不安(感)　避けること
seen by others. ⑩ In some countries, for some religious reasons,
　　　　　　　　　　　国々　　　　　　　　宗教(上)の

14

women cover their face and/or body with a piece of cloth and they
　　　　　　　　顔と体の両方またはどちらか　　　一片の　　　　布
don't expose their skin to the public. ⑪ But, generally, foreigners
　　　さらす　　　　肌　　　　公衆　　　　　　　一般的に
don't wear a mask on their face unless they get seriously ill.
　　　　　　　　　　　　　　　　　…でない限り　　　深刻に　病気
⑫ Foreigners visiting Japan seem to wonder what kind of awful
　　　　　　　　　　　　　　　　　不思議に思う　　　　　　恐ろしい
diseases on earth are spreading throughout Japan when they see
病気　　いったい(全体)　広まっている　〜のいたるところに
some Japanese walking on the street wearing a mask.

※①日本人が通常つけている「マスク」は、英語では "surgical mask"（外科［手術］用のマスク）と
　表現します。単に "mask" だと、レスラーの覆面等のイメージがあるようです。ただし、ここでは、
　タイトルと初出以外は "mask" で統一してあります。

和訳

01. なぜ、いつも「マスク」をしている人がいるのか？

①多くの外国人が日本に来て不思議に感じることの一つは、一部の日本人が「マスク」をして生活していることだといいます。②道を歩いていても、電車に乗っていても、また人と話をするときも、常にマスクをしているからです。③さすがに、食事をするときはマスクをとったり、ずらしたりしますが、それ以外にはいつもマスクをつけています。④風邪の予防、花粉症の予防、防寒用など、いろいろ理由で使われるようです。⑤確かに、最近、いろいろな花粉が一年を通して飛んでいます。⑥そのため、花粉症を発症する人が多く、彼らの多くはマスクが欠かせないといいます。⑦しかし、それだけではないようです。⑧女性のなかには、時間がなくて化粧をしていないのを隠すためとか、目だけを見せて、他人から美しく見られたいという人もいるようです。
⑨また、顔をマスクでおおうことで、他人の視線から逃れて、不安感を和らげたいという人もいます。⑩宗教上の理由から、女性が顔や体を布などで隠して肌を露出させないという国はあります。⑪しかし、一般的に、外国人は病気などでよほどの重症でもない限り、マスクはつけません。⑫日本を訪れている外国人は、街を歩いていて、マスクをつけている日本人を見て、いったい、日本ではどんなひどい病気が流行しているのかと、驚くようです。

Why do the Japanese make a pose with the "peace sign" for a picture?

① When the Japanese have pictures taken, many of us make a pose with a V-shaped hand sign, thrusting out one or both hands, raising our index and middle fingers only, and bending our thumb and other two fingers. ② In Japan, generally, this is called the "peace sign." ③ It is also called the "V-sign," because this sign makes the shape of a "V" in the English alphabet. ④ This comes from the shape of the initial letter V of the English word "Victory." ⑤ This is used as a pose which expresses victory, peace and antiwar in Europe and the United States of America. ⑥ These meanings extend from there, and this pose is used to express joy and happiness in Japan. ⑦ According to a popular tradition, they say that it is the first time when, in the hundred-year war which started in 1337, bow soldiers of the English Army used this pose to provoke the enemy, the French Army. ⑧ They say that, because bow soldiers of the English Army used longbows and were successful in the war against the French, the French Army cut off the fingers of English Army prisoners of war so they could not draw bows anymore. ⑨ It is said that the English Army soldiers

16

dared to show off their fingers to the French Army soldiers with
　　あえて〜した　見せつける
this pose as a way to provoke the French Army soldiers as if
　　　　　　　　　　　　　　　　　　　　　　　　　　　　　　　　　〜かのように
saying, "We dare you to cut off our fingers!" so it came to be used
as a way of showing off their triumph proudly. ⑩ However, it
　　　　　　　　　　　　　　　　　　　　　 勝利　　 誇らしげに　　　 しかし
seems that, in some countries, showing the inside of the palm with
　　　　　　　　　　　　　　　　　　　　　　　　　　　内側　　　　　　手のひら
this pose indicates contempt.
　　　　　　　　 示す　　 侮蔑

和訳

02. なぜ、写真を撮るとき、「ピース・サイン」のポーズをとるのか？

①日本人は写真を撮られるとき、多くの人が片手または両手を前につき出し、人さし指と中指だけを立て、残りの3本の指を曲げるVの字のポーズをします。②日本では一般的に「ピース・サイン」と呼ばれています。③また、Vの形をつくることから「Vサイン」とも呼ばれています。④これは、勝利を意味する英語「Victory」の頭文字Vの形からきています。⑤欧米では勝利、平和、反戦を表わすポーズとして用いられています。⑥そこから意味が広がり、日本では歓喜や幸福感を示すときに使われています。⑦俗説によると、1337年に始まった百年戦争において、イギリス軍の弓兵が、敵のフランス軍を挑発するポーズとして使ったのが始まりとされています。⑧イギリス軍の弓兵は長弓を用いて、フランス軍に対して大きな戦果を上げたため、フランス軍はイギリス軍の兵士を捕虜にすると、二度と弓が引けないよう、指を切り落としたといいます。⑨イギリス軍の兵士がフランス軍の兵士にあえて彼らの指を見せつけて、「切り落とせるものなら切り落としてみろ」と挑発して、このポーズをとったことから、勝利を誇示する意味として使われるようになったといわれています。⑩しかし、一部の国では、手のひらを内側に向けてこのポーズをとると、侮蔑を意味するようです。

03. Why do the Japanese hold our "dishes" when having a meal?

① We can say（…という） that the eating（食べる） style（スタイル） of holding（持つこと） chopsticks（箸） in one（片方の） hand（手） and a dish（食器） like（～のような） a rice bowl（茶碗） in the other（もう一方の） hand is part（一部） of the food culture（食文化） that is unique（～に独特な） to Japan. ② In many European（ヨーロッパの） and American（アメリカの） countries（国々）, generally（一般的に）, people（人々） have meals using a knife（ナイフ）, a fork（フォーク） or a spoon（スプーン） in hand, but leave（置いておく） the dishes on the table（テーブル）. ③ Even（～さえ） in countries where people eat food with their hands, they usually don't hold dishes. ④ The people in South Korea（韓国） don't hold dishes, though（…でも） they use chopsticks like（～のように） the we do. ⑤ Why do we hold dishes while（…のときに） we have a meal? ⑥ It is said that（…といわれている） the Japanese used to（～するのが常だった） sit on our heels（正座する） in the Japanese style and eat foods on a small（小さな） and low（低い） tray（お膳） with legs（脚） for one person（一人用の） called a "hakozen" (individual（個々人の） dining table（食卓）). ⑦ Because（…なので） the distance（距離） between the food and our mouth（口） is far（遠い）, we used to dine holding our bowls of rice and miso soup in order not to（～しないために） drop（落とす） food. ⑧ It is also believed（…と信じられている） by some that rice and other foods are important（重要な） gifts（贈り物） from god（神） (kami-sama（神様）) which should not be（～するべきではない） neglected（おろそかにされる）, so holding the dishes expresses（表現する） gratitude（感謝の気持ち） when eating. ⑨ However（しかし）, we don't eat every kind of food with dishes in hand. ⑩ We eat fish and other foods

which are on <u>large</u> <u>plates</u> with chopsticks, leaving the plates on
the table. ⑪ <u>Today</u>, in many <u>occasions</u>, we have meals at the table
where we eat rice <u>served</u> on a plate, so we don't <u>always</u> hold a
dish in hand.

和訳

03. なぜ、「食器」を手にもって食事をするのか？

①片手に箸を持ち、もう一方の手で茶碗などの食器を持って食事をするスタイルは日本独特の食文化といえます。②欧米の多くの国では一般的にナイフ・フォーク・スプーンを使って、食器はテーブルに置いたまま食事をします。③片手でじかに食べ物をつかんで食べる国でも、基本的に食器は手に持ちません。④日本と同じ箸を使う韓国でも食器は手に持ちません。⑤なぜ、日本では食器を手に持って食事をするのでしょうか。⑥もともと、日本人は「箱膳」と呼ばれる一人用の小さくて低いお膳に載せられた食べ物を日本式に正座して食べていました。⑦食べ物と口との距離が遠いので、こぼさないように主にごはんやみそ汁などを入れた茶碗を手に持って食べていたのです。⑧米などは神様からいただいた大切な食べ物であり、おろそかにできないという考え方から、食器を手に持って、ありがたくいただくという感謝の気持ちの表われだともいわれます。⑨しかし、なんでもかんでも食器を手で持って食べるのではありません。⑩大きな皿に載せられた魚などのその他の食べ物は、置いたまま、箸を使って食べます。⑪今日では、日本人もテーブルで食事をすることが多く、また、ごはんを皿に盛って食べることがあるため、食器を手に持たない場合があります。

04. Why do the Japanese slurp "noodles"?

① When we eat "soba" (buckwheat) noodles, a typical Japanese noodle, we generally slurp and make a noise. ② Slurping not only soba noodles but also other noodles is part of Japanese food culture. ③ However, from a foreigners' perspective, it is considered bad manners to slurp noodles, and it seems that many foreigners feel uncomfortable when someone slurps something. ④ For a while, this was called "noodle harassment," and slurping noodles around other people makes them feel uncomfortable, so it has been a much talked-about negative topic. ⑤ It is considered good manners not to slurp noodles, especially pasta. ⑥ When eating pasta, it is good manners to wind a mouthful of pasta on a fork, move them to the mouth supporting them with a spoon, and eat them without making any noise. ⑦ Then, why do we generally slurp noodles? ⑧ The main reason is that we can taste the stock and noodles at the same time by slurping. ⑨ For that reason, we think, when we eat noodles there's no choice but to slurp. ⑩ Soba connoisseurs say that we can enjoy the aroma much more in our mouths by slurping especially when it comes to soba noodles.

⑪ However, it seems that modern Japanese are globalized: not
<u>グローバル化されている</u>
making any noise when eating noodles is elegant and graceful to
<u>上品な</u>　　　<u>優雅な</u>
them. ⑫ So, meeting the world standard, the number of noodle
<u>〜に合わせて</u>　<u>世界の基準</u>　　　　　　　　　　　　　<u>麺類好きな人</u>
eaters who don't slurp and don't make noise when eating them is

getting higher.
<u>多くなりつつある</u>

04. なぜ、「麺類」をすすって食べるのか？

①日本独自の「そば」を食べるとき、日本人は一般的に音を立てて、すすって食べます。②そばに限らず、麺類はすすって食べるのが、日本人の食文化です。③しかし、外国人からすると、麺類をすすって食べるのはマナー違反で、音を立てて食べることに不快感をいだく人が多いようです。④一時期、「ヌードル・ハラスメント」と呼ばれ、麺類をすすって食べることは、周りに不快感を与える行為として、よくネガティブな話題とされることもありました。⑤麺類の中でも、特にパスタは、すすらないで食べるのがマナーだとされています。⑥パスタを食べるときは、フォークで一口分のパスタをクルクル巻き取り、スプーンを添えて、口まで運び、音を立てずに食べるのが正しいマナーだとされています。⑦それでは、なぜ、日本人は一般的に麺類をすすって食べるのでしょうか。⑧すすることによって、つゆと麺を同時に味わって食べられるというのが一番の理由です。⑨そのためには、麺をすするのは、仕方がないことと考えています。⑩特にそばは、すすることで、香りを口の中で存分に楽しむことができると、そば通はいいます。⑪ただ、現代の日本人は、グローバル化されて、音を立てないことが上品で優雅だとしています。⑫そのため、世界の基準に合わせて、麺類をすすらず、音を立てずに食べる人も多くなってきています。

05. Why are many Japanese people glued to a cell phone on the train?

① Every city and town in Japan are full of people who talk with
すべての　都市　　　町　　日本　　〜であふれている　人々　　　　　〜と話す

somebody, enjoy games, take pictures or videos, or search the
ある人　　　楽しむ　ゲーム　撮る　写真　　　動画　　　検索する

Internet using a cell phone. ② Incidentally, speaking of a cell
インターネット　　　携帯電話　　　　ちなみに　　　〜についていえば

phone, there are two major kinds "smapho" and "galakei" in Japan.
　　　〜がある　2つの　主な　種類　スマホ　　　　ガラケー　　日本

③ Smapho is short for smartphone in Japanese, and it is an
　　　　　　〜の略である　　　　　　　日本語で

evolved cell phone which has various functions, like searching
進化した　　　　　　　　　　　　さまざまな　機能　　　〜などの

the Internet and schedule management, besides conventional
　　　　　　　　スケジュール　管理　　　〜のほか　従来の

communication functions such as making telephone calls and
通話　　　　　　　　　　〜などの　　　　　　通話

sending and receiving emails. ④ Galakei (flip phone) is short
送信する　　　受信する　　メール　　　　　　パタパタとふたを開閉する〜

for a Galapagosnized cell phone in Japanese, and this phone is
　　ガラパゴス化した　　　　　　日本語で

unique to Japan and it is named after the Galapagos Islands due
〜に特有の　　　　　　〜になぞらえて名づけられる　ガラパゴス島　　　〜のために

to the fact that living things have independently evolved there
　　　　　　　生き物たち　　　　独自に

remote from others. ⑤ By comparing the cell phone contracts of
遠い　　　　　　　〜によって比較する　　　　　　　契約者(数)

other countries in the world, usage is almost proportional to their
　　　　　　　　　　　　　利用(率)　ほぼ　比例した

populations. ⑥ Then, why do many people are glued to their cell
人口　　　　それでは　　　　　　　　　〜に夢中になっている

phones in Japan? ⑦ We can point out that there seems to be a
　　　　　　　　　　　　指摘する

behavioral disposition of modern Japanese: that is, we don't want
行動の　　　性向　　　　　　　　　　　　つまり

to interact with strangers, therefore we leave ourselves to our
〜と関わり合いになる　見知らぬ人　そこで　　ゆだねる

cell phones <u>so that</u> we can stay in our own world. ⑧ <u>Also</u>, <u>it is</u>
　　　　　　…するように　　　　　　　　　　　　　　　　　　また
<u>thought that</u> some of us <u>stay on</u> our cell phones because they are
…と思われる　　　　　　　　　　～に集中している
<u>convenient</u> and <u>light</u> <u>tools</u> to <u>kill time</u> with. ⑨ However, we cannot
便利な　　　　　　手軽な　　ツール　　時間つぶしをする
<u>overlook</u> the fact that the number of "cell phone <u>addicts</u>" who are
看過する　　　　　　　　　　　　　　　　　　　　　　依存症
<u>uneasy</u> and cannot <u>spend</u> <u>even</u> one <u>moment</u> without a cell phone
不安な　　　　　　　過ごす　～さえも　一時
<u>has been increasing</u>.
　　　　増えてきている

和訳

05. なぜ、多くの人が電車の中で携帯電話に夢中になっているのか？

①日本では町じゅうに、携帯電話を持って、誰かと電話しているか、ゲームをしているか、写真や動画を撮っているか、インターネットで何かを検索している人であふれています。②ちなみに、携帯電話といえば、日本では「スマホ」と「ガラケー」と呼ばれる2種類に大別することができます。③スマホとは、スマートフォンの略で、従来の通話やメールなどの通信機能のほか、インターネット検索やスケジュール管理などの多様な機能を備えた、進化した携帯電話のことです。④ガラケーとは、「ガラパゴス化した携帯電話」の略で、ガラパゴス島の生物が他と隔絶して独自の進化を遂げたことになぞらえて名づけられた、日本特有の携帯電話のことです。⑤世界各国の携帯電話の契約者数でみてみると、やはり人口にほぼ比例しています。⑥それでは、なぜ、日本では多くの人が携帯電話に夢中になるのでしょうか。⑦現代の日本人の行動性向があると指摘できます。つまり、知らない他人と関わらなくてすむので、自分一人の世界にひたれる携帯電話にわが身をゆだねるということです。⑧また、ひまな時間に手軽でちょうどいい時間つぶしのツールとして携帯電話をいじるケースもあると思われます。⑨ただし、携帯電話がないと不安で、一時も過ごせない「携帯電話依存症」の人が増えていることも看過できない事実です。

06. Why do some Japanese women put on "makeup" on the train?

① There are some japanese women who put on makeup on the
　　　　　　　　 日本(人)の　　　女性たち　　　　　 化粧をする
train shamelessly despite the fact it is a public space. ② Foreigners
電車　 臆面もなく　　～にもかかわらず 事実　　　 公共の場　　　　　 外国人(たち)
seem to be surprised by the women who put on makeup without
～のようである 驚く　　　　　　　　　　　　　　　　　　　　　 ～なしに
worrying about other passengers or where they sit in a row of
～を気にする　　　　　 乗客　　　　　　　　　　　　　　　　　　　 列
seven seats. ③ Some of the Japanese, regardless of sex and age,
7つの 席　　　　　　　　 日本人(たち)　 ～にかかわりなく 性別　　 年齢
feel uncomfortable with such a sight. ④ This is because it is
　　　 不快な　　　　　　 そのような 光景　　　 …だからである
generally thought that they should put on makeup at home or
一般的に …と考えられる　　　　　　　　　　　　　　　　 家で
touch up makeup in a public powder room, not in front of other
～を直す　　　　　　 公共の　 化粧室　　　　 ～の前で
people. ⑤ This act is not prohibited in public, but it is considered
　　　　　　　 行為　　　　 禁止されている 公衆の面前で　　 ～と考えられる
shameful as a public manner. ⑥ Many of the women who put on
恥ずかしい
makeup on the train don't have enough time to do so at home in
　　　　　　　　　　　　　　　　　十分な
the morning; therefore, it seems that, in many cases, they do so
朝に　　　　 それで　　　 …のようである
on the train reluctantly. ⑦ It seems that even those women put on
　　　 しぶしぶ
makeup swiftly, feeling a little embarrassed. ⑧ Let's analyze the
　　　 素早く　　　　　 少し　　　 恥ずかしい　　 ～しましょう 分析する
feelings of those women who put on makeup on the train.

⑨ Being made up is part of a woman's appearance, and there are
　　　　　　　　　　　　　　　　　　　 身だしなみ
some who think it is shameful to show their face without makeup
to their acquaintances. ⑩ However, on the other hand, it seems
　　　 知り合い(の人たち)　　 しかし　 その一方で

24

that they don't feel ashamed to show their face without makeup
（〜するのが）恥ずかしい

and the process of putting on makeup in front of strangers.
過程

⑪ These are complex feelings some women have. ⑫ But, it seems
複雑な　感情

that, recently, the mentality and senses are changing among
最近　心理　意識

women, and the number of women who put on makeup on the

train is smaller than before.
より少ない　以前より

06. なぜ、電車の中で「メイク（化粧）」をする女性がいるのか？

①電車の中という公衆の面前で、何のてらいもなく、化粧をしている女性がいます。②他の乗客や7人掛けの横一列の座席のどこに座ろうが気にせず化粧をしている女性に、外国人は驚くようです。③性別・年齢を問わず、日本人の中には、こうした光景をいぶかる人もいます。④化粧は人前でするものではなく、家でしたり、公共の化粧室などで直すものと一般的に考えられているからです。⑤特に禁止されていることではないのですが、公共のマナーとして恥ずかしい行為というわけです。⑥電車の中で化粧をする女性の多くは、朝、家で化粧をする時間がなく、仕方なく電車の中で化粧をしているというケースが多いようです。⑦彼女たちにしても、多少の恥ずかしさを感じながら、素早く化粧をすませているようです。⑧電車の中で化粧をする女性の心理を分析してみましょう。⑨化粧をすることは、女性の身だしなみの1つであり、知っている人に自分の素顔を見られるのは恥ずかしいとする考え方があります。⑩ただ、その一方で、知らない人の前では素顔や化粧をしている過程を見せることは恥ずかしくないということのようです。⑪複雑な女性心理です。⑫ただ、最近では、そうした女性の心理や意識も変わってきたのか、電車の中で化粧をしている女性を見かけることが、以前よりも少なくなっています。

07. Why do we take a public bath or soak in a hot spring "in the nude" in Japan?

① It is well-known that the Japanese love taking baths, and it seems that some foreigners who visit Japan often experience bathing facilities such as a public bath or a hot spring. ② However, in that case, what foreigners are surprised at is that we take a bath in the nude. ③ Foreigners, especially men, feel uncomfortable about the thought of appearing in the nude when we take a bath together with many unspecified persons. ④ Foreigners think that bathing facilities like public baths or hot springs are similar to a "heated swimming pool" which, we imagine, they go into a mixed bath in a swimsuit. ⑤ Those foreigners who get naked in public are, they think, the same as the nudists who are naked on a nudist beach, and this behavior is not easily acceptable in general. ⑥ And it seems they don't think that, as we do, taking a bath helps them relax and shake off fatigue. ⑦ That's why many foreigners just take a shower. ⑧ In Japan, there has been a sense of being "completely open with others" for a long time, and wearing no clothes in facilities like public bathes implies our sincerity that we don't have anything to hide. ⑨ Lately we can see that foreigners visiting

Japan can take off their clothes with a sense of being open with
　　　　　　　脱ぐ　　　　衣服
others, and they seem to enjoy taking a bath with Japanese people
　　　　　　　　　　　　　　楽しむ　　　　　　　　　　　日本の　　　　人々
happily. ⑩ They might observe the proverb: "When in Japan, do
幸せそうに　　　　　〜するかもしれない　気づく　　　諺
as the Japanese do."

※上記⑩の When in Japan, do as the Japanese do. は、When in Rome, do as the Romans do. と
いうことわざをもじったものです。

和訳

07. なぜ、銭湯や温泉でタオルを持たず「すっ裸」になって入るのか？

①日本人のお風呂好きはよく知られており、日本を訪れる外国人が銭湯や温泉など
の入浴施設を体験することも多いようです。②ただし、その際、外国人が驚くのは、
日本人がそうした入浴施設にすっ裸になって入ることです。③外国人、特に男性は、
不特定多数の人間と入浴する場合、すっ裸になることに抵抗感があるようです。
④外国人にとっては、銭湯や温泉などの入浴施設は、日本人が考える「温水プール」
のようなもので、男女混浴で水着等を着たまま入るものと考えているようです。⑤彼
らにとっては、公共の場で裸になるというのは、ヌーディストたちがヌーディスト・ビー
チ等で裸になっているのと同じと考えており、一般的には受け入れにくいことのよう
です。⑥また、日本人のように、入浴することで、のんびりリラックスができ、疲れも
とれるとは思っていないようです。⑦外国人の中でシャワーですましてしまう人が多い
のは、そのためです。⑧日本には、昔から「裸のつき合い」という考え方があり、公
共の入浴施設で何も付けていない、着ていないことで、他人に対して、自分が何も包
み隠していないという誠実さを示しているのです。⑨最近では、日本を訪れる外国人
も、この裸のつき合い精神からすっ裸になって、日本人の入浴客と和気あいあい、仲
よく入浴している光景が見受けられます。⑩「郷に入っては郷に従え」ということに気
づいたのかもしれません。

08. Why do Japanese parents sleep "together with" their small children?

① In foreign movies, we often watch scenes where, at night,
外国の　　　　　映画　　　　しばしば　観る　シーン　　　　　夜に
parents take their small child to the child's room, kiss him/her
両親　　　　　　　　小さな　子ども　　　　　　部屋　　　(〜に)おやすみのキスをする
good night, and put him/her to sleep. ② However, many Japanese
(〜を)寝かしつける　　　　　しかし　　　　日本人
feel it is strange when we watch those scenes. ③ In Japan,
感じる　　不思議な
parents, especially mothers, sleep alongside their small children
特に　　　　　母親　　　　　　そばに
in most cases. ④ And, in Japan, some families have slept and still
たいていの場合は　　　　　　　　　家族　　　　　　　　　　　いまだに
sleep in the shape of the Chinese character for "river (kawa)."
形　　　　　漢字　　　　　川　　川
⑤ The style in which a child sleeps between his/her father on one
父親　　　片側
side and mother on the other side looks like the Chinese character
反対側　　　　　〜のように見える
for "river," so we use this expression in Japanese. ⑥ This has
表現　　　　　日本語で
been inevitable due to the traditionally small Japanese living
必然的な　　〜のために　　伝統的に　　　　　　　　　住環境
environments. ⑦ However, on the other hand, parents, especailly
その一方で
mothers, think it is more efficient and a relief to sleep alongside
効率的な　　　　安心
their small child. ⑧ This is because there are things that need
〜だから　　　　　　　　　　　　　必要とする
attention in the night like breastfeeding, coping with night-time
注意　　　　　　　〜などの　授乳すること　〜に対応すること　夜間の
crying, and their own anxiety in letting the child sleep alone. ⑨ In
泣くこと　　　　不安　　　　〜させること
general in foreign countries, the "individual" is respected.
一般に　　　　　　　　　　　　個(人)　　　尊重される
⑩ Coming from the perspective that parents should foster a sense
〜からすると　　観点　　　　　　　　　養う　意識

of independence in their children and protect their own privacy,
独立　　　　　　　　　　　　　　　　　　　　　保護する　　　　　プライバシー

the custom of putting a small child to sleep in the child's room

from an early age takes root. ⑪ Even in Japan, you may think
幼少のころ　　　定着する　　　　　　　～でさえ

that parents and their small children always sleep together in one
いつも

room, but we don't. ⑫ When a child grows up to some extent,
成長する　　　ある程度まで

parents and children sleep in different rooms.
異なる

08. なぜ、親は幼い子どもと「一緒」に寝るのか？

①外国映画を観ていると、夜になると、親が幼い子どもを子ども部屋に連れて行き、おやすみのキスをして寝かしつけるというシーンがよくあります。②しかし、多くの日本人はそれを観て、違和感をいだきます。③日本では、親、特に母親が子どもと添い寝することが多いのです。④また、日本には昔から、そして今でも、親子が「川」の字になって寝るという家族がいます。⑤父親と母親の真ん中に子どもが寝るスタイルが、「川」という漢字の形に似ているところから、日本語ではそういう表現をします。⑥これは、昔ながらの日本の狭い住環境から必然的にそうせざるを得ないという事情もありました。⑦ただ、その一方で、親、特に母親が子どもと添い寝するほうが効率的で安心であると考えているようです。⑧これは、夜間の授乳の必要性や夜泣きへの対応、一人で寝かせることへの不安など、夜に注意を払うべき事柄があるからです。⑨外国では、一般的に「個」を尊重します。⑩子どもの自立性を養うことや、両親のプライバシーを確保するという観点から、子どもを早い段階から子ども部屋で寝かせる習慣が定着しているのです。⑪日本でも、親と子どもがずっと同じ部屋で一緒に寝るかというと、そうではありません。⑫子どもがある程度大きくなったら、親と子どもは別々の部屋で寝ます。

① Japan is a country with a seal culture. ② We have to use a seal to receive home delivery service and registered mail. ③ This also includes important documents such as contracts, so using a seal has spread into our daily lives as well as important business situations. ④ It is required to match the imprint of a registered seal in a bankbook and a life insurance policy. ⑤ Also, we have to use a legal seal previously registered at a government office for the legal procedures of large sum transactions including the buying/selling of real estate and the agreement for division of inherited property. ⑥ There are various kinds of seal which are used depending on different circumstances: a correction approval seal, a private seal and a self-inking stamp, including a registered seal which is required to use for formal (or legal) documents.

⑦ This custom is much different from the one in which an individual uses his/her signature in European and American countries. ⑧ What they need in important situations dealing with such things as contracts and money is their signature. ⑨ A signature means to handwrite one's own name on the documents,

and it is uniquely written by oneself, not someone else. ⑩ A seal
　　　独特に　　　　　　自分で

can be put on paper by someone else. ⑪ In contrast, a signature
　　（ハンコが）押される　　　　その他の人　　　　　対照的に

is written by oneself, and the handwriting differs from individual
　　　　　　　　　　　　　　　　　筆跡　　　　　　　　　～によって…と異なる

to individual. ⑫ Even if someone imitate your handwriting, it
　　　　　　　　　　たとえ～でも　　　　　　まねする

is easily judged that it is not written by you, if others verify the
　　容易に　判断される　　　　　　　　　　　　　　　　　　　　　～を実証する

handwriting, and it helps you prevent and avoid trouble. ⑬ Even
　　　　　　　　（～が…するのに）助けとなる　予防する　　回避する　トラブル

in Japan, lately, the number of situations in which signatures are
　　　　　最近

required without needing a seal has been increasing.
　　　　　　　　　　　　　　　　　　　増えてきている

09. なぜ、書類等に自筆のサインではなく、「ハンコ」を押すのか？

①日本はハンコ文化の国です。②宅配便や書留郵便などの受け取りにハンコを使わなければなりません。③また、契約書などの重要書類を含め、仕事の重要な場面から日常生活にいたるまでハンコが浸透しています。④預金通帳や生命保険証券などの届出印制度ではハンコの印影の一致が求められます。⑤また、不動産取引をはじめとする高額取引や遺産分割協議などの法的な手続きにも、あらかじめ役所に登録している実印を用いなければなりません。⑥ハンコには、公式な書類に必要な実印のほか、訂正印や認印、シャチハタ印など、用途に応じて、いろいろなハンコが使われています。⑦欧米の国々で個人がサインをするのとは、大きな違いです。⑧契約などの取引や金銭を扱うような重要な場面で必要なのはサインです。⑨サインとは、自分の手で自分の名前を署名することであり、唯一無二、本人以外は書けないものです。⑩ハンコは、その人以外でも押せるものです。⑪それに対して、サインというのは、その人自身が書くので、筆跡は人によってそれぞれ異なります。⑫いかにまねて書いても、筆跡鑑定すれば、容易に本人でないと判断され、トラブルの予防や回避になります。⑬日本でも、最近では、ハンコではなくサインが求められる場面が増えています。

Why do the Japanese have different concepts called "hon-ne" and "tatemae" depending on the situation?

① The Japanese are sometimes called the people who have different concepts of "hon-ne" and "tatemae" depending on the situation. ② "Hon-ne" means personal feelings and sense of values, and sometimes these are not accepted by the general public. ③ On the other hand, "tatemae" is the response which the general public looks for, and in many cases this makes them keep a good relationship with the other person. ④ Even if they want to say "NO" in hon-ne on their sides, they sometimes respond in tatemae in a way such as "I'll think it over again." or "I'll consider it." ⑤ Therefore, foreigners are apt to interpret that hon-ne is real, and tatemae is false. ⑥ We sometimes hear the expression "archaic smile." ⑦ That is, Japanese smile vaguely, and do not express their real feelings (hon-ne). ⑧ However, it is considered that having hon-ne and tatemae shows consideration and thoughtfulness to others depending on the situation and is peculiar to the Japanese. ⑨ Even Europeans and Americans who express their own opinions straightforward in a businesslike manner may have hon-ne and tatemae more or less depending on the situation.

なぜ、「本音」と「建て前」を使い分けるのか

①日本人は「本音」と「建て前」を使い分ける国民だと、往々にしていわれることがあります。②「本音」とは、個人がもっている感情や価値観のことで、社会一般に受け入れられない場合があります。③一方の「建て前」は、社会一般が求めている答えであり、相手との関係なども存続させてくれる場合が多いものです。④こちらの本音では「NO」であっても、「もう一度考えてみます」とか「検討してみます」と建て前で応えてしまう場合があります。⑤そのため、外国人には、本音は本当のこと、建て前は嘘のことだと解釈されがちです。⑥「アルカイック・スマイル」という言葉も聞かれます。⑦日本人はあいまいな微笑を浮かべ、本音を隠していわないというのです。⑧しかし、本音と建て前の使い分けは、相手に対する日本人特有の思いやりや気づかいといえるものです。⑨ビジネスライクにストレートに自分の意見をいうといわれる欧米人でも、大なり小なり「本音」と「建て前」を使い分けることでしょう。

第 **2** 章

英語対訳でわかる
ニッポンと日本人の不思議

「慣習」のなぜ？

Wonders of Japan and the Japanese
Customs

10. Why do the Japanese say "Kampai!" when drinking alcoholic drinks?

① A sight you often see at various celebratory events and parties and so on, is one where we hold glasses or cups of alcoholic drinks with one hand, then drink it after clinking our glasses and saying "Kampai!" with each other. ② "Kampai!" means drinking up a glass or a cup of an alcoholic drink and emptying it. ③ According to one theory, the first kampai was made at the time of the Treaty of Friendship and Amity between the United Kingdom and Japan in the Bakumatsu period. ④ From the delegations of the United Kingdom, some officials of the Edo shogunate heard that there was a custom in the country, at happy occasions, to have alcoholic drinks which are poured for one another, in order to toast to the King's health. ⑤ They followed this custom, and it is said that this is the beginning of kampai in Japan. ⑥ It is said that, at that time, the Japanese delegates used the phrase "Kampai!" for the first time, and they emptied glasses of alcoholic drinks. ⑦ They say that, in the period of ancient Europe, when they drank a toast, they lightly clinked their glasses or cups with each other, in order to drive devils out of the room with the sound of the clink the glasses.

34

⑧ And, in the Medieval period, it is also said that clinking glasses
　　　　　　　　中世の
made the alcoholic drinks mix in both glasses, so they could taste
　　　　　　　　　　　　　　　　　　　　　　　　　　　　　　　　　　～を毒味する
the drinks for poison. ⑨ When we use thin glasses, the toasters
　　　　　　　for poison.　　　　　　　　　　　　　　　　　　　　　　　　　　乾杯する人たち
may raise them to the height of our eyes without clicking our
　　　持ち上げる　　　　　　　　高さ　　　　　　目
glasses, and we drink a toast making eye contact and giving a
　　　　　　　　　　　　　　　　　　　　　　　アイコンタクト
slight bow to each other.
軽い　　お辞儀すること

10. なぜ、お酒を飲むとき、「乾杯！」というのか？

①いろいろなお祝いの席やパーティーなどで、最初に周りの人たちとお酒の入ったグラスや杯(さかずき)を片手に持ち、互いにそれらを軽くぶつけ合いながら「乾杯！」といってお酒を飲む光景をよく目にします。②乾杯とは、お酒の入っているグラスや杯を飲み干してカラにするという意味です。③日本で最初に乾杯が行なわれたのは、一説によると、幕末時代、日英和親条約の協約のときだったといわれています。④江戸幕府の要人たちは、イギリスの派遣団から、イギリスではおめでたい席で国王の健康を祝して、杯をくみ交わし、お酒を飲む慣習があると聞きました。⑤彼らは、その習慣にならい、これが日本での乾杯の始まりとされています。⑥その際、日本側の代表が「乾杯！」という言葉を初めて使い、お酒を飲み干したといいます。⑦乾杯するとき、お互いのグラスや杯を軽くぶつけ合うのは、古代ヨーロッパ時代に、グラスをぶつけ合う音で部屋の中にいる悪魔を追い払うためだとされています。⑧また、中世になって、ぶつけ合うことで、互いのグラスの中のお酒が混じり合い、毒見ができたともいわれています。⑨薄い(うす)グラスの場合は、ぶつけ合わずに目の高さまでグラスを持ち上げ、周りの人とアイコンタクトや会釈で乾杯する場合もあります。

11.

Why do the Japanese say "moshi, moshi" when making a phone call?

① Most Japanese start speaking with the phrase "moshi, moshi" when we make a phone call, regardless of the kinds of phones: a fixed-line telephone and a cell phone. ② Foreigners seem to think that this phrase is some kind of code, or a set phrase in a telephone conversation. ③ They say that the Japanese used to say "mousu, mousu" two times: "mousu" was originally an old Japanese word which meant "say" or "speak." ④ The phrase is used to say something to the other party that means "OK, let's talk over the phone from now." ⑤ Long ago in Japan, there was one superstition that said that when a specter or a ghost tried to call to a human being, they called to them only once, and if you responded to this, your life was taken. ⑥ So, it seems that saying "mousu, mousu" two times proves to the party that the speaker is neither a specter nor a ghost. ⑦ Telephone service in Japan started in 1890 between Tokyo and Yokohama. ⑧ It is said that, a little later, the style to start a telephone conversation with "mousu, mousu" spread widely throughout Japan and took root. ⑨ And, it seems that this "mousu, mousu" changed into "moshi, moshi"

without anyone noticing. ⑩ This phrase "moshi, moshi" is now
<u>誰も気づかずに</u>
used only in telephone conversations. ⑪ <u>Until</u> <u>a short while ago</u>,
        <u>~まで</u>   <u>少し前</u>
when we would <u>hail someone</u>, we used to say "moshi, moshi" to
        <u>~を呼び止める</u>
him/her, but this phrase is <u>not used any more</u>. ⑫ When we hail a
                        <u>もはや～ない</u>
<u>stranger</u>, we say "<u>Sumimasen</u>" which <u>is equivalent to</u> "<u>Excuse me</u>"
<u>見知らぬ人</u>   <u>すみません</u>   <u>～に相当する</u>   <u>すみません</u>
in <u>English</u>, and when we hail our <u>acquaintance(s)</u>, we say "<u>Ne-e</u>" or
<u>英語で</u>   <u>知り合い(の人)</u>   <u>ねぇ</u>
"<u>Chotto</u>" which is equivalent to "Hello" or "Hi" in English.
<u>ちょっと</u>

和訳

11．なぜ、電話をかけるとき、「もしもし」というのか？

①たいていの日本人は、固定電話・携帯電話にかかわらず、電話で人と話しをするとき、「もしもし」という言葉から始めます。②外国人からすると、何かの暗号か電話での会話の決まり文句と思うようです。③もともと「いう」とか「話す」などの意味の古い日本語である「申す」を重ねて「申す申す」といっていたようです。④「さあ、これから電話でお話ししましょう」と相手に呼びかけるものです。⑤昔の日本では、妖怪や幽霊が人間に話しかけるとき、一度しか呼ばないという説があり、それに返事をすると、命を奪われたという迷信がありました。⑥そのため、「申す申す」と二度重ねることで、自分が妖怪や幽霊ではないということを相手に証明しているのだそうです。⑦日本で最初に電話が開通したのは、１８９０年のことで、東京と横浜間だとされています。⑧それからしばらくして、「申す申す」という言葉で電話での会話を始めるという形が一般に広がり、定着したのだといわれています。⑨そして、この「申す申す」がいつしか「もしもし」に変化したようです。⑩この「もしもし」という言葉は、いまでは電話でしか使いません。⑪少し前までは、人を呼びとめるときに、「もしもし」といっていましたが、いまでは、使われなくなりました。⑫知らない人なら、英語の "Excuse me" にあたる「すみません！」とか、知り合いなら英語で "Hello" や "Hi" を意味する「ねぇ」とか「ちょっと」と呼びかけます。

12.

Why do the Japanese say "Sumimasen" to mean both "appreciation" and "apology"?

① For foreigners, the phrase "sumimasen" which we often use sounds quite strange. ② This is because we use the same phrase "sumimasen" in both apology and appreciation. ③ The one who steps on someone's shoe in a crowded train says "sumimasen" to the other party. ④ And, the one who gets on an elevator after someone says "sumimasen" to the other party who got on before for pressing the "open" button and waiting. ⑤ Clearly, the former is an apology and the latter shows "appreciation." ⑥ Nevertheless, why do we express our feelings to the other party using the same phrase, "Sumimasen," in both situations? ⑦ The Japanese phrase "Sumimasen" has three different meanings. ⑧ They are "apology," "appreciation," and "call for request." ⑨ "Sumimasen" is a compound word of "sumu" and "masen" which is a negative. ⑩ This word denies the word "sumu" which means "something is completed" and "feeling refreshed." ⑪ In other words, one meaning is an "apology" for when one could not complete something, and he/she didn't feel good about it. ⑫ The second meaning is one of "appreciation" for someone who has done

something for the other party, but there is regret that the favor
　　　　　相手から　　　　　　　　　　　　　　　　　　後悔　　　　　親切
cannot be returned. ⑬ The third is the combination of "apology"
　　お返しする　　　　　　　　　　　　　　　　　組み合わせ
and "appreciation" meaning, when you ask the other party for
　　　　　　　　　　　　　　　　　　　　　　　　　〜に…を頼む
something, we feel sorry to impose on him/her. ⑭ For example,
　　　　　〜をすまなく思う　　〜に負担をかける　　　　　　たとえば
when we ask someone for directions, we first say "Sumimasen" to
　　　　　　〜に…を尋ねる　　　方角
him/her.

和訳

12. なぜ、お礼も謝罪も「すみません」というのか？

①外国人にとって、日本人がよく使う「すみません」という言葉はとても不思議なようです。②日本人は相手に謝（あやま）るときも感謝する場合も「すみません」という同じ言葉を使うからです。③満員電車で他人の靴を踏んでしまったとき、相手に「すみません」といいます。④また、エレベーターで先に乗った人が「開く」のボタンを押して、あとから乗ってくる人を待ってくれている場合も、相手に「すみません」といいます。⑤明らかに、前者は謝る場面だし、後者は感謝の気持ちを伝えるシーンです。⑥それなのに、どちらも同じ「すみません」という言葉を使って、相手にこちらの気持ちを伝えるのは、どうしてなのでしょうか。⑦「すみません」という日本語には、大きく3つの意味があります。⑧「謝る」、「感謝する」、「呼びかけて依頼する」の3つです。⑨「すみません」とは、「すむ」という言葉とそれを否定する「ません」という言葉の複合体です。⑩「物事が完了する」とか「心が晴れる」という意味の「すむ」を否定しているのです。⑪つまり、物事を完了できなくて、自分の気持ちがすっきりしないという「謝罪」の意味がその1つです。⑫2つめは、相手から何かをしてもらったのに、そのお返しもできず、自分の気持ちがすっきりしないという「感謝」の意味です。⑬3つめは、相手に何かを依頼するとき、相手に何かしらの負担をかけることが申し訳ないという「謝罪」と「感謝」を合わせた意味です。⑭たとえば、街で道を尋ねるときなどに、相手にまず「すみません」と声をかけます。

13. Why do the Japanese say "Tsumaranai-mono-desuga … " when giving someone a present?

① When we give someone a gift or a present, we often say
誰か　　　　　　　　贈り物　　　プレゼント　　　しばしば
"Tsumaranai-mono-desuga…, " (This is a trifling thing, but….)
つまらないものですが　　　　　　　　　　　　　つまらない
as an introductory remark. ② "Tsumaranai" means worthless,
　　前置きの　　　言葉　　　　　　　　　　意味する　価値のない
unattractive, meaningless and insignificant in Japanese. ③ It
興味を引かない　意味のない　　　とるに足りない　日本語で
seems to be difficult for foreigners to understand why we take the
～のようである　難しい　　　外国人(たち)　　　理解する　　　　わざわざ(～)する
trouble to give him/her such a trifling gift. ④ This is an expression
　　　　　　　　　　　　　　　　　　　　　　　　　　　　表現
which derives from a spirit of humility peculiar to the Japanese.
　～に由来する　　気持ち　謙譲　　　　～に特有の
⑤ This spirit of humility is taken up in "Bushido" (the Way of the
　　　　　　　　　　　　～にとり上げられる　武士道　　　道
Samurai) written by Nitobe Inazo. ⑥ Nitobe Inazo was a Japanese
さむらい(→武士)　書かれた　新渡戸稲造　　　　　　　　　　　　日本の
educator who played an active part from the Meiji period to the
教育者　　　　　　(役割を)果たした　活発な　役割　　　明治時代
Taisho period, and served as Under-Secretary-General of the
大正時代　　　　　任務を果たした　　　事務次官
League of Nations (at present, the United Nations). ⑦ The book
国際連盟　　　　　　　現在(では)　　　国際連合
"Bushido" explains the Japanese thinking and way of life, and this
　　　説明する　　　　　　　考え方　　　生き方
book has been given a high rating in foreign countries such as
　　　　　　　　　　　　　　評価する　外国の　国々　　　～などの
the United States. ⑧ He mentions that "Tsumaranai-mono-desuga
アメリカ合衆国　　　　述べている
…," shows a feeling of humility implying that "this is a thoughtful
　　　　　　　　　　　　　　示す　　　　　　　　　　よく考えられた～
present which I have chosen, but this may not be so much for
　　　　　　　選んだ　　　　　たぶん～だろう　十分な
you." ⑨ Many Japanese think that this is a modest and beautiful
　　　　　　　　　　　　　　　　　　　　　　　　奥ゆかしく　美しい

remark. ⑩ However, lately, this kind of modest remark is not
　　　　　　　 しかし　　　 最近では
used very often. ⑪ When giving a gift, many convey our feelings
　　　 しばしば　　　　　　　　　　　　　　　　 伝える
directly, and we give someone a present with phrases that express
直接的に　　　　　　　　　　　　　　　　　　　　　　　　　　 表現する
our real intentions like "This is just a token of my goodwill." or "I
　 真の　 意志　　 ～のような　　　 象徴　　　 善意
hope you like this." ⑫ Lately, many books on Japanese manners
advise that we had better not use the phrase "Tsumaranai-mono-
忠告する　　　　 ～しないほうがよい
desuga…"

和訳

13. なぜ、贈り物をするとき、「つまらないものですが……」というのか？

①日本人は人に物を贈ったり、プレゼントする際に、よく「つまらないものですが……」
と前置きしてから渡します。②「つまらない」とは、日本語で価値がない、興味をひかない、
意味がない、得るものがないといった意味です。③外国人からすると、日本人はなぜ、
そんなつまらないものをわざわざ渡すのか、理解しがたいようです。④これは、日本人
独特の謙譲の気持ちから生じる言葉です。⑤この謙譲の精神については、新渡戸稲造
が著した『武士道』でもとり上げられています。⑥新渡戸稲造とは、明治時代から大正
時代に活躍した日本の教育者で、国際連盟(いまの国際連合)の事務次官も務めた人
です。⑦『武士道』という書物は、日本人の思想や生き方を示したもので、アメリカな
どでも評価の高い本です。⑧「つまらないものですが……」は、「自分としては、精い
っぱい心を込めて選んだものですが、あなたにとってはそれほどでもないかもしれませ
ん」という、謙譲の気持ちを表わしたものだと述べています。⑨奥ゆかしく、美しい言
葉だと、多くの日本人は思っています。⑩ただし、最近では、こうした謙遜の言葉もあ
まり使われなくなってきています。⑪贈り物をするとき、素直に自分の気持ちを伝えて、
「ほんの心ばかりのものですが……」、「気に入ってもらえるとうれしいのですが……」と
いった、こちらの本音を表わした言葉を添えて渡します。⑫多くの日本のマナー本でも、
最近では「つまらないものですが……」という言葉は控えたほうがよいとしています。

14. Why do the Japanese "bow" rather than shake hands when they greet?

① There seems to be a notion that we often bow politely to others, not only when we meet and exchange greetings, but also in many other situations. ② Some foreigners seem to feel humbled when seeing such Japanese people. ③ When and for what reason did this Japanese conduct of bowing start? ④ There is a view that this conduct came to Japan about 500 years ago, when Buddhism was introduced from China. ⑤ It is said that bowing is proper etiquette when one worships the Buddha, and trying to show himself/herself as more timid than others implies that he/she doesn't have any hostility toward them. ⑥ It seems that, hearing this, many foreigners nod in agreement, but they still feel that we bow too much, like bowing to an unseen party on the phone. ⑦ However, this conduct shows respect to others, so we can say that it is not strange to bow when speaking to someone on the phone.

⑧ We can see this bowing custom not only in Japan but also in East Asian countries like China and Thailand. ⑨ On the contrary, Europeans and Americans generally shake hands when they greet. ⑩ It is said that, by controlling each other's dominant hands,

they show that they aren't hiding any weapons, and express their
　　　　　　　　　　隠している　　　　武器　　　　　　表現する

intentions to build friendship with respect toward their partner.
意図　　　　　　築く　友好（関係）　　　　　　　　　　　相手

⑪ Lately, in business and other situations, we also shake hands,
　最近では　　　　　　　　　　　場面

not bow, as Europeans and Americans do.
お辞儀をするのではなく　～と同じく

14. なぜ、挨拶するとき、握手よりも「おじぎ」をするのか？

①日本人は挨拶するときはもちろん、相手に対してよく頭をペコペコ下げているイメージがあるようです。②外国人の中には、そんな日本人を見て、卑屈に感じる人もいるようです。③このすぐおじぎをする日本人の行動は、いつどういう理由で始まったのでしょうか。④中国から仏教が伝わった約５００年前からだという説があります。⑤おじぎをすることは、仏様を拝む作法であり、また、身分の高い人に対して、相手より自分が小さくなることで、相手に敵意を持っていないことを表わしているのだといわれています。

⑥それを聞くと、なるほどとうなずく外国人も多いようですが、相手の姿が見えない電話でも、おじぎをするのはやりすぎではないかと感じているようです。⑦ただ、相手に対する敬意からとる行動なので、電話でお辞儀をするのもおかしなことではないといえます。⑧このおじぎをする習慣は日本だけではなく、中国やタイなどの東アジアでも広くみられます。⑨これに対して、欧米人の場合は、挨拶などをするとき、一般的には握手をします。⑩これは、利き手をお互い制することで、武器を隠し持っていないことを示し、相手に対して敬意をもって友好関係を築きたいという意思表示であるといわれています。⑪最近では、日本人もビジネスの場などで、欧米人と同じく、おじぎではなく、握手で挨拶しています。

15. Why do the Japanese say "arigatou" when expressing their thanks?

① First of all, what does the Japanese phrase "arigatou" mean?
第一に　　　　　　　　　　　　　　　　日本語　　　言葉　　ありがとう　　意味する

② In breaking down this phrase, it means that something is rare.
分解すると　　　　　　　　　　　　　　　　　　　何か　　　　まれな

③ It is said that this phrase originally comes from Buddhism.
…といわれている　　　　　　　　もともと　　〜に由来する　　仏教

④ Oshaka-sama (the Buddha) who is the founder of Buddhism
お釈迦様　　　　仏（様）　　　　　　　　　創始者（→教祖）
once had a dialog with one of his pupils. ⑤ He mentions that
ある時　　　対話　　　　　　　　　弟子たち　　　　　述べる
being born in this world is quite rare; that is, it is impossible to
生まれること　　　　　　　　かなり　　　　つまり　　　不可能な
do, so we can never be grateful enough for it. ⑥ He preached
そのため　　　　　　〜に感謝している　十分に　　　　　　　説いた
that it was impossible in the same way as if a blind turtle which
同じように　　　　　　　　目の見えないカメ
lived at the bottom of the boundless great ocean took his/her own
底　　　　果てしない　大きな　海洋　　〜を…から出した
head out of the surface of the ocean every one hundred years,
頭　　　　　　表面　　　　　　　100年ごとに
and each time he/she stuck his/her head into the hole of a log
毎回　　　　　　〜を…にさし込んだ　　　　穴　　　丸太
which by chance was drifting above the ocean. ⑦ It is said that
たまたま　　　漂っている　上に
being born is such a precious matter, so we should say our thanks
貴重な　こと　　〜すべきである　感謝の言葉
every day: this is the original meaning of "arigatou" in Japanese.
もともとの　意味　　　　　　　　日本語で

⑧ By the way, what is the antonym of "arigatou"? ⑨ Some say
ところで　　　　　　　　反対語　　　　　　　　　　　一部の人々
that the answer to this question is "atarimae." ⑩ They say that the
答え　　　質問　　　当たり前　　　…といわれている
antonym of rareness and preciousness is a common and natural
めったにないこと　貴重なこと　　　ありふれた　当たり前の
matter. ⑪ People just don't feel grateful for what is common.
人々

44

⑫ Buddha <u>might</u> have told us that being born in this world is <u>not</u>
　　　　　～だったのかもしれない　　　　　　　　　　　　　　　　　　　～ではなく…

common, but we should think it is very precious, and we should

live with <u>appreciation</u> every day. ⑬ <u>Incidentally</u>, <u>according to</u> a
　　　　　　感謝　　　　　　　　　　　　　　ちなみに　　　～によれば

survey, the phrase "arigatou" ranks <u>by far</u> the <u>highest</u> among the
調査　　　　　　　　　　　　　　　　　　位置する　断然　　一番高い

<u>favorite</u> phrases to hear from others <u>for</u> the <u>Japanese</u> people.
好みの　　　　　　　　　　　　　　　　　　～にとって　日本の

15. なぜ、感謝の気持ちを述べるとき、「ありがとう」というのか？

①そもそも、日本語の「ありがとう」とは、どういう意味なのでしょうか。②この日本語を分解すると、あることが難しいという意味になります。③この言葉は、もともと仏教に由来するといわれています。④仏教の教祖であるお釈迦様があるとき、弟子の一人と問答をします。⑤人がこの世に生まれることは、あることがとても難しい、つまりありえないことなので、感謝してもし足りないと述べています。⑥それは、あたかも、果てしない大海原の底深くにいる目の見えないカメが１００年に一度海面に頭を出し、その際、たまたま海面を漂っている丸太の穴に頭をつっ込むくらいにありえないことだと説きました。⑦人が生まれるということはそれほど貴重なことなので、日々、感謝すべきであるというのが、日本語の「ありがとう」のもともとの意味だといわれています。⑧ところで、「ありがとう」の反対語は、何でしょうか。⑨答えは、「当たり前」だという人がいます。⑩めったにない、貴重なことの反対語は、ありふれた、当たり前のことだというわけです。⑪人はつい、ありふれたことには感謝の気持ちを感じません。⑫人はこの世に生まれてきたことをありふれたことではなく、とても貴重なことだと思い、日々、心から感謝して、生きていくべきであるとお釈迦様はいっているのでしょう。⑬ちなみに、ある調査で「ありがとう」という言葉は、日本人が人からいわれて好きな言葉の、断トツ一位だそうです。

16. Why do we stand in a "line" and wait with patience in Japan?

① A common sight in Japan is that many Japanese stand in a long line in front of popular ramen noodle shops and/or sweets stores in the news waiting to eat. ② There seems to be no data to prove scientifically that only the Japanese like to stand in a line. ③ However, we cannot deny the fact that we like to stand in a line. ④ Then, why do we eat popular ramen and sweets in the news going as far as standing in line? ⑤ According to a psychologist's analysis, human beings are social creatures, and, when faced with uncertainty, they try to get a sense of security by following the same behavior as others. ⑥ It seems that if we see a line of guests and customers in front of restaurants and stores, we may stand in a line and take the same action as others. ⑦ And, we don't cut into a line. ⑧ We keep the line straight and wait in line with patience. ⑨ It is thought that the sense of "harmony" peculiar to the Japanese still exists. ⑩ We think that it is a virtue to observe social rules without causing others any troubles. ⑪ It is often said that the British do not go as far as standing in a line to buy or eat food . ⑫ They treasure the "individual," and the idea that "I am

myself and others are themselves." takes root in the country.
私自身 _他人_ _彼ら自身_ _根づいている_

⑬ There are also many Japanese who don't like to stand in a
〜もまた

line. ⑭ They are not cross-grained, but they dislike following
あまのじゃくな(←木目の不規則な) _〜に従う_

others.

16. なぜ、「行列」を作って、辛抱強く並ぶのか？

①人気のラーメン店や話題のスウィーツの店など、日本人は長蛇の行列を作って、並んで待ってでも食べるという光景をよく目にします。②日本人だけが行列好きという科学的な裏づけのあるデータは、特にないようです。③ただし、日本人が行列好きであることは否定できないでしょう。④それでは、なぜ、人はわざわざ行列をしてまで、人気のラーメンや話題のスウィーツを食べるのでしょうか。⑤ある心理学者の分析によると、人は社会的な生き物で、不確かなことについては、他人と同じ行動をとって確かめることで、安心感を得ようとするとのことです。⑥店の前で行列ができていると、つい自分も並んで他人と同じ行動をとってしまうことがあるらしいのです。⑦そして、日本人は横入りなどしません。⑧日本人は、その行列を乱すことなく、辛抱強く並んで待っています。⑨これは、日本独自の「和」の精神が生きているものと思われます。⑩他人に迷惑をかけないで、きちんとルールを守ることが美徳であると考えているのです。⑪イギリス人は、行列を作ってまで、ものを食べたり、買ったりしないとよくいわれます。⑫「個」を大切にしており、「他人は他人、自分は自分」という考え方が根づいているのです。⑬行列が好きではないという日本人も多くいます。⑭天邪鬼なのではなく、他人に同調することをよしとしない人たちです。

Why do the Japanese say "Itadakimasu" and "Gochisosama" when having meals?

① We often say "Itadakimasu" when we start a meal and "Gochisousama" when we finish eating. ② Some put our hands together even if we do not say these words aloud. ③ "Itadakimasu" is a humble expression which means "receiving something" or "having a meal" in Japanese. ④ "Gochisosama" is a phrase of gratitude for hospitality. ⑤ When children have a meal, if they do not say "Itadakimasu" and "Gochisosama," some of their parents scold them for having bad manners. ⑥ It is said that there are two meanings for these. ⑦ One of them implies that people should thank all of those who prepare meals and those who are involved with the ingredients. ⑧ The other is to thank the ingredients themselves. ⑨ It implies that people should thank living creatures such as cows, pigs, chickens and fish, and gifts from the land like vegetables and grains.

なぜ、食事をするとき、 「いただきます」「ごちそうさま」というのか？

①日本人はよく食事をするときに「いただきます」といい、終えると「ごちそうさま」といいます。②声に出していわなくても、手を合わせるなど、態度で表わす人もいます。③「いただきます」とは、日本語で「もらう」「食べる」という意味の謙譲語です。④「ごちそうさま」は、もてなしに対するお礼の言葉です。⑤自分の子どもが食事をする際、それらをしないと、行儀が悪いと注意する親もいます。
⑥これには２つの意味があるといわれています。⑦１つは、食事をつくってくれた人はもちろん、食材に関わったすべての人に感謝するという意味合いです。
⑧もう１つは、食材そのものへの感謝です。⑨牛・豚・鶏・魚などの生き物、野菜や穀類などの大地の恵みに対して、感謝をするという意味合いです

第 **3** 章

英語対訳でわかる
ニッポンと日本人の不思議

「しきたり」のなぜ？

Wonders of Japan and the Japanese
Conventions

17. Why do the Japanese "bow two times, clap hands two times and bow one more time" at a Shinto shrine?

① When we visit a shrine, we bow two times, clap our hands two times and bow one more time. ② When we visit a temple, the manners are different. ③ We don't clap our hands, but we place our hands together once in prayer. ④ Where do these differences come from? ⑤ First of all, bowing two times at the altar in a shrine means that we do this to respect the god (kami) and treat the god with the utmost courtesy. ⑥ Next, clapping our hands two times expels evil spirits around and invites the god at the same time. ⑦ It is thought that, when we clap our hands two times, we should shift our right hand down a little. ⑧ The right hand represents the god's pure hand, and the left hand represents the human's impure hand at this stage, this proves that the god and the human are not connected yet. ⑨ And, we make a wish upon the god, under the condition that the god and we become one with our hands placed together. ⑩ It is thought that, lastly, bowing one more time sends the god away. ⑪ Depending upon shrines like Izumo Taisha Shrine, we are urged to clap our hands four times, instead of two times. ⑫ On the other hand, at a temple, we

don't clap our hands. ⑬ We place our hands together only once and make a wish upon the Buddha. ⑭ <u>By the way</u>, we <u>throw</u> an
ところで　　　　　　　　　投げ入れる

<u>offering</u> of <u>money</u> into the <u>offering box</u>, both at a shrine and at a
お供え（物）　お金　　　　　賽銭箱

temple. ⑮ Many of us <u>mistakenly</u> <u>believe</u> that this offering is for
勘違いして　　　信じる

<u>granting</u> our <u>wishes</u>. ⑯ <u>To tell the truth</u>, we should throw the
かなえてもらう　願いごと　　実をいうと

offering as our thanks for a <u>previous</u> wish being granted.
前回の

和訳

17. なぜ、神社では「二礼二拍一礼」をするのか？

①神社に参拝するとき、「二礼二拍一礼」をします。②お寺に参拝するときは、作法が異なります。③拍手をせず、両手を一度だけ合わせて合掌します。④この違いは、いったいどこにあるのでしょうか。⑤まず、神社の神前で二礼するのは、神様に敬意を示し、礼を尽くす行為です。⑥続いて、二拍するのは、両手を音を立ててたたくことで、周りの邪気を祓うのと同時に神様を招きます。⑦二拍の際には、右手を少し下にずらすようにしてたたくとされています。⑧右手は清浄な神様の手、左手は不浄な人間の手を暗示し、その段階では神様と人間がまだつながっていないことを示します。⑨そして、両手をそろえて神様と一体になった状態で、神様に願いごとをします。⑩最後に、一礼することで神様をお送りするというわけです。⑪神社によっては、出雲大社のように二拍ではなく、四拍するところもあります。⑫一方、お寺では、神社のように柏手を打ちません。⑬両手を一度だけ合わせて合掌し、仏様にお願いごとをします。⑭ところで、神社でもお寺でも、お賽銭を賽銭箱に入れます。⑮このお賽銭は、願いごとをかなえてもらうために入れると勘違いしている人が多くいます。⑯本当は、前回にした願いごとをかなえてもらったお礼に入れるものなのです。

18. Why do the Japanese put a "noshi" on a present?

① In Japan, when we give a gift to someone, we formally put a
日本　　　　　　　　与える　贈り物　誰か　　　　　　正式には　　　　〜に…をかける
mizuhiki on a gift-wrapped box and then put a noshi on it.
水引　　　　　贈り物用に包装した　箱　　　　　　　　　熨斗

② What do a mizuhiki and a noshi mean? ③ A mizuhiki is a
　　　　　　　　　　　　　　　　意味する

red-and-white or white-and-black webbing which is put on a gift-
紅白　　　　　　白黒　　　　　　帯

wrapped present or an envelope when we give a formal present to
　　　　　プレゼント　　　　封筒　　　　　　　　　　正式な

someone. ④ It is thought that the custom of putting on a mizuhiki
誰か　　　　　　…と考えられている　　慣習

originally started when all the imported goods from China were
もともと　　　　　　　　　　　　　　輸入品　　　　　中国

tied with a red-and-white cord in the Muromachi period. ⑤ In
結ばれた　　　　　　　　　　縄　　　　室町時代

China, it is said that this cord was used to differentiate the exports
　　　…といわれている　　　　　　　　区別する　　　　輸出品

from others, but the Japanese at that time mistook them as gifts.
その他の品物　　　日本人　　　　　　　〜と…を勘違いした

⑥ Since then, in Japan, it is said that we put this kind of cord on
それ以来

a formal present. ⑦ A mizuhiki has three different ways of tying
　　　　　　　　　　　　　　　　3つの　異なる　　方法

the cord, and there are other color combinations besides red-and-
　　　　　　　　　　　　　　　　　　　　組み合わせ　〜以外の

white. ⑧ These are used in different ways in accordance to the
　　　　　　　　　　　　　　　　　　　　　〜に応じて

use. ⑨ On the other hand, a noshi was originally thinly-stretched
使用　　　一方　　　　　　　　　　　　　　　　　薄くのした

and dried abalone, and this is pasted on the right upper corner
　　乾燥した　あわび(貝)　　　　　貼られている　　右の　上のほう　角

of the wrapped gift as a symbol of enjoying longevity. ⑩ The
　　包装された　　　　　象徴　　　享受する　長寿

starting point seems to be the idea that a gift was originally an
出発点　　　　〜のようである　　考え

52

offering made to the gods of Shinto and Buddhism. ⑪ A paper
お供え(物) なされた   神道   仏教

printed mizuhiki and noshi are called noshi-gami (noshi paper).
印刷された   熨斗紙   熨斗紙

⑫ Actually, there is an informal way to give a gift whichi is
実際には   略式の

wrapped with a noshi gami without a mizuhiki and a noshi.
                    〜なしに

⑬ However, in the case of an important present or a very valuable
ただし   〜の場合には   大切な   意味のある

present, we should be careful when giving a present to someone
            〜すべきである 注意深い

because it may be rude to put only a noshi gami on the present.
                    失礼な

18. なぜ、贈答品に「熨斗」をつけるのか?

①日本では、贈り物をするとき、正式には贈り物用の包装をした箱に水引をかけ、熨斗をつけます。②水引と熨斗には、どんな意味があるのでしょうか。③水引とは、正式な贈り物をするときの品物の包み紙や封筒などにかける紅白や白黒などの帯のことです。④水引をかけるのは、室町時代に中国からの輸入品のすべてに紅白の縄がかけてあったことが始まりとされています。⑤中国側では輸出品とその他を区別するために使っていましたが、日本側がこの縄を贈答用に使用するものと勘違いしたといわれています。

⑥ それ以来、日本では正式な贈答品にかけるようになったようです。⑦ 水引には3種類の結び方があり、紅白以外の色の組み合わせもあります。⑧ 用途に応じて、それぞれ使い分けられています。⑨ 一方、熨斗とは、もともとはあわび貝を薄くのして干したもので、長寿をもたらすものの象徴として、包装の上から右肩に貼られます。⑩ これは、贈り物がもともと神仏への供え物という思想が原点にあるようです。⑪ 水引と熨斗を印刷した紙のことを熨斗紙といいます。⑫ 実際には水引や熨斗をつけていなくても、熨斗紙で贈答品を包んで贈るという略式の方法もあります。⑬ ただし、大切な贈り物や意味のある品を贈る場合には、熨斗紙では失礼になることがあるので、注意が必要です。

19. Why do the Japanese exchange "san-san-ku-do" cups at a wedding ceremony?

① At a wedding ceremony according to Shinto ritual peculiar to Japan, there is a ritual to exchange "san-san-ku-do" cups.
② The wedding ceremony is given by a Shinto priest and Shinto priestesses. ③ The groom and bride share the same three sake cups, and they exchange the sake which is called omiki with each other. ④ They say that this omiki has two meanings, "prosperity" and "talisman." ⑤ They sip the omiki to pray for the god's protection over those two persons who are going to be a couple.
⑥ They use three different sizes of cups: a small one, a medium-sized one, and a large one, and they have meanings of "prosperity of descendants," "marriage vows of the two," and "appreciation to ancestors" respectively. ⑦ The order of this ceremony is as follows: starting from a small cup, a priestess pours the omiki into a small cup for the groom first, then he sips it three times.

⑧ The priestess pours the omiki into the same cup for the bride too, and she sips it three times. ⑨ The bride and groom sip the omiki three times from three different cups which totals nine times in all, so this custom is called "san-san-ku-do" (san means

three, and ku means nine respectively, and do means the number
of times). ⑩ The reason why they sip three times each from three
different cups is that, the odd numbers, three, five, seven, and
nine, have been thought to be happy numbers, since ancient times
in Japan. ⑪ The order in which the groom and bride sip the omiki
is that the groom sips first and the bride sips next, but only in the
case of the second cup, the bride sips first, and the groom sips
next.

19. なぜ、神式の結婚式では「三三九度」の盃を交わすのか?

①日本独自の神前での結婚式では、「三三九度」と呼ばれる儀式があります。②神官と巫女によってとり行なわれます。③新郎と新婦が三つの同じ盃を共に使って、お神酒と呼ばれる日本酒を飲み交わします。④お神酒には「繁栄」、「魔除け」の意味があるとされています。⑤これは、夫婦となる二人への神様のご加護を願うために飲むものです。⑥使われる三つの盃は大、中、小があり、「子孫繁栄」、「二人の誓い」、「先祖への感謝」とそれぞれの意味を持っています。⑦儀式のやり方は、小さな盃から始めて巫女が新郎にお神酒を注ぎ、盃ごとに三度にわたってそのお神酒を飲みます。⑧新婦にも巫女がお神酒を注ぎ、同じく盃ごとに三度にわたって飲みます。⑨三つの盃でそれぞれ三度にわたって合計九度、飲むことから「三三九度」と呼ばれています。⑩なぜ、三つの盃で三度にわたって飲むのかについては、日本では昔から三や五、七、九の奇数はおめでたい数とされてきたことによるとされているからです。⑪新郎と新婦がお神酒を飲む順番は、新郎が先、新婦が後ですが、二番めの中盃の場合のみ、新婦が先、新郎が後です。

20. Why do the Japanese strike wooden clappers for "Fire patrol"?

① The Japanese used to patrol their neighborhood on a cold
winter night shouting "Hino-youjin!" (Fire patrol!) in Japanese
and striking wooden clappers two times in order to echo sound
through the clear sky, though such a sight cannot be seen so often
any more today. ② It is thought that this custom began in the Edo
period, when the government put out an official notice in order
to prevent fires in towns. ③ It is said that shouting "Fire patrol!"
came from the letter which Honda Shigetsugu, who was a follower
of Tokugawa Ieyasu (one of the famous warlords in the Sengoku
period), sent to his family when he was in the field of The Battle
of Nagashino (1575). ④ The letter said: "Just a brief note: Guard
against fire; Don't let the baby Osen cry; Feed the horses well."
⑤ The content of this letter means that "I'm writing this letter to
you. Please beware of fire! Please take good care of Senchiyo
(at that time, three years old) who is the only boy among our five
children. Please don't fail to care for horses which are precious
to samurais." ⑥ This letter became famous as the shortest one in
Japan, so it seems that this phrase was adopted later as a shout of

night patrol. ⑦ There are various theories about why the wooden
　　　　　　　　　　　　 いろいろな　　 説
clappers were struck two times, but it is said that this custom
　　　　　　　　　　　　 2回
came from the Chinese thought of yin and yang. ⑧ This means
　　　　　　　　　　　 考え方　　　　 陰と陽
that all matters have two sides: yin and yang, and striking wooden
　　　　 物事　　　　　 側面
clappers two times implies a pair of yin and yang, so these matters
　　　　　　　　　 表わす　 一対の
would be neatly completed. ⑩ That is, this means that both
　　　　 きちんと 完成している　　 つまり
bewaring of fire and night patrol make matters complete, safe and
　　　　　　　　　　　　　　　　　　　　　　　　　　　　　　　　　 無事に
sound.

和訳

20. なぜ、「火の用心」で拍子木を鳴らすのか?

①今ではあまり見られなくなりましたが、冬の寒い夜、「火の用心!」と声をかけ、澄んだ空に響くように拍子木を二回、打ち鳴らして見回りをする人たちがいました。②これは、江戸時代に幕府から町の火事を防ぐ目的でお触れがあり、そこから始まったものとされています。③「火の用心」というかけ声は、徳川家康の家臣であった本多重次が、長篠の戦い(1575年)の陣中から家族にあてた手紙が由来だとされています。④手紙の内容は、次の通りです。「一筆啓上 火の用心 おせん泣かすな 馬肥やせ」⑤手紙の内容は、「お手紙をさし上げます。火事には気をつけるように。五人の子供のうち、男子は仙千代(当時3歳)だけだから大事に育てるように。武士にとって大切な馬の世話を怠らないように」というものです。⑥日本一短い手紙として有名になったことから、のちに夜回りのかけ声に採用されたようです。⑦拍子木をなぜ二回鳴らすかについては諸説がありますが、中国の陰陽思想からきているといわれています。⑧すべての物事には陰と陽の二つの側面があり、二回鳴らすことで、陰と陽の一対を表わし、物事がきちんと完成するという意味です。⑨つまり、火の用心も夜回りも無事完成させるということです。

21. Why do the Japanese close a banquet with "ippon-jime"?

① As one of the manners and customs, all persons who are involved clap their hands in unison, which is the so-called "tejime" in Japanese, after the successful end of some activity or at the end of a banquet. ② A general one is called "ippon-jime" and, shouting in unison, all the participants clap their hands rhythmically ten times in all : three times, three times, three times, and one time. ③ Three sets of this "ippon-jime" are called "sambon-jime" (ippon means one set, and sambon means three sets). ④ Even some Japanese make the mistake of clapping their hands only once for "ippon-jime", but this one is called "iccho-jime". ⑤ Then, why do we do "tejime" after the successful end of some activity or events? ⑥ "Tejime" was originally the act of opening the hands and clapping in order to show others that there are no weapons in anyone's hands. ⑦ That is, this is a ritual for strengthening unity and becoming friendly with others. ⑧ This "tejima" has a long history, and this is a joyful act which is also introduced in myths about the transfer of land. ⑨ Hands are clapped nine times at first, which consists of a set of three claps three times each.

⑩ This gives us the number 9 (nine), and in Japanese it is
　　　　　示す
connected with "worry." ⑪ So, we clap ten times in all, because
〜とつながる　　　　　　　苦労　　　　　　　　　　　　　　　　　　　なぜなら…だから
there is an idea that adding one more clap makes everything go
　　　　　　　　　　　　加えること　　　　　　　　　　　　　すべて
well. ⑫ Sambon-jime is done with the intention to strengthen its
うまくいく　　　　　　　　　なされる　　　　　　意図
effects more, and iccho-jime is done to simplify the ippon-jime
効果　　　よりよく　　　　　　　　　　　　　　　　簡素化する
ritual with all our heart.
　　　　心を込めて

和訳

21. なぜ、宴会の最後に「一本締め」をするのか？

①日本の風習の一つに、物事が無事に終わったときや宴会の終わりなどに、その関係者が全員で「手締め」と呼ばれる行為をします。②一般的なのが「一本締め」と呼ばれ、全員がかけ声に合わせて、三回・三回・三回・一回の合計十回、リズミカルに手を打ちます。③この「一本締め」を3セット続けて行なうのを「三本締め」といいます（日本語で一本は一セット、三本は三セットを意味します）。④日本人でも、よく一回だけ手を打つのを「一本締め」と勘違いしている場合が多いのですが、それは「一丁締め」といいます。⑤それでは、なぜ、日本人は物事が無事に終わったときなどに、こうした手締めを行なうのでしょうか。⑥手締めは、もともと、互いに武器などを手に持っていないことを見せ合う意味から両手を広げて打つという行為です。⑦つまり、お互いにうちとけ合って、結束を固めるための儀式なのです。⑧手締めの歴史は古く、日本の国譲り神話の中でも紹介されているおめでたい行為です。⑨三回ずつ三度、計九回手を打つことになります。⑩「九」という数字が日本語では「苦」につながるとされています。⑪それに一回足すことで、すべてがうまくいくという考え方があるため、計十回手を打つのです。⑫三本締めは、その効果をより強めたいという意思で行ない、一丁締めは、心を込めることで、一本締めの儀式を簡素化する場合です。

22. Why do the Japanese bind a "hachimaki" (headband) around their head at festivals?

① In Japan, the participants at festivals bind "hachimaki" around their heads, and they lively carry a stand with the so-called "mikoshi," a portable Shinto shrine, on their shoulders, and/or hold festivals peculiar to the location. ② Hachimaki is a cloth or string which one binds around his/her head, or such behavior.

③ Originally, when Buddhist priests did practice called "takuhatsu" (mendicancy), they had a container called "hachi" in their hands and it looked like a human's skull. ④ That's why they say this binding around one's head came to be called hachimaki. ⑤ Then, why do we bind a hachimaki around our heads at festivals?

⑥ By tying one's head with a hachimaki, it has the effect of spiritual unity, and it motivates him/her. ⑦ This act indicates one's intention to hold festivals in earnest. ⑧ One binds a hachimaki around his/her head not only at festivals, but also for preparing for examinations and on sports days. ⑨ Binding a hachimaki around one's head shows his/her intention to study with all of his/her might, and it means to boost the morale of a team. ⑩ It is said that the hachimaki has a long history, and it

dates back to the mythical age. ⑪ When Sun Goddess (Amaterasu
~にさかのぼる　　　　　神話の　　　　時代　　　　　　　　　　　　　　　　太陽の女神　　　　　天照大神

O-omikami) hid in Amano Iwato (Cave of Heaven), the land
　　　　　　隠れた　　　天岩戸　　　　　　　洞窟　　　神（天国）　　　　土地

became completely dark. ⑫ As a result, people around the cave
　　　　完全に　　　暗い　　　　その結果として　　人々

hoped to take her out of the cave and bring light back to the land,
(〜したいと)思う〜を…から連れ出す　　　　　　　　　　　〜を…に戻す 明かり

so they bound ivy around their heads and they danced like crazy
　　　　　巻いた　蔦　　　　　　　　　　　　　　　　踊った　　　　　気が狂った

and fascinated her. ⑬ It is said that this is the origin of hachimaki.
　　〜の興味を引いた　　　　　　　　　　　　　　　　　　　　起源

和訳

22. なぜ、お祭りのとき、「鉢巻き」をするのか？

①日本では、祭りのときに参加者が頭に「鉢巻き」をして、威勢よく神輿と呼ばれる神様を乗せた台を担いだり、その土地独自の祭り行事をとり行ないます。②鉢巻きとは、人の頭に巻く布や紐もしくはその行為のことをいいます。③もともと、仏教僧が托鉢という修行をする際に手に持っていた「鉢」と呼ばれる器の形が人の頭蓋骨に似ていました。④そんなところから、頭に巻くことを鉢巻きと呼ぶようになったといいます。⑤それでは、なぜ、祭りのとき、頭に鉢巻きをするのでしょうか。⑥頭を縛ることで、精神統一や気合を入れる効果があります。⑦この行為は、本気で祭りをとり行なうという意思表示なのです。⑧祭りのときだけではなく、試験勉強をするときや運動会などでも鉢巻きをします。⑨鉢巻きをすることで、気合を入れて勉強することを態度で示したり、チームの士気を高める意味があるのです。⑩鉢巻きの歴史は古く、神話の時代にさかのぼるといわれています。⑪天照大神が天岩戸に隠れたとき、地上が真っ暗になりました。⑫その結果、なんとか外へ連れ出して地上を明るくしようと考えた周りの者が頭に蔦を巻き、踊りまくって興味を引きました。⑬これが、鉢巻きの由来といわれています。

Why do the Japanese celebrate "kanreki" wearing red chanchan-ko when they become sixty years old?

① In Japan, when people turn sixty years old, called "kanreki" (the celebration of one's 60th birthday) in the traditional Japanese system, they celebrate their long life. ② "Kanreki" means "the calendar returns to the origin" in Japanese. ③ This originates in the calendar from Ancient China, and this view states that after sixty years, it returns to the origin, and starts from the beginning of the new year. ④ When someone becomes sixty years old, he/she wears a red "chanchan-ko," and is celebrated by his/her family, friends and so on. ⑤ Chanchan-ko is originally clothing which they make a newborn baby wear. ⑥ From the point of view that when someone becomes sixty years old, he/she returns to the original one year old, the person who is sixty years old also wears chanchan-ko. ⑦ Of course, he/she wears a larger size chanchan-ko for adults. ⑧ It is considered that the color red has the power to keep away evil spirits and wearing red chanchan-ko means praying for health and longevity. ⑨ In modern times, they say that not all wear red chanchan-ko to celebrate their sixtieth birthday, but they celebrate it in the way which matches their taste.

....

なぜ、60歳になると、赤いちゃんちゃんこを着て「還暦」の祝いをするのか？

①日本では、伝統的に「還暦」と呼ばれる満60歳を迎えると、長寿のお祝いをします。②「還暦」とは、日本語で「暦が元に還える」という意味です。③古代中国から伝わった暦の考え方で、60年経つと、元に還って、また1年目から始まるとする理論です。④60歳になったら、その人は赤い「ちゃんちゃんこ」を着て、家族や知り合いなどから祝ってもらいます。⑤ちゃんちゃんことは、本来、生まれたばかりの赤ちゃんに着せる着物です。⑥60歳になったら、元の1歳に還るという考え方から60歳の人もちゃんちゃんこを着るのです。⑦もちろん、大人用に大きくしたちゃんちゃんこを着ます。⑧赤い色は、昔から魔除けの力があるとされ、赤いちゃんちゃんこを着るのは、健康と長寿を祈願する意味があります。⑨現代では、みんながみんな、赤いちゃんちゃんを着てお祝いすることはなくなり、個人の好みに合ったお祝いをするようになったようです。

英語対訳でわかる
ニッポンと日本人の不思議

「社会」のなぜ？

Wonders of Japan and the Japanese
Life in Society

23. Why do we drive on the left side of the street in Japan?

① It is normal in Japan that cars keep left on the street, but throughout the world overwhelmingly more cars keep right. ② The main countries where cars keep left like Japan are the United Kingdom (U.K.) and countries historically related to the U.K. such as Australia, India and South France. ③ On the other hand, the countries where cars keep right are Canada, France, Germany, Italy, China, South Korea, Russia and Brazil including the United States. ④ In the UK, it is thought that it began when the Pope decided to keep left in the 14th century. ⑤ It is said that Japan also followed this system. ⑥ However, according to another view, they say that it dates back to the age when samurais wore swords at their waists in Japan. ⑦ Right-handed samurais who were generally in the majority wore their swords at their left waist which made it easy to draw their swords with their right hand. ⑧ Therefore, if they walked or rode horseback, they had trouble avoiding bumping their sheaths against samurais coming from the other side. ⑨ In order to avoid this, it is said that they decided to ride on the left side. ⑩ However, some insist that all of these

are just <u>folklore</u>, and they say it is based on the <u>fact</u> that this was
俗説　　　　　　　　　　　~に基づいている　　　事実

<u>baselessly</u> written in the <u>road regulations</u> in the <u>Meiji period</u>.
根拠なく　　　　　　　　　　道路取締規則　　　　　　明治時代

⑪ On the other hand, they say that France started to drive on the

right side. ⑫ It is said that, <u>as a result of</u> the <u>French Revolution</u>
　　　　　　　　　　　　　　~の結果として　　　　フランス革命

which <u>broke out</u> in the 18th century, they decided to drive on the
勤発した

right, <u>due to</u> the fact that <u>anti-Catholics</u> didn't <u>want to</u> be <u>the same</u>
~のために　　　　　　　　反カトリック派　　　　~したい　　　~と同じに

<u>as the Catholics</u>.

和訳

23. なぜ、日本ではクルマは「左側通行」なのか？

①日本では当たり前のように、クルマは左側通行をしていますが、世界では圧倒的に右側通行が多いのです。②日本と同じ左側通行している主な国はイギリスとそのイギリスと歴史的に関係が深いオーストラリアやインド、南フランスなどです。③一方、右側通行の国は、アメリカをはじめ、カナダ、フランス、ドイツ、イタリア、中国、韓国、ロシア、ブラジルなどです。④イギリスでは、14世紀にローマ教皇が左側通行にすると決めたことが始まりとされています。⑤日本もそれに倣ったといわれています。⑥しかし、他説によると、日本では武士が刀を腰にさしていた時代までさかのぼるといいます。⑦一般的に多かった右利きの武士は左手で抜きやすいように左の腰に刀をさしておりました。⑧そのため、右側通行で歩いたり、馬に乗っていると、対向からくる武士と刀の鞘がぶつかるのを避けるのが大変でした。⑨これを避けるために、左側通行するようになったのが始まりともいわれています。⑩ただし、それらはいずれも単に俗説で、明治時代の道路取締規則において、根拠もなく明文化されたものがもとになっていると主張する人もいます。⑪一方、右側通行はフランスがその端緒といわれています。⑫18世紀に起こったフランス革命により、反カトリック派がカトリック派と同じにしたくないという事実から右側通行にしたのが始まりといわれています。

24. Why are there so many "sotobiraki" (out-swinging doors) which we have to pull in Japan?

① A long time ago, a "sliding door" was common in a Japanese house, but the "swinging door" which opens back and forth, has become mainstream, because Japanese life has been Westernized. ② However, in contrast to European and American doors, the "uchibiraki" (in-swinging doors), Japan has by far the largest number of "sotobiraki" (out-swinging doors). ③ Why is that so? ④ It is said that the reason why the European and American doors are "in-swinging doors" is for security. ⑤ Even if a suspicious person tries to force himself/herself into a home, if the door opens inward, the people in the house can protect themselves against the invasion by applying their whole weight on the door or leaning some pieces of furniture against it to prevent entry. ⑥ That makes sense. ⑦ Nevertheless, the reason why there are many "out-swinging doors" in Japan is because our way of life is different from the way of life in Western and American countries. ⑧ In Japan, we have to take off our shoes at a space which is called "tataki" in Japanese inside the front door before we enter. ⑨ It is also thought that if the front door opens inward, it is not easy to

open and shut the door, because those shoes taken off already on
<u>閉じる</u>   <u>それらの</u>   <u>すでに</u>

the tataki may be an obstacle for the front door and the door may
<u>邪魔もの</u>

damage those shoes. ⑩ And, if the door opens inward, the space
<u>傷つける</u>

in the tataki will be narrower, and it might be difficult to take off
<u>より狭い</u>   <u>かもしれない</u>   <u>～することが難しい</u>

shoes there. ⑪ Security issues are the main reason in European
<u>その場所で</u>   <u>問題</u>   <u>主たる</u>

and American countries, but the reason why it has not been a big

issue in Japan might be because Japan is a relatively safe country.
<u>比較的に</u>   <u>安全な</u>

和訳

24. なぜ、日本の家のドアは手前に引く「外開き」が多いのか？

①昔は、日本の家屋は「引き戸」が一般的でしたが、生活全般の欧米化により、引き戸から前後に開閉するスタイルの「ドア」が主流となりました。②しかし、欧米のドアが「内開き」なのに対して、日本では、特に玄関のドアは圧倒的に「外開き」が多いようです。③それは、いったいなぜでしょうか。④欧米のドアが内開きである理由は、防犯上の問題だといわれています。⑤不審者が無理やり中に入ってこようとしても、内開きなら、内側にいる人が全体重をかけて押しとめたり、家具などをもたせかけることで、侵入を防ぐことができるからです。⑥理にかなった理由です。⑦にもかかわらず、日本で外開きが多いのは、欧米との生活様式の違いがあります。⑧日本では、玄関のドアの内側にある「たたき」と呼ばれる靴を脱ぐスペースで、靴を脱いでから中に入ります。⑨もし、内側にドアが開いてしまうと、たたきに先に脱いである靴が邪魔をしてドアの開閉がしにくかったり、その靴をドアが傷つけることも考えられます。⑩また、内側にドアが開くと、たたきのスペースが小さくなり、靴を脱ぐことが困難にもなりかねません。⑪欧米では防犯が大きな理由なのに対して、日本では、それがあまり問題にならなかったのは、日本が比較的安全な国であるということかもしれません。

25. Why is the Japanese currency "yen"?

① It is well-known in history textbooks, period novels, samurai TV dramas and samurai movies that the Japanese currency was called "ryo" or "mon" in the Edo period. ② Then, when and for what reason did the present "yen" start? ③ It was not until the beginning of the Meiji period that "yen" first appeared in Japan. ④ Until then in Japan, many kinds of currency were mixed together: golden coins and silver coins which were minted by the Edo Shogunate, various local currencies issued by each han (now prefecture), and foreign currency which came into Japan after opening its borders to the outside world. ⑤ Then, Ookuma Shigenobu who was in charge of monetary policy at that time became engaged in it, and after the sequences of events, "yen" finally became the unified currency in Japan. ⑥ Coins made of several shapes like oval and square used until then were made round because round coins are easier to carry and the corners would not wear out. ⑦ As the Japanese word "yen" has the meaning of round, they named round coins "yen." ⑧ By the way, why do they write "yen" instead of "en" in English? ⑨ It is said

that this is related to its pronunciation. ⑩ They pronounce "yen"
　　　　　　　　　　　～と関連している　　　　　　発音　　　　　　　　　　　　　　　　　　　～を…と発音する

as "en" in English. ⑪ Originally, when the Japanese pronounced
　　　　　　英語で　　　　　　　もともと

"en," foreigners in English-speaking countries heard it as "yen."
　　　　　　　　　　　　　　　　英語を話す～

⑫ As the holdover of that, it is said that, even now, they write "yen"
　　　～として　　　名残　　　　　　　　　　　　　　いまでも

as "en" in English.

25. なぜ、日本の通貨単位は「円」なのか?

①日本の通貨単位が江戸時代には「両」や「文」などと呼ばれていたことは、歴史の教科書や時代小説、テレビや映画の時代劇などで知られています。②それでは、いまの「円」になったのはいつ頃からで、どういう理由からなのでしょうか。③日本に初めて「円」が登場したのは、明治時代の初頭です。④それまで日本には、江戸幕府が発行していた金貨や銀貨、各地の藩(いまの県)ごとに発行していた地域の通貨、開国後に入って来たさまざまな外国通貨などが入り乱れていました。⑤そこで、当時、通貨政策を担当していた大隈重信が関わり、いろいろ経緯があった後、最終的に「円」に通貨が統一されたのでした。⑥それまで楕円形や四角形など、複数あった貨幣の形を、持ち運びやすく、角が摩耗することもない、丸い形にしようとしました。⑦日本語の「円」には、丸いという意味があるので、丸い貨幣イコール「円」という呼び名にしたのです。⑧ところで、「円」を英語などで表記するとき、「en」ではなくて、「yen」と書くのは、どうしてでしょうか。⑨これは発音の問題だといいます。⑩英語では、「円」を「yen」と発音します。⑪もともと、日本人が「円」と発音したとき、英語圏の外国人には「yen」と聞こえたといいます。⑫その名残から、いまでも「円」は英語表記で「yen」と書くのだそうです。

26. Why do only Japanese 5 yen and 50 yen coins have a hole?

① Japanese currency has the following kinds of bills and coins: four kinds of bills (1,000 yen, 2,000 yen, 5,000 yen, and 10,000 yen) and six kinds of coins (1 yen, 5 yen, 10 yen, 50 yen, 100 yen, and 500 yen). ② Why do only the 5 yen and 50 yen coins among these have a hole in the middle? ③ The 5 yen coin was first minted in Showa 23 (1948). ④ The then 5 yen coin was minted without a hole in it. ⑤ It is said that Japan experienced runaway inflation in the following year, Showa 24 (1949), so they made a hole which was five millimeters in diameter in the middle of the coin in order to save the raw materials. ⑥ They say that the reduction in cost of raw materials was five percent. ⑦ Also, it was in Showa 30 (1955) when the 50 yen coin was first minted, and the size was bigger than the present 50 yen coin. ⑧ It was made from white copper which was a mixed metal of copper and nickel, and it had no hole. ⑨ The 50 yen coin was confusingly similar to the 100-yen coin which was minted in Showa 32 (1957) in both the shape and the color, so in order to differentiate these two, a hole was drilled in the middle of the coin in Showa 34 (1959).

⑩ By the way, among these six kinds of coins, only the 5 yen coin
ところで　　　　　　　〜の中で

has a Chinese numeral "five" on it. ⑪ This bears witness to us that
　　　　漢数字　　　　　　　　五　　　　　　　　(…の)証拠となる

the design has not been changed since the 24th year of Showa

when the present 50 yen coin was minted. ⑫ The coins with a

hole in the middle are quite rare, and especially the 5 yen coin
　　　　　　　　　　　　かなり　珍しい　　　　　特に

that looks golden, so they seem to be popular among foreigners.
　　　　　金色　　　　　　　　　　　　　　　人気がある

※③の Showa23 は、そのまま Showa twenty-three と音読します。

和訳

26. なぜ、日本の硬貨は５円と50円だけ穴があいているのか？

①日本の貨幣には、４種類の紙幣（1000円・2000円・5000円・10000円）と６種類の硬貨（１円・５円・10円・50円・100円・500円）があります。②硬貨のなかで、５円と50円だけが真ん中に穴があいているのは、なぜでしょうか。③５円硬貨は、昭和23年（1948年）に初めてつくられました。④当時の５円硬貨は穴なしでつくられていました。⑤翌年の昭和24年（1949）に急激なインフレに見舞われたことから、原材料を節約するために真ん中に５ミリの穴をあけたといわれています。⑥その原材料費のコストダウンは５％だったといわれています。⑦また、50円硬貨が初めてつくられたのは昭和30年（1955）で、いまの50円硬貨よりもサイズが大きいものでした。⑧これは、銅とニッケルの合金である白銅からできていて、穴なしでした。⑨その50円硬貨が、昭和32年（1957）に発行された100円硬貨と形も色も紛らわしかったことから、区別するために、昭和34年（1959）に真ん中に穴があけられたというわけです。⑩ところで、６種類ある硬貨のうち、５円硬貨だけが漢数字の「五」が使われています。⑪これは、いまの５円硬貨がつくられた昭和24年からデザインが変わっていない という証拠 です。⑫真ん中に穴があいている硬貨は世界でも珍しく、特に５円硬貨は金色をしているために外国人には人気があるようです。

① According to a recent survey by the Ministry of Land, Infrastructure, Transportation and Tourism, the most commonly used as roadside trees in Japan are gingko trees, the second most commonly used are different kinds of cherry trees, the third most is zelkova, and the fourth most is dogwood. ② What kind of role do these roadside trees play? ③ The roadside trees not only let us know the changes of the seasons and enrich the townscape view, but also become homes for wild birds and insects, absorb carbon dioxide and exhaust gas and give off oxygen. ④ Also, they give shade to avoid strong sunshine, hold down the rise in temperature on the roads, separate the sidewalk and the street, and enhance the safety for pedestrians and driving cars. ⑤ Why is gingko used much among roadside trees? ⑥ Roadside trees are exposed to the exhaust gas of vehicles in many cases, and moreover they are forced to survive in harsh environments, as they are planted in the openings of hard asphalt-paved grounds. ⑦ Gingko trees are vigorous and long-lived, so they are suitable for roadside trees, as we don't have to replant them often. ⑧ Also, from a long time

72

ago, gingko trees are supposed not to burn easily. ⑨ It is also
～しないと考えれている

said that sixty percent of Edo city was reduced to ash in the Great
江戸の町　　　　焼失した　　　　　　大火

Fire in the Meireki period (Meireki-no-taika) in 1657, and in this
明暦時代　　　　明暦の大火

incident, many gingko trees were planted as fire protection.
出来事　　　　　　　　　　　　　　　　　防火対策

⑩ However, in fall, smells of fallen nuts of gingko trees on the
しかし　　　秋　臭い　　落ちた　イチョウの実(→ぎんなん)

street get avoided by people, so only male strains without nuts are
雄　株

planted in many places. ⑪ According to another recent survey,
別の

gingko has lost the number one position to dogwood as roadside
譲った　　1位の座

trees.

和訳

27. なぜ、日本の街路樹には「イチョウ」が多いのか？

①近年の国土交通省の調査によると、日本で街路樹として最も使われているのは、1位イチョウ、2位サクラ類、3位ケヤキ、4位ハナミズキとのことです。②街路樹の役割とは、いったい何でしょうか。③季節の変化を知らせ、街の景観を豊かにするほか、野鳥や昆虫の棲み家となる、二酸化炭素や排気ガスを吸収して酸素を放出します。④また、強い日ざしを防ぐ木かげをつくり、路面の温度上昇をおさえ、歩道と車道を分け、歩行者と車の通行の安全性を高めます。⑤街路樹のなかで、イチョウが多いのは、なぜでしょうか。⑥街路樹はクルマの排気ガスにさらされることが多いうえに、硬いアスファルトのすき間の地面に植えられるなど、過酷な環境が強いられます。⑦イチョウは丈夫で寿命が長く、たびたび植え替えなくてすむので、街路樹に適しています。⑧また、イチョウは昔から燃えにくい木とされています。⑨1657年に発生した「明暦の大火」で江戸の街の6割が焼失した際にその防火対策としてイチョウが多く植えられたことによるともいわれています。⑩ただ、秋になって路面に落ちるぎんなんの臭いが近年、敬遠されて、実をつけない雄株のみを植えることが多いそうです。⑪最近のほかの調査では、街路樹の多さ1位の座をハナミズキに譲ったといいます。

Why are there so many "cedar" trees on the grounds of a shrine and "pine" trees on the grounds of a castle in Japan?

① When we step into the grounds of a shrine, we may have a
　　　　足を踏み入れる　　　境内　　　　神社　　　　　　かもしれない
solemn feeling, and at the same time, you will be surprised at
厳かな　気分　　　　　　同時に　　　　　　　　　　　　　～に驚く
the number of "cedar" trees. ② The reason why many cedar
　　　　　　　　杉(の木)　　　　　なぜ…なのかの理由
trees are planted on the grounds of a shrine is that, in ancient
　　　　植えられている　　　　　　　　　　　　　～はつまり…　　古代の
mythology, tradition has it that when a god first climbed down
神話　　　…という言い伝えがある　　　　神　　最初に　降りてきた
to the Takachiho District in Kyushu from Takamagahara where
高千穂　　地方　　九州　　　　高天原
gods lived, he climbed down cedar trees. ③ Cedar trees play an
　　　　　　　　　　　　　　　　　　　　　　　　　　　　果たす
important role for the gods who come and go between the Heaven
重要な　　役割　　　　　　　行き来する　　～と…の間　　　天上界
and the Earth. ④ In addition, it is said that the bark of cedar trees
地上界　　　加えて　　　…といわれている　　樹皮
were used to repair roofs, and they were used to compensate for
～することに使われた　修理する　屋根　　　　　　　　　　　補てんする
the operating cost of a shrine, because they sold at a good price.
　　維持する～　費用　　　　　　　　　　　売った　高い値段で
⑤ On the other hand, do you know there are many "pine" trees
　　一方　　　　　　　　　　　　　　　　　　　　　　　松(の木)
in the grounds of a castle? ⑥ In the Sengoku period (the age of
　　　　　　　　城　　　　　　戦国時代　　　　　　　時代
Civil Wars), the inferior soldiers sometimes barricaded themselves
内乱　　　　下級の　戦士　　ときどき　障壁で守る
in a castle to offer resistance to their enemy. ⑦ In that case, it
　　　　～に抗戦する　　　　　　敵
was natural to have a prolonged war until their food supplies
当然である　　持久戦　　…まで　　食糧の供給
ran out in the castle. ⑧ At that time, "pine" trees were valued as
尽きる　　　　　　　　　　　　　　　　　　　　　　　重宝された
emergency foods. ⑨ You cannot eat the hard outer bark, but if
非常食　　　　　　　　　　　　　　　　　　　　外側の

you boil the soft thin skins inside the bark, they say you can eat
煮る　　柔らかい 薄い 皮　　内側の　　　　…といわれている
them. ⑩ And, it is said that, if you dry them and grind them into
　　　…といわれている　　　　乾かす　　　粉に挽く
powder and mix them with wheat flour and rice flour, you can
　　　　混ぜる　　　　　麦粉　　　　米粉
make rice cakes. ⑪ They say that pine trees grow in poor soil
餅　　　　　　　　　　　　　　　　　　　　　　貧弱な 土地
that doesn't have many nutrients, and they keep green leaves all
　　　　　　　　栄養分　　　　　　　　保つ　緑の葉
year around. ⑫ Moreover, it seems that they were used as fuel,
1年中　　　　　さらに　…のようである　　　　　　　　燃料
because pine trees have much pine resin which is vegetable oil
　　　　　　　　　　　　　　　　　　やに　　　　植物樹脂
and fat, and even green wood of pine trees burn easily.
　　　　～でさえ 緑の木(→生木)　　　　　　　燃える 容易に

和訳

28. なぜ、神社には「杉」の木、城には「松」の木が多いのか？

①神社に一歩足を踏み入れると、厳かな気分になるのと同時に、「杉」の木が多いことに驚かされます。②神社に杉が多く植えられている理由は、古代神話において、神々が住む高天原から最初に九州の高千穂地方に神が降り立ったとき、杉の木をつたってきたという言い伝えによります。③神様が天上界と地上界を行き来するための大切な役割を担っているわけです。④そのほか、屋根などの修理に杉の樹皮が使われたとか、杉材は高く売れるので、神社を運営するための費用の補てんに使われたなどといわれています。⑤一方、城に「松」の木が多いことをご存知でしょうか。⑥戦国時代には城に立てこもって抗戦することがしばしばありました。⑦その際は、城内の食糧が尽きるまで戦うという持久戦も当然想定されました。⑧そのときの非常食として、「松」の木が重宝されました。⑨硬い外側の皮は食べられませんが、その内側にある柔らかい薄皮を煮れば、食用になるようです。⑩また、それを干して粉にし、麦粉や米粉と混ぜれば、餅をつくるといいます。⑪松は、養分の少ないやせた土地でも育つといわれ、一年中緑の葉をつけているので、敵からの目隠しにもなりました。⑫さらに、植物油脂である松やにが多いので生木でもよく燃えることから、燃料にもなったようです。

29. Why does "machiya" in Kyoto have a narrow frontage and a wide depth?

① Speaking of streets lined with houses in Kyoto, the houses
~といえば　　　車道　　　　　～が並んでいる　　家屋　　　　京都

called "machiya" meaning townspeople's houses are arranged
町家　　　　意味している　　町人たち　　　　　　　　配置された

in an orderly checkerboard pattern. ② Also, there is a structural
きちんと　碁盤の目状の　模様　　　　また　　　　　　構造上の

feature of wide depth, though the frontage called "maguchi" is
特徴　　　広い　奥行き　…にもかかわらず　入り口　　　間口

narrow. ③ The machiya is sometimes called "unagi-no-nedoko"
狭い　　　　　　　　　　ときどき　　　　　　うなぎの寝床

(bed for eel in Japanese), too. ④ Why is the structure narrow in
ベッド　うなぎ　日本語で　　～も　　　　　　　構造

the front but with a wide depth? ⑤ Somehow, it seems to be
間口　　　　　　　　　　　　　　　さらに　　　～のようである

concerned with the history of Kyoto. ⑥ The capital was moved
～と関わりがある　　　歴史　　　　　　　　首都　　　　　～に移った

to Kyoto in the Heian period, and the city was designed like a
平安時代　　　　　　　　　　　　　デザインされた　～のように

checkerboard pattern modeling the Changan of China (then, Tang).
　　　　　　　　～をモデルにして　チャンアン　中国　当時は　唐
　　　　　　　　　　　　　　　　　長安

⑦ When the capital prospered, the population increased due to
繁栄した　　　人口　　　増加した　～のために

its active foreign trading. ⑧ For that reason, they tried to build
活発な　外国との　貿易　　そのため　　　　　　～しようとした　建てる

as many houses as possible in narrow spaces, and people started
～をできるだけ…する　　空間　　　　　　　　　～し始めた

moving into Kyoto. ⑨ As a result, the houses with a narrow
その結果

frontage lined facing the street. ⑩ Moreover, as time passed by
～に面して　　　さらに　　～したころ　～が過ぎた

in the Edo period in Kyoto, a tax on the house called "maguchi-
江戸時代　　　　　　　　　　税金　　　　　　　　　間口税

zei" (frontage tax) was enforced, and the tax amount was decided
施行された　　　　　　税金額　　　決められた

depending on the width of the frontage. ⑪ For that purpose, it is
～に応じて　　　広さ　　　　　　　　　　　そのため

76

said that a larger merchant family would build a narrow and long
・といわれている　より大きな　商家

house equivalent to the narrower frontage and the wider depth.
　　　　　～に等しい

⑫ There is another idea that maguchi-zei was modeled on the tax
　　　　　　別の　　説　　　　　　　　　　　　　　　　　　　　税

system of Toyotomi Hideyoshi (one of the famous warlords of the
制度　　豊臣秀吉　　　　　　　　　　　　　　有名な　　武将

Sengoku period) during and before the Edo period. ⑬ In any case,
戦国時代　　　　　～の前とその間じゅう　　　江戸時代　　　いずれにせよ

they say that the remainders are still alive in the present houses in
…といわれている　　名残　　　　　　いまだに 生きている　　現在の

Kyoto.

和訳

29. なぜ、京都の「町家」は間口（入り口）が狭く、奥行きが広いのか？

①京都の町並みといえば、町人たちの家という意味の「町家」と呼ばれ、碁盤目状に整然と家屋が建ち並んでいます。②それと、「間口」と呼ばれる入り口が狭いわりに、奥行きが広いという構造上の特徴があります。③「うなぎの寝床」などとも呼ばれています。④なぜ、間口が狭く、奥行きが広い造りになっているのでしょうか。⑤どうやら、京都の歴史がかかわっているようです。⑥平安時代に京都に遷都され、中国（当時は唐）の長安をモデルにして碁盤目状の都市がつくられました。⑦都が栄えるようになると交易が盛んになり、人口も増えました。⑧そのため、狭い空間にできる限り多くの家屋をつくって、人々が移り住むようになりました。⑨その結果、通りに面して、入り口の狭い家屋が建ち並ぶことになりました。⑩さらに、時は移り、江戸時代に入って、京都では家屋に課せられる税金は間口税と呼ばれ、間口の広さで決められました。⑪そのため、大きな商家ほど、間口を狭くして、その分、奥行きの広い細長い家を建てたといいます。⑫間口税については、江戸時代以前の豊臣秀吉の税制によるという説もあります。⑬いずれにせよ、その名残がいまの京都の家屋に息づいているというわけです。

30. Why is "shachi-hoko" set on the top of a castle in Japan?

① As to a Japanese castle, we might imagine a magnificent castle
~といえば 日本の 城 ~(した)かもしれないイメージする 荘厳な 城の塔
tower called "tenshu (commonly called "tenshukaku") which soars
天守 通例として ~と呼ばれた 天守閣 そびえ立つ
in the center of the fort, and a pair of shachi-hoko (a fabulous
中央 城郭 一対の~ しゃちほこ すばらしい
dolphin-like fish) are attached on both sides of the roof. ② A
イルカに似た 魚 取り付けられている 両側 屋根
tenshu is a special building which symbolizes the castle with
特別な 建物 象徴する
functions of interviewing key persons, overlooking lands near a
機能 ~と接見すること 要人 ~を見渡すこと 土地 ~に近い
castle, and stockpiling weapons and foods for emergencies.
~を貯蔵すること 武器 食糧 緊急時の
③ However, not all castles have a tenshu. ④ Many castles don't
しかし すべての~が…ではない
have even a shachi-hoko on the top. ⑤ There is a strange castle
てっぺんに ~がある 変わり種の
like the Shibata Castle in Niigata prefecture, which doesn't have
新発田城 新潟県
a tenshu, but has three shachi-hokos on the top. ⑥ What kind of
meaning does shachi-hoko on the tenshu have in general?
意味 一般に
⑦ Shachi-hoko is not an imitation of a killer whale we can see
かたどったもの シャチ
often in an aquarium. ⑧ This is an imagined monster whose head
しばしば 水族館 想像上の 怪獣 その~が 頭
is a tiger and whose body is fish, with many sharp spines on its
虎 体 鋭い とげ
back. ⑨ It is thought that this monster drinks all the water of the
背中 …と思われている 飲む
ocean in one gulp, and protects buildings from fires. ⑩ It is said
大海 一飲みに ~を…から守る 建物 火事 …といわれている
that it was Oda Nobunaga who made a tenshu at a castle and put
織田信長

a shachi-hoko on it first in Japan. ⑪ Generally, when looking at
a castle from the front, a male shachi-hoko and a female one are
enshrined at the right and left side respectively on the roof.
⑫ The one with an open mouth is a male and the one with a
closed mouth is a female. ⑬ There is a unique castle like Himeji
Castle in Hyogo prefecture, which has two large ones and nine
small ones, all females, on the tenshu.

和訳

30. なぜ、お城のてっぺんには「しゃちほこ」が付いているのか？

①日本の城といえば、城郭の中央に高々とそびえる「天守」と呼ばれる（「天守閣」は俗称）壮麗な櫓と、その屋根の左右に1対とり付けられた2体の「しゃちほこ」をイメージするのではないでしょうか。②天守は、要人との接見、城下の物見、緊急時の武器や食糧の貯蔵の機能をもった、城を象徴する特別な建物です。③しかし、全部の城に天守があるわけではありません。④しゃちほこが鎮座していない城も多くあります。⑤新潟にある新発田城のように、天守がないのに、3体のしゃちほこを載せた変わりだねの城もあります。⑥一般的に天守にとり付けられたしゃちほこには、いったいどんな意味があるのでしょうか。⑦しゃちほこは、水族館でよく見かけるシャチをかたどったものではありません。⑧頭が虎で姿は魚、背中にいくつもの鋭いとげを持っている、想像上の海獣です。⑨海の水を一気に飲み干すといわれ、建物を火災から守るとされています。⑩日本で最初に、城に天守をつくり、しゃちほこを載せたのは織田信長だといわれています。⑪通常、雄と雌が正面から見て屋根の右と左に鎮座しています。⑫口をあけているほうが雄で、口を閉じているほうが雌です。⑬兵庫の姫路城のように、天守に大きな2体のほか、9体の小さなものまで、すべてが雌という珍しいケースもあります。

31. Why do we call the small characters attached to kanji "rubi" in Japanese printing terms?

① For some kanji (Chinese characters) in a sentence, we attach
〜に対して　いくつかの　漢字　中国の　文字　文章　付ける
small characters which are called "rubi" when the kanji is read
小さい　ルビ
difficultly or differently than usual. ② Usually, in the case of
困難で　異なって　普段よりも　通常は
vertical writing, the rubi is put on the right side of the kanji, and
タテ書き　〜に付ける
in the case of horizontal writing, the rubi is put above the kanji.
ヨコ書き　上に付けられる

③ Originally, this is a term which comes from letterpress printing.
もともと　言葉　活版　印刷
④ Letterpress printing is printing using typesetting which was
組版
made from a combination of letters. ⑤ This is a relief printing
組み合わせ　活字　凸版印刷
in which they put some printing ink on the projection of a print
突起部分
version with an uneven surface like a seal. ⑥ Rubi refers to ruby,
版　凸凹の　表面　〜のことである　ルビー
which is a kind of gem. ⑦ A long time ago, mainly in the United
宝石　昔　主に　イギリス(連合王国)
Kingdom, the size of the type was indicated in "points", and they
サイズ　活字　表わされた　ポイント
had different names depending on the size. ⑧ For instance, the
異なる〜　〜に応じて　たとえば
4.0-point type was called "diamond," the 5.0-point type was called
ダイヤモンド
"pearl" and the 6.5-point type was called "emerald." ⑨ And, the
パール(真珠)　エメラルド
5.5-point type was called "ruby." ⑩ When using a 10.5-point type,
ルビー　〜するとき(場合)
a typical character size, it was common to put another character
通常の　一般的な
(the original Japanese character "hiragana") on it which was about
もともとの　ひらがな　ほぼ〜

half the size of the kanji. ⑪ So this size has been called "rubi" in
半分　　　　　　　　　　　　　　　　　　　　　　そこで

Japan. ⑫ By the way, there are several kinds of printing besides
ところで　　　　　　　　　　　　　　　　　　　　　　　　　　〜のほかに

letterpress printing: intaglio printing (gravure printing) in which
凹版印刷　　　　　　グラビア印刷

they put printing ink in the recess, stencil printing (silk-screen
凹んだ部分　　　　孔版印刷　　　　シルク・スクリーン

printing) in which they put printing ink in the hole they made on
印刷

the printing plate, and lithographic printing (offset printing) in
印刷版　　　　　　　　　　　平版印刷　　　　　オフセット印刷

which they use the thin printing plate without unevenness. ⑬ At
薄い　　　　　　　　凸凹のない

present, offset printing and on-demand printing are mainstream.
現在では　　　　　　　　　　　オンデマンド印刷　　　　主流

和訳

31. なぜ、漢字に付ける小さな文字のことを印刷用語で「ルビ」というのか？

①文章内のある漢字に対して、その読み方が難しい場合や異なる読み方をする場合などに付ける小さな文字のことを「ルビ」といいます。②通常、タテ書きの場合は文字の右側、ヨコ書きの際は文字の上側に付けます。③もともと、活版印刷から生まれた言葉です。④活版印刷とは、活字を組み合わせてつくった組版を使う印刷のことです。⑤これは、ハンコのような凸凹のある印刷版の凸部分にインクをつけて紙に転写する凸版印刷です。⑥ルビとは、宝石のルビーのことです。⑦昔、英国を中心に活字の大きさを「ポイント」で表わしており、そのサイズによって、別称がありました。⑧たとえば、4.0ポイントなら「ダイヤモンド」、5.0ポイントなら「パール（真珠）」、6.5なら「エメラルド」と呼ばれていました。⑨そして、5.5ポイントのことを「ルビー」と呼んでいました。⑩一般的な文字サイズである10.5ポイントの文字を用いる際には、漢字にその約半分の大きさの別の文字（ひらがな）を付けるのが普通だったのです。⑪それで、日本でそのサイズの文字のことを「ルビ」と呼んだのです。⑫ところで、印刷には活版印刷のほか、凹部分にインクをつける凹版印刷（グラビア印刷）、印刷版に孔をあけてその孔にインクを通す孔版印刷（シルクスクリーン印刷）、凸凹のない薄い印刷版を使う平版印刷（オフセット印刷）などがあります。⑬現在では、オフセット印刷やオンデマンド印刷が主流です。

32. Why are there two paper sizes, size A and size B, only in Japan?

① Do you <u>know</u> there are two <u>paper</u> sizes in <u>Japan</u>: <u>size A</u> and
　　　知る　　　　〜がある　　　　用紙　　　　　　　日本　　　　A判

<u>size B</u>? ② <u>Among</u> these, size A is an international <u>standard</u> which
B判　　　　　〜の中で　　　　　　　国際的な　　　規格

<u>circulates</u> in the world, but size B is a <u>domestic</u> standard used
流通している　　　　　　　　　　　　　　国内の

only in Japan. ③ Size A was <u>originally</u> the size which a <u>German</u>
　　　　　　　　　　　　　　もともと　　　　　　　　　　　　　ドイツの

<u>physicist</u>, <u>Oswald</u>, <u>proposed</u> in the 19th <u>century</u>, and the size of
物理学者　オズワルド　提唱した　　　　　　世紀

<u>one square meter</u> is called AO, and the <u>half</u> size of this is called
1平方メートル　　　　　　　　　　　　　半分

A1, <u>and then</u> the half size of A1 is A2, <u>and so on</u>. ④ <u>On the other</u>
　　さらに　　　　　　　　　　　　　〜などなど　　　　　一方

<u>hand</u>, the size B <u>is based on</u>" <u>Minogami</u>" in Japan, and the size of
　　　　　　　　〜に基づく　　　美濃紙

five square meters is called BO, and the half size of this is B1 and

then the half size of B1 is B2, and so on. ⑤ <u>Around</u> the <u>beginning</u>
　　　　　　　　　　　　　　　　　　　　　　〜の頃　　　　初頭

of the <u>Showa period</u>, there was an <u>increasing</u> <u>momentum</u> that the
　　　昭和時代　　　　　　　　　　　高まりつつある　機運

<u>unified</u> standard size of paper <u>is convenient to</u> print, <u>carry</u>, and
統一した　　　　　　　　　　　　　〜に便利で　　　　　携行する

<u>store</u>. ⑥ <u>Therefore</u>, they <u>investigated</u> the printing <u>circumstances</u>
収納する　　　そこで　　　　　調べた　　　　　　　　　　事情

in <u>various</u> <u>foreign</u> countries, and <u>decided to</u> <u>adopt</u> the size A which
いろいろな　外国の　国々　　　　決めた　　　採用する

<u>had taken root</u> in Germany. ⑦ Among size A, the size A5 was
定着した

<u>close to the</u>" <u>kikuban</u>" (220 millimeters × 150 millimeters) which
〜に近い　　　菊判

had been used as the standard size of <u>magazines</u> in Japan <u>until</u>
　　　　　　　　　　　　　　　　　雑誌　　　　　　　　〜まで

then. ⑧ <u>On the other hand</u>, the "shirokuban" (188 millimeters ×
　　　　その一方で　　　　　　　　　　四六判

128 millimeters) widely used in general for books until then was not good for size A, so there were fears that if only size A would be the standardized paper size, it might cause confusion. ⑨ Then, the newly designed size, size B, which is a vertical and horizontal 1.5 times larger in the square measure like size A, was also adopted because the size B6 is close to the shirokuban.

対応する — not good
懸念 — fears
統一した — standardized
原因となる — cause
混乱 — confusion
新たに — newly
倍の — times

和訳

32. なぜ、日本だけA判・B判の2種類の用紙があるのか？

①日本では、用紙のサイズがA判とB判の2種類あるのをご存知でしょうか。②このうち、A判は世界に流通する国際規格ですが、B判は日本のみの国内規格です。③A判はもともと19世紀末にドイツの物理学者オズワルドが提唱したサイズで、面積が1平方メートルをA0として、その半分がA1、そのまた半分がA2…となっています。④一方、B判は日本の美濃紙をもとにしており、面積が5平方メートルをB0として、その半分がB1、そのまた半分がB2…となっています。⑤昭和の初め頃、紙の統一規格があったほうが、印刷にも携行にも収納にも便利という機運が高まりました。⑥そこで、諸外国の出版事情を調べ、ドイツで定着していたA判を採用することになったのでした。⑦A判の中のA5判が、それまで日本で採用されていた雑誌の標準サイズである菊判（220ミリ×150ミリ）に近いということもありました。⑧その一方で、それまで一般の本のサイズとして広く使われていた四六判（188ミリ×128ミリ）にA判では対応できないため、A判のみに紙の規格を統一するのは混乱を招きかねないという懸念がなされました。⑨そこで考案されたのが、A判と同じタテヨコ比で面積を1.5倍にしたB判なら、B6判が四六判に近いということで、B判もあわせて採用されることになったのでした。

Why do the Japanese call the Kyoto and Osaka areas "Kinki"?

① In dividing Japan into larger districts, we refer to Kyoto, Osaka and its neighboring areas as Kansai or "Kinki." ② The origin of the name "Kansai" will be introduced in item 81 in this book, so you can learn about "Kinki" here. ③ Long ago, the capital of Japan was Kyoto. ④ "Ki" of "Kinki" means the capital. ⑤ They referred to the area around Kyoto, the capital, namely the country near Ki (capital) as "Kinai" or "Kinki." ⑥ Then, what is the difference between Kinki and Kansai of today? ⑦ Kinki indicates two "fu" (metropolitan prefecture), Kyoto-fu and Osaka-fu, and the five prefectures Hyogo, Nara, Shiga, Wakayama and Mie. ⑧ On the other hand, "Kansai" indicates two "fu", Kyoto-fu and Osaka-fu, and the four prefectures Hyogo, Nara, Shiga and Wakayama. ⑨ That is, we call the area including Mie Prefecture "Kinki," and we call the area excluding Mie Prefecture "Kansai."

....

なぜ、京都や大阪などのことを「近畿」と呼ぶのか？

①日本を大きく地域に分けるとき、京都や大阪とその近隣地域を関西または「近畿」と呼びます。②「関西」の名称の由来については、81項で紹介しますので、ここでは、「近畿」について知っておきましょう。③日本の都は昔、京都でした。
④近畿の「畿」とは、都のことです。⑤都である京都の周辺、つまり、畿から近い国を「畿内」とか「近畿」と呼んでいたわけです。⑥それでは、現在の近畿と関西の違いは何でしょうか。⑦近畿は京都府・大阪府・兵庫県・奈良県・滋賀県・和歌山県・三重県の2府5県のことを指します。⑧一方、「関西」は京都府、大阪府、兵庫県、奈良県、滋賀県、和歌山県の2府4県のことです。⑨つまり、三重県を含めると「近畿」となり、三重県を除くと「関西」ということになるわけです。

第**5**章

英語対訳でわかる
ニッポンと日本人の不思議

「伝統」のなぜ？

Wonders of Japan and the Japanese
Traditions

33. Why is "Gengo" (the Japanese Imperial era name) used besides the Christian era in Japan?

① There are two kinds of dating systems are used in Japan.
種類　　　　　年代の数え方　　　　　　日本

② They are the Western dating system and the "Gengo" dating
欧米の　　　　　　　　　　　　　　　　　元号

system. ③ The western dating system is based on the birth year of
～に基づく　　　　誕生　年

Jesus Christ who is called the Savior in Christianity. ④ Not only in
イエス・キリスト　～と呼ばれている　救世主　　キリスト教　　　　　～ばかりでなく～もまた

the Christian blocks, but also in many other countries in the world,
区画

this western system is widely adopted. ⑤ Of course, this is used
広く　　採用されている　　　もちろん

even in Japan. ⑥ On the other hand, in Japan, "Gengo" shows the
…でも　　　　他方

name of the Imperial era. ⑦ "Gengo" has its own dating system
それ自体の～

characteristic of Japan, and a name is given to the particular
特有の　　　　　　　　　　　　　　　　　　　　　特定の

era. ⑧ When the Reformation of Taika was carried out in 645
大化の改新　　　　行なわれた

and Emperor Kotoku succeeded to the throne, the first Gengo was
孝徳天皇　　～を継承した　　　王位　　最初の

named "Taika." ⑨ There are 248 Imperial era names from Taika
大化

to the present Reiwa. ⑩ In modern times, through "the Law of the
現在の　令和　　　　　現代　　～によって　元号法

Imperial Era Name," it is stipulated that only when the new emperor
規定される

succeeds to the throne, a new Imperial era name is established.
制定される

⑪ It is said that there are six conditions to be an Imperial era
…といわれている　　　　　　条件

name: (1) one which should have a meaning that is ideal for the
もの　　～するべきである　　意味　　　　理想的な

Japanese people, (2) one which should consist of two Chinese
日本国民　　　　　　　　　　　　～からなる　　　漢字

characters, (3) one which should be easy to write, (4) one which
～しやすい　書く

should be easy to <u>read</u>, (5) one which has not been used in the <u>past</u>,
　　　　　　　　　読む　　　　　　　　　　　　　　　　　　　　　　　過去
and (6) one which is not <u>commonly</u> used. ⑫ The Imperial era name
　　　　　　　　　　　　　一般に
"Reiwa" which <u>was set up</u> on <u>May 1st</u>, 2019, is <u>taken</u> from the
　　　　　　　　　施行された　　　5月1日　　　　　　採用される
<u>oldest</u> <u>existing</u> Japanese <u>anthology</u>, "<u>Man-yo-shu</u>". ⑬ It is the first
最も古い　現存する　　　　　　名詩選　　　　万葉集
time when an era name <u>comes from</u> Japanese <u>classical literature</u>.
　　　　　　　　　　　　　～に由来する　　　　　　古典文学
⑭ It means that "a new <u>culture</u> <u>is born</u> and <u>grows</u> when the
　　　　　　　　　　　　文化　　生まれる　　　育つ
<u>Japanese</u> <u>come together</u> and <u>care for</u> each other <u>beautifully</u>."
日本人　　寄り添う　　　　　　気づかう　　　　　　　　　美しく

和訳

33. なぜ、西暦年号以外に「元号」があるのか？

①日本では、年号を表わす場合に2種類の数え方があります。②西暦年号と元号（げんごう）です。③西暦年号とは、キリスト教において救世主といわれるイエス・キリストが生まれたとされる年を元年とする数え方です。④キリスト教圏をはじめ、世界の多くの国で採用されている年号の数え方です。⑤もちろん、日本でも採用されています。⑥その一方で、日本では元号でも年号を表わします。⑦元号とは、日本独自の数え方で、特定の年代に付けられる称号のことです。⑧大化（たいか）の改新（かいしん）が645年に行なわれ、孝徳天皇が即位したとき、最初の元号が「大化」と名づけられました。⑨その大化から今度（こんど）の令和（れいわ）まで、248の元号があります。⑩現代では、『元号法』により、皇位の継承（天皇の代替わり）があった場合に限り、新元号を定めると規定されています。⑪元号になる条件は、(1) 国民の理想としての意味を持つ、(2) 漢字2文字である、(3) 書きやすい、(4) 読みやすい、(5) これまでに元号として用いられていない、(6) 俗用されていないの6つがあるとされています。⑫2019年5月1日に施行された「令和」という元号は、現存する日本最古の和歌集『万葉集』の一節から採（と）られました。⑬元号が日本の古典に由来するのは、今回が初めてです。⑭ 意味は、「日本人が寄り添い、互いに美しく気づかうとき、新しい文化が生まれ、育つ」ということです。

34. Why do the Japanese respect the "Emperor" as the national symbol?

① In Japan, since ancient times, there has been a point of view that the Emperor was the ultimate authority of the country. ② In the Meiji period, in the Constitution of the Emperor of Japan, it was provided that the Emperor had the supreme power as the sovereign of the country. ③ In the age of Showa, after the Pacific War (the Second World War), the machinery that the Emperor reigned the country changed to the one that the Japanese people govern the country. ④ The Constitution of Japan was enforced in 1946, and, in article 1, it is prescribed that the Emperor shall be the symbol of the State and of the unity of the people. ⑤ It is also prescribed that the Emperor doesn't have any political powers at all, and carries out only the Emperor's constitutional functions in the Constitution of Japan. ⑥ In the present "Imperial House Act" which is the basic code of the Imperial Household, it is provided that only when the Emperor dies the crown prince will succeed to the throne by heredity. ⑦ However, under the pretext of coming advanced age and losing his health, the former 125th Emperor Akihito abdicated while living and the crown prince

Naruhito succeeded to become the 126th Emperor. ⑧ There are some apprehensions concerning abdication during the Emperor's
恐れ　　　　　　～に関する　　退位　　　　　～の間に
lifetime, as it was pointed out that it may bring political power to
生涯　　…のように　指摘された
the retired Emperor, or the Emperor may be forced to abdicate
退位した　　　　　　　　　　　　　　強制的に～させられる
against his will. ⑨ After the Second World War, this abdication
～に反して　意思
is the first case under the present Constitution, and "A special
　　　　　　　　　　　　　　　　　　　　　　　　　　　　特別な
provision to the Imperial House Law allowing the Abdication of
規定　　　　　　　　　　　　　　　　　　　　～を考慮する
the Emperor" which is permitted to only Emperor Akihito was
　　　　　　　　　　　　　～に認められる
enacted.
施行された

和訳

34. なぜ、「天皇」を国の象徴として敬愛するのか？

①日本には、古来より天皇を国の最高権力者とする考え方がありました。②明治時代には、大日本帝国憲法に天皇は国の元首として、国の統治権を有すると定められていました。③昭和に入り、太平洋戦争後、天皇が国を統治するしくみから国民が統治するしくみに変わりました。④ 1946 年に日本国憲法が制定され、第1条に天皇は日本国および日本国民統合の「象徴」と定められました。⑤天皇は国の政治に関する一切の権限を持たず、憲法が定めた国事行為のみを行なうとも規定されています。⑥皇室に関する基本法典である現在の『皇室典範（こうしつてんぱん）』には、天皇が崩御（ほうぎょ）した場合にのみ、皇太子が世襲（せしゅう）（子孫が継承すること）で即位することが定められています。⑦しかし、高齢や健康悪化を理由に、先の第 125 代天皇明仁（あきひと）の生前退位により、皇太子徳仁（なるひと）が第 126 代天皇に即位しました。⑧生前退位は、天皇が退位後もその地位から政治的な影響力を持つことになるかもしれないという恐れや、本人の意思に反して強制的に天皇が退位させられかねないという恐れがあることが指摘されました。⑨戦後、今の憲法のもとで初めてとなる今回の生前退位に際しては、明仁に限り認められるとする『天皇の退位等に関する皇室典範特例法（しこう）』が施行されました。

35. Why is the Japanese national flag "hinomaru"?

① The Japanese national flag is formally called "Nisshoki" in Japanese, and is also called "Hinomaru" (the Rising Sun Flag).
② "Nissho" is a design in the shape of the sun, and the designed flag is called "Nisshoki". ③ "Hinomaru" means the round sun.
④ Then, why is the sun used for the national flag? ⑤ As it will be introduced the original name of Japan in this book (No. 72), Japan is the country where the sun rises, so it is used for the flag.
⑥ Moreover, it is also said that, for the Japanese, who used to be an agricultural people, the sun was quite important as the object of faith. ⑦ The Japanese national flag was designed as red round mark on a white background. ⑧ The red round mark symbolizes the Sun. ⑨ Then, what does the white background mean?
⑩ One of the reasons is that, during the ancient times in Japan, the combination of the colors, red and white was supposed to bring good luck. ⑪ It is also said that, at the Gempei Gassen (the battle between the Minamoto family [Genji] and the Taira family [Heishi]) (1180-85) in the end of the Heian period, Genji, the winner, used this Hinomaru which is the combination of these two

colors. ⑫ According to "the Law about the National Flag and the
　　　　　　　　　～によれば　　　　　　　　法律　　　～に関する
National Anthem" which was enacted in 1999, it is provided as
国歌　　　　　　　　　　　施行された　　　　　　　　規定されている
follows: (1) the flag is a rectangle whose width is two-thirds of its
次のように　　　　　　　　長方形　　　　　　縦　　　　3分の2
length, (2) the diameter of the "nissho" is three-fifths of its width
横　　　　　　直径　　　　　　　　　　　　5分の3
and is located in the center of the flag, and (3) the background is
　　　～にある　　　　　　中心
white and the nissho is red, and it is symmetrical in both up and
　　　　　　　　　　　　　　　　　　　　対称で　　　　両方　上下
down and left to right positions.
　　　　　左右　　　　位置

和訳

35. なぜ、日本の国旗は「日の丸」なのか？

①日本の国旗は、日本語で正式には「日章旗」と呼ばれ、「日の丸」ともいいます。
② 日章とは太陽をかたどったデザインのことで、そのデザインの旗が日章旗ということです。 ③ 日の丸とは、丸い太陽という意味です。 ④ それでは、なぜ、国旗に太陽が用いられているのでしょうか。 ⑤ 72 項で日本の国名について紹介しますが、太陽がそこから昇る国というところから、国旗に太陽が使われています。 ⑥ また、農耕民族であった日本人にとって、太陽は信仰の対象として、とても大切な存在であったことも挙げられます。 ⑦白地に赤い丸が日本の国旗のデザインです。 ⑧ 赤い丸は太陽です。 ⑨ それでは、白地はいったい何を意味しているのでしょうか。 ⑩ 日本では古来、赤と白の紅白2色の組み合わせは縁起がいいとされてきたことが理由の1つとして挙げられます。
⑪ 平安時代末期の源平合戦（1180 ～ 1185 年）の時、勝者の源氏がこの2つの配色の日の丸の旗を使っていたからともいわれています。 ⑫ 1999 年に施行された「国旗および国歌に関する法律」によれば、次のように規定されています：(1) 旗の形は縦が横3分の2の長さの長方形である、(2) 日章の直径は縦の5分の3、円の中心は旗の中心である、(3) 地色は白色、日章は赤色、上下・左右対称とする。

36. Why do we celebrate children who are seven, five, and three years old ("shichi-go-san") in Japan?

① In Japan, in celebrating the growth of children, those who turn three, five, and seven years old visit a shrine in that year (shichi-go-san-mode) on November 15th. ② Both boys and girls aged three, only boys aged five, and only girls aged seven take part in this festival. ③ In a shrine, we receive "oharai" (purification) in order to avoid disasters, and "norito" (Shinto ritual prayer) is recited by a Shinto priest in order to pray to a Shinto god.
④ This is a ritual celebration of boys and girls who turn three in which the children ,who in earlier times used to keep their heads shaved, begin to grow their hair after this ritual. ⑤ This is a ritual celebration of boys who turn five years old in which they wear a hakama (a man's formal divided skirt). ⑥ This is a ritual celebration in which seven-year-old girls who tied their kimono with a string start to put on a wide sash instead. ⑦ This custom continued among court nobles from the Muromachi period, and in the mid-Edo period, it became common among samurai families and rich merchants, and eventually it took root among ordinary people. ⑧ It is said that the celebration date of November 15th

is related with the day when Tokugawa Tsunayoshi, the fifth
　～と関係する　　　　　　　　　　　徳川綱吉

shogun, prayed for his first son Tokumatsu's health. ⑨ Moreover,
将軍　　 ～を祈る　　　　　長男　　徳松　　　健康　　　　　　ほかに

there is another view that November in the old calendar is the
　　　　 別の　　 説　　　　　　　　　　　旧暦

month when we give thanks to the gods for the autumn harvest,
　　　　　　　 ～に…を感謝する　　　　　　　　　秋の　　　収穫

and seven plus five plus three is 15. ⑩ However, lately, when
　　　　　　足す　　　　　　　　　　　　　しかし　　最近

November 15th falls on a weekday, in many cases, the ceremony
　　　　　　　～にあたる　　平日

will be held on a convenient day around Saturday or Sunday and a
　～に行なわれる　　都合のいい　　　～あたりの　　土曜日　　　日曜日

national holiday.
祝祭日

36. なぜ、「七五三」でお祝いをするのか？

①日本では、子どもの成長を祝って、3歳、5歳、7歳になった年の11月15日に、神社で「七五三詣で」を行ないます。② 3歳は男女とも、5歳は男の子、7歳は女の子だけが行ないます。③ 神社では、災いなどを退けるための「お祓い」を受け、神様にお祈りするための「祝詞」をあげてもらいます。④ 3歳は男女がそれまで剃っていた髪を伸ばし始めるのを祝う儀式です。⑤ 5歳は男の子が袴を身につけるのを祝う儀式です。⑥ 7歳は女の子がそれまで着物を着るとき、紐を結んでいたのにかわり、幅広な帯をつけるようになるのを祝う儀式です。⑦ 室町時代から公家を中心に行なわれてきたもので、それが江戸時代中期になり、武家や裕福な商人の間で広まり、やがて庶民の間でも定着したものです。⑧ 11月15日にお祝いするのは、五代将軍・徳川綱吉が自分の長男である徳松の健康を祈った日に関係しているといいます。⑨ ほかに、旧暦の11月は秋の実りを神様に感謝する月でもあり、七五三を足せば15になるからという説もあります。⑩ ただし、近年では11月15日が平日の場合、その周辺の土日や祝日などで、それぞれの都合がつく日に行なうことが多くなりました。

37. Why do we call an attractive guy an "otoko-mae" (handsome man) or a "nimaime" (good-looking man) in Japanese?

① Originally, the word "ike-men" means a "attractive man." ② It is said that this word is a combination of "iketeru" which means "attractive" in Japanese and "men" meaning a male in English or "men" from "face" in Japanese meaning "facial appearance." ③ In Japanese, there are other expressions such as "otoko-mae" (handsome man) or "nimaime" (good-looking man) which means an "attractive man." ④ If we translate the Japanese word "otoko-mae" word for word, it means the front of a man, but it is not clear why "otoko-mae" implies attractive. ⑤ "Mae" (the front) is a word which comes from Kabuki, a Japanese traditional performance art, and this expresses "action" to move forward. ⑥ It is said that an "otoko-mae" came to mean an attractive man, because the action to move forward was based on the standard of male actors' beauty. ⑦ On the other hand, a "nimaime" doesn't mean the number one, but it means the number two in Japanese. ⑧ In Kabuki, they hung out eight signs in a playhouse, and they wrote an actor's name on each sign. ⑨ On this occasion, they put the leading actor's name on the first sign, the name of the young attractive man plays the

love interest on the second sign, and the name of the clown who
恋愛もの   二枚目の   道化師

makes audience laugh and smile on the third sign. ⑩ Because of
～させる 観客 笑う ほほえむ 三枚目の   ～のため

that, "nimaime" (the second sign) is used to mean an attractive guy
                            使われる ～するために   男

and "sammaime" (the third sign) is used to mean a clumsy man.
                                            ブサイクな

⑪ The leading actor is a skilled entertainer beyond his beauty or
                    熟練した 芸(能)人 ～を超えて 美しさ

ugliness, because he plays various roles as a central actor.
醜さ   いろいろな 役   中心的な

37. なぜ、イケメンを「男前」とか「二枚目」というのか？

①もともと、「イケメン」という言葉は、「ハンサムな男性」という意味です。②「魅力的な」という意味の日本語である「イケてる」と「男性」を意味する英語 (men) または「顔立ち」を意味する日本語 (面) の「メン」が合体してできた言葉ともいわれています。③日本語にはこのほか、「魅力的な男性」という意味の言葉に「男前」とか「二枚目」というのがあります。④「男前」という日本語を直訳すると、「男の前」ということで、なぜ、男の前がハンサムになるのかが判然としません。⑤「前」とは、日本の伝統芸能である歌舞伎の言葉で、前に出る「動き」を表わしています。⑥この前に出る動きが男の役者の美しさの基準だったことから「男前」が魅力的な男性という意味になったといわれています。⑦ 他方、「二枚目」とは、日本語で一番ではなく、二番目という意味です。⑧ 歌舞伎では、芝居小屋に八枚の看板を掲げ、出演する役者のそれぞれの名前を載せます。⑨その際、一枚目の看板に主役の名前、二枚目には男女の恋愛ものを担当する若い魅力的な役者、三枚目には観客を笑わせる道化役の名前を載せました。⑩そんなところから、二枚目が魅力的、三枚目がブサイクの意味で使われています。⑪主役は、中心役者としていろいろな役を演じ分けるので、美醜を超えた芸達者ということになるわけです。

38.

Why is a special skill called the "number eighteen"(jyu-hachi-ban) instead of the number one in Japan?

① In Japan, in performing arts and sports, the artistic skill and
技巧　　　　芸能　　　　　　　スポーツ　　芸術的な　技術
technique which a person is best at is called his/her "number
日本　　　　人　　　　最も得意である　　　　　　　　　　ナンバー・
eighteen" (jyu-hachi-ban). ② You may believe that, if a person is
エイティーン　十八番　　　　　　　　～かもしれない　信じる
best at it, it must be the "number one." ③ The "number eighteen"
　　　　　　～に違いない
doesn't mean the 18th. ④ This is the word which originally comes
　　　　　　　18番目　　　　　　　　言葉　　　もともと　　～に由来する
from Kabuki, a traditional Japanese performance art, in the middle
～から　　　伝統的な　　日本の　　芸能　　　　中期の
of the Edo period. ⑤ This is because Ichikawa Dan-jyuro (the
江戸時代　　　　　　～なので　市川團十郎
seventh) selected 18 plays known as "Kabuki jyu-hachi-ban" (18
七代目　　　～を選定した　演目(種類)　～として知られている　歌舞伎十八番
kabuki plays) from the programs which the Ichikawa family, the
　　　　　　　　　　　演目　　　　　　　市川家
well-known family in the Kabuki world, inherited from generation
名門　　　　　　　　　　　　　　　　　受け継いだ　代々
to generation. ⑥ In Japanese, we write Chinese characters which
　　　　　　　　　日本語で　　　　書く　　漢字
express the "number eighteen" and we pronounce them as they
表現する
are written. ⑦ On the other hand, we sometimes refer to these
　　　　　　その一方で　　　　　　ときどき　　　～のことをいう
Chinese characters as "ohako" which we usually don't read.
　　　　　　　おはこ　　　　　　通常　　　読む
⑧ They called this eighteen "ohako" with a prefix "o" which
～を…と呼んだ　　　　　　　　　　　　接頭辞　　お
expresses politeness and respect, because they carefully kept the
　　　　丁寧　　　　尊敬　　　　　　　　大切に　保管した
scripts of "18 kabuki plays" (kabuki jyu-hachi-ban) in a box (hako).
台本　　　　　　　　　　　　　　　　　　　　　　箱
⑨ There is another view on the origin of the "number eighteen."
　　　　　別の　　説　　　起源

96

⑩ When Amida-nyorai (one Buddha) was practicing to become
阿弥陀如来　　　　一人の仏　　　　修行していた
a Buddha, he swore 48 oaths. ⑪ It is said that this word comes
（誓いなどを）立てた 誓い　　　…といわれている
from a wish which is more welcome than any other : that is, the
願い　　　…よりもっと〜 ありがたい ほかの何か つまり
eighteenth of them relieves those who chant a prayer to Amida
救済する 〜する人 唱える 念仏 〜に対して
Buddha. ⑫ In this view, the number eighteen means the number
説
one. ⑬ Lately, not only in performing arts and sports, but also
最近では 〜ばかりでなく…もまた
in karaoke, we call the song which anyone is best at the number
誰もが
eighteen.

和訳

38. なぜ、得意わざを一番ではなく、「十八番」というのか？

①日本では、芸能やスポーツなどで、最も得意な芸や技のことを「十八番」といいます。② 最も得意ならば、「一番」にちがいないと信じているかもしれません。③「十八番」というのは、十八番目ということではありません。④ これは、もともと江戸時代中期に日本の伝統芸能である歌舞伎から生まれた言葉です。⑤ 歌舞伎の名門である市川家が代々受け継いでいる演目の中から十八種類を、七代目市川団十郎が『歌舞伎十八番』として選定したことによるものです。⑥ 日本語では、「十八番」という数字を表わす漢字を書いて、そのまま数字として読みます。⑦ その一方で、この漢字をふつうでは読まない「おはこ」とも呼びます。⑧『歌舞伎十八番』の台本を箱に入れて大切に保管していたことから、丁寧や尊敬の意味を表わす接頭辞の「お」をつけて、「おはこ」と呼びました。⑨「十八番」の由来には他説もあります。⑩ 阿弥陀如来が仏になるための修行をしているときに、四十八種類の誓いを立てました。⑪ その十八番目が念仏を唱える人は必ず救済するという、何よりもありがたい発願であったことから生まれた言葉だといいます。⑫ この説では、十八番がナンバー・ワンであるという意味です。⑫ 最近では、芸能やスポーツだけでなく、たとえば、カラオケなどで、誰もが得意でよく歌う歌のことも「十八番」などといったりします。

39. Why do we turn "chawan" (teacup) two times to drink tea in a tea party in Japan?

① In the tea ceremony which is also called "cha-no-yu," when we have tea, we drink tea after we turn our chawan (teacup) two times or two and a half times in our palms. ② Why do we do so? ③ A chawan has a part which is called "shoumen" (the front): it is the most flowery painted part if it has a pattern, and it is the best shaped part if it doesn't have a pattern. ④ After the host called "teishu" in the tea ceremony makes tea, he/she puts the chawan facing its front looking from the guest. ⑤ At that time, after the guest holds the chawan up, he/she drinks tea after turning it two times or two and a half times in his/her palms. ⑥ This means that they drink tea showing respect to the teishu by avoiding the best part of the chawan. ⑦ The reason why the guest turns the chawan two times or two and a half times is that, although the number of turns is not important, there is a strong sense to avoid the front of the chawan. ⑧ The direction of turning the chawan (clockwise or counterclockwise) depends on the school of thought. ⑨ The number of sips from one chawan is often said to be three and a half, but it seems the guest doesn't have to do so forcibly. ⑩ After

drinking it up, the guest puts the chawan down facing the front of
the teishu. ⑪ When having tea, Japanese sweets are sometimes
served. ⑫ In that case, the guest eats the sweets before having
tea. ⑬ It is poor etiquette to have tea and the sweets in turn.
⑭ The guest can taste the tea more if he/she has the sweets first,
because sweetness remains in his/her mouth, and the sweets
reduce the tea stimulus to his/her stomach.

和訳

39. なぜ、茶会で二回「茶碗」をまわしてから飲むのか？

①「茶の湯」とも呼ばれる茶道では、お茶をいただくとき、茶碗を手の中で二回とか二回半とかまわしてから飲みます。② なぜ、そうするのでしょうか。③ 茶碗には、絵柄がある場合は一番華やかに絵づけされている部分、絵柄がない場合は一番形がよい部分があり、それを「正面」と呼びます。④「亭主」と呼ばれる茶会のもてなし役は茶を点てると、もてなした客から見て「正面」が前にくるように、茶碗を置きます。⑤ その際、客は茶碗を持つと、手の中で二回ないし二回半まわしてから、茶をいただきます。⑥ これは、亭主に敬意を表わし、茶碗の一番よい部分を避けて飲むという意味があります。⑦ 二回ないし二回半まわすというのは、その回数が大事なのではなく、茶碗の正面を避けるという意味合いが強いのです。⑧ まわす方向も流派によって、右まわしと左まわしがあります。⑨ 飲む回数はよく三口半といわれますが、無理にそうすることはないようです。⑩ 飲み終わると、客は茶碗を亭主から見て正面が向くように戻します。⑪ 茶をいただく際に、和菓子を一緒にすすめられることがあります。⑫ その場合は、茶をいただく前に和菓子を食べます。⑬ 茶と和菓子を交互にいただくのは、マナー違反です。⑭ 先に和菓子をいただくことで口に甘みが残り、茶をよりおいしくいただけるのと、茶による胃への刺激を軽減させるのです。

40. Why do males play "female roles" too in Kabuki in Japan?

① Many foreigners feel it is strange that all the actors are males
外国人(たち)　感じる　　　奇異な　　　　　　　役者　　　男性
in "Kabuki," a traditional Japanese performance art. ② This is
歌舞伎　　伝統的な　　　日本の　　芸能
due to the long history of Kabuki. ③ Izumo-no Okuni, who used
〜による　　長い　歴史　　　　　　出雲阿国　　　　　かつて〜したものだった
to be a Shinto priestess at Izumo Taisha Shrine, organized an
巫女　　　　　　　出雲大社　　　　　組織した
entertainment group and went from place to place to perform.
芸能集団　　　　　　　　行った　各地へ　　　　　芸を演じる
④ The "Kabuki Odori" which they performed in 1603 at Kyoto
かぶき踊り　　　　　　　　演じた
Shijyo no Kawara (riverside) gained popularity. ⑤ It is said
四条の川原　　　　　　　川岸　　（人気などを）博した　人気　　…といわれている
that this is the origin of Kabuki. ⑥ The Kabuki Odori was
始まり
called "Okuni Kabuki," and after that, this became the basis of
阿国歌舞伎　　　　　　　　　　　　　　　〜になった　　基礎
"On-na Kabuki (female kabuki)." ⑦ On-na Kabuki was the style
女歌舞伎　　　　女性の　　　　　　　　　　　　　　　　　流儀
of kabuki in which some female prostitutes (yu-jyo) imitated
売春婦　　　遊女　　真似た
Okuni Kabuki. ⑧ This was also called "Yu-jyo Kabuki." ⑨ They
遊女歌舞伎
performed sensual dances, and they had sex with males after
官能的な　踊り　　　　　　　〜と性交渉をもった
their performances, so this kabuki was prohibited because they
禁止された
would corrupt social morals. ⑩ After this, through the time of
〜するだろう　〜を乱す　風紀　　　　　　　　〜を経て　　　時代
"Wakashu Kabuki" performed by young handsome men and "Yarou
若衆歌舞伎　　　　　　　　若い　ハンサムな　男性
Kabuki" performed by adult males, the prototype of the current
成人した　　　　　原型　　　　　現代の
kabuki performed by only males was born. ⑪ The kabuki plays

performed by Ichikawa Dan-jyuro I (the first) and Sakata Tou-jyuro I (the first) gained popularity and spread like wildfire.
⑫ By the way, the kabuki world is also called "rien" (pear garden) in Japanese. ⑬ This word comes from the fact that Emperor Xuan Zong of the Tang dynasty in China gathered people who were outstanding in performance of song and dance entertainment at pear gardens in the northwestern suburbs of Changan, the capital, and gave them the lessons in singing and dancing.

和訳

40. なぜ、歌舞伎では「女役」も男が演じるのか？

①日本の伝統芸能である「歌舞伎」の役者が全員男性であることに奇異に感じる外国人が多いようです。②これは歌舞伎の長い歴史によるものです。③出雲大社の巫女であったとされる出雲阿国が芸能集団を組織し各地を巡りました。④彼女たちが1603年に京都四条の川原で演じた「かぶき踊り」は人気を博しました。⑤これが歌舞伎の始まりといわれています。⑥そのかぶき踊りは「阿国歌舞伎」と呼ばれ、その後の「女歌舞伎」のもとになりました。⑦女歌舞伎は遊女が阿国歌舞伎を真似たものです。⑧これは、「遊女歌舞伎」とも呼ばれました。⑨彼女たちは扇情的な踊りを演じたり、演目後、男性と性交渉をするなどしたため、風紀を乱すということで禁止になりました。⑩その後、美少年による「若衆歌舞伎」や成年男性による「野郎歌舞伎」などの変遷をたどり、現代の男性だけの歌舞伎の原型が生まれました。⑪初代・市川團十郎や初代・坂田藤十郎が演じた歌舞伎が評判を呼び、人気に火がついたのでした。⑫ところで、歌舞伎界のことを日本語で「梨園」ともいいます。⑬中国・唐の皇帝・玄宗が都である長安の西北郊外にあった梨園に歌舞音曲に秀でた者たちを集めて教習したところから生まれた言葉です。

41. Why do many Shinto shrines have a red "tori-i gate" in Japan?

① It seems that a large number of red "tori-i gates (sembon-tori-i)
　…のようである　　たくさんの～　　　　　　赤い　鳥居(の門)　千本鳥居
in Fushimi-Inari Shrine, Kyoto, which are arranged to overlap with
　伏見稲荷神社　　　京都　　　　　　　　　～するように配列されている　重なる
each other, are popular with foreigners. ② Originally, a tori-i gate
互いに　　　　人気がある　　外国人(たち)　　　もともと
stands at the entrance of the divine space, and this is the border of
立つ　　　　入り口　　　　　　神の　領域　　　　　　　　　境界(線)
the world where human beings live. ③ In the ancient mythology,
　　　　　　　　　　人間　　　　　　　　　　　　　古代の　神話
tradition has it that when Amaterasu O-omikami (Sun Goddess) hid
…という言い伝えがある　　　　　天照大神　　　　太陽の女神　　　　隠れた
in Amano Iwato (Cave of Heaven) and it became completely dark
　天岩戸　　　天国の洞窟　　　　　　　　　　　すっかり　暗い
throughout the country, the people wanted her to come out in one
～のいたる所で　　　　　　　人々　　　～に…させたがった　出てくる　何とかして
way or another, and they put a naganakidori (cock) on the tree at
　　　　　　　　　　　　　～に乗せる　長鳴鳥　　　鶏　　　　　　　木
the gate of Amano Iwato and made it crow. ④ Judging from this
　　　　　　　　　　　　　　～に…させる　鳴く　　　～から判断すると
legend, the view that the place where the cock (tori)was set was
言い伝え　　説　　　　　場所　　　　　　　鳥　　置かれた(→居た)
named "tori-i gate" seems to be influential. ⑤ Many of tori-i gates
名づけられた　　　　　～のようである　有力な
are made of wood and rocks, but in modern times, some of them
～からつくられている　木　　　石　　　　　　現代
are constructed with reinforced concrete. ⑥ The color of the tori-i
建てられている　　　　鉄筋コンクリート　　　　　　　　色
gates is accurately vermilion, but many of them are painted red.
　　　正確には　　　朱色　　　　　　　　　　　　　　塗られている
⑦ This is because it is believed that the red color represents the
　…だからである　　…と信じられている　　　　　　　　　　表わす
sun, fire and our life, and therefore it has the power to avoid evil
太陽　火　　　　生命　　　　それで　　　　　　　　力　　避ける　悪霊
spirits and disasters. ⑧ Besides the red color, white, blue and
　　　　　災厄　　　　　　～のほかに　　　　　　　　白　　青

black are also used. ⑨ The white tori-i gates are not painted
黒　　　　　〜もまた　　　　　　　　　　　　　　　　　　　　　〜でなく…である
white, but mainly the color of bark-stripped wood. ⑩ The white
但し　　主に　　　　　　　樹皮を剥いだ〜
tori-i gates in Izumo Taisha Shrine and Ise Grand Shrine are
　　　　　　　　　　　　　　　　　　　　　　伊勢神宮
famous. ⑪ The way of counting tori-i gates is "ikki, niki…" in
有名な　　　〜の数え方　　　　　　　　　　　　　　一基　二基
Japanese. ⑫ When you pass the tori-i gate, it is advised that you
日本語で　　　　　　　　　　　通る　　　　　　　…と忠告される
must bow once in order to express your feeling of respect to the
おじぎする 一度 〜するために 表現する　　　感情　　　敬意
Shinto gods. ⑬ In addition, it is better for you if you tell your
神様　　　　　あわせて　　　　よりよい　　　　　　　〜を…に伝える
name and address to the gods.

41. なぜ、神社には赤い「鳥居」が立っていることが多いのか？

①京都の伏見稲荷神社にいくつも重なるように立っている赤い「鳥居」（千本鳥居という）が外国人に人気のようです。②そもそも鳥居は、神様の領域への入り口に立っており、人間が住む俗界との境界線になっています。③古代神話には、天照大神が天岩戸に閉じこもり、国中が真っ暗になったとき、なんとか外へ出てきてもらおうと、天岩戸の入り口にあった木に長鳴鳥（鶏）を乗せて鳴かせたという言い伝えがあります。④この言い伝えから、鳥が居たところという意味で、「鳥居」と名づけられたという説が有力なようです。⑤木や石でつくられたものが多く、現代では鉄筋コンクリート製もあります。
⑥鳥居の色は正確には朱色なのですが、赤色が多いです。⑦その理由は、太陽や火、生命を表わす色とされ、悪霊や災厄を退ける力があると信じられているからです。⑧赤色のほかには、白色や青色、黒色などもあります。⑨白色といっても、白い塗料をぬるのではなく、樹皮を剥いた木の色が主です。⑩白色の鳥居は、出雲大社や伊勢神宮が有名です⑪鳥居の数え方は、日本語では「一基、二基……」と数えます。⑫鳥居をくぐるときは、神様に畏敬の念を表わし、必ず一礼してからくぐるようにします。⑬あわせて、名前と住所を神さまに伝えると、さらによいといわれています。

42. Why do sumo wrestlers put on mawashi and tie a topknot in the "o-ozumo" (grand sumo wrestling) in Japan?

① One of the great (大きな) surprises (驚き) to foreigners (外国人(たち)) is the sumo wrestler's (相撲の力士) appearance (いで立ち) in the "o-ozumo" (大相撲) (grand (壮大な) sumo (相撲) wrestling (レスリング)), the Japanese (日本の) national sport (国技). ② Because (〜なので) they wrestle (戦う) in a hairstyle (髪型) that they tie (結ぶ) in a "mage" (髷) (topknot (トプノト)) with his bound (頭頂の結び目) hair (結ばれた〜), and wear (身につける) a "mawashi" (まわし) (loincloth (腰布)). ③ The "topknot" is transmitted (〜から伝承された) from Kanjin-Zumo (勧進相撲) which was held (行なわれた) during the (〜の間じゅう) Edo period (江戸時代) in order to (〜するために) make money (お金) for the construction (建設) and repair (修理) of shrines (神社) and temples (寺院). ④ At that time, not only (〜だけでなく…もまた) sumo wrestlers but also samurai (武士) and townspeople (町人) tied their hair in a topknot (this is also called a "chon-mage" (丁髷)), and it was passed on to (〜へ引き継がれた) the present (現代の) time as it is (そのまま). ⑤ In the Sengoku (戦国) (the civil war (内乱)) period (時代), the warlords (武将) shaved (剃った) the top of their head, in order to (〜するために) keep (〜が…しないようにする) their heads from getting musty (むれる) when they wore a war helmet (兜(←戦闘ヘルメット)) and to prevent (〜が…することを防ぐ) their bangs (前髪) from hanging (たれ下がる). ⑥ This is called "sakayaki" (月代) in Japanese (日本語で). ⑦ However (しかし), in the Edo period (江戸時代), when peace (平和) came, the style of bound hair which laid forward (前に寝かせた) became fashionable (流行した), and it decorated (飾った) the top of their heads which was shaved in the past (過去に). ⑧ This is the so-called (いわゆる) a "chon-mage." ⑨ In grand sumo wrestling, the topknot called "o-oichou" (大銀杏)

104

(big gingko leaf)which looks like a widely opened gingko leaf
　　　　　　　　　　　　～のように見える　　大きく　　開いた　　イチョウ　　葉

is the mainstream hairstyle. ⑩ On the other hand, as for the
　　　　主流の　　　髪型　　　　　　一方　　　　　　　　　～に関しては

"mawashi," they say that the mawashi began to worn in order to
　まわし　　　…といわれている　　　　　　　　　　　身につける

show that they weren't carrying any weapons like a sword at all.
示す　　　　　　　　　　　持っている　　　武器　　　　～などの　　刀　　全く～ない

⑪ In Japanese, we refer to putting on a mawashi as "tightening a
　　日本語で　　～を…と呼ぶ　身につける(こと)　　　　　　　締める(こと)

mawashi." ⑫ Tightening means that it makes both their mind and
　　　　　　　　　　　　意味する　　　　～にさせる　　　　　　　心

body tense, and frees themselves of evil thoughts and dirty hearts.
身体　　緊張した(状態)　　～を…から自由にする　　　　邪悪な　考え　　　　汚れた　心情

和訳

42. なぜ、「大相撲」では力士がまわしをつけて、髷を結うのか？

①外国人がとても驚くことの一つに、日本の国技である大相撲の力士たちのいで立ちがあります。②頭は髪を束ねた「髷」を結い、腰には「まわし」をつけたスタイルで、競技をするからです。③「髷」は、江戸時代に寺社の諸費用を捻出するために開催した勧進相撲からの伝承です。④その頃、力士はもちろん、武士や町人も髷（丁髷ともいう）を結っていて、そのまま現代に引き継がれました。⑤戦国時代には、武将たちは兜をかぶったときに頭がむれないよう、また前髪が落ちてこないように頭頂部を剃っていました。⑥これを「月代」といいます。⑦しかし、江戸時代に入り、平時になると、束ねた髪を前に寝かせた形が流行し、以前なら剃り上げていた頭頂部を飾るようになりました。⑧これがいわゆる「丁髷」といわれるものです。⑨大相撲では、イチョウの葉が大きく開いたような「大銀杏」と呼ばれる髷が主流になっています。

⑩一方、「まわし」ですが、刀などの武器を一切持っていないことを証明するために、なるべくほかのものを身につけないことを示すためにまわしを締め始めたといわれています。⑪日本語では、まわしをつけることを「まわしを締める」といいます。⑫「締める」ことで、心身ともに緊張させ、邪念や汚心をとり去る意味があります。

43. Why do the Japanese feel a sense of beauty in "wabi" and "sabi"?

① It seems to be difficult for foreigners to understand "wabi" and "sabi", the sense of beauty peculiar to the Japanese. ② This is a concept that is not easy to explain even for the Japanese. ③ "Wabi" has meanings of feeling depressed, feeling lonely and helpless, and going down in the world. ④ "Wabi" is a feeling toward something simple and frugal and poor, not glorious, and we consciously try to enrich the heart in something insufficient, not something sufficient. ⑤ It is said that this feeling developed uniting with the tea ceremony (cha-no-yu) at the late Muromachi period. ⑥ In contrast to the tea things made in China called "karamono" which were expensive, the people turned their eyes on commonplace and poor tea things, and Sen-no-Rikyu deepened its flow. ⑦ In the Edo period, Matsuo Basho in the world of haiku (Japanese poems of seventeen [5-7-5] syllables) pursued the "bi" (beauty) which wabi has. ⑧ On the other hand, "sabi" has meanings of getting old and withering. ⑨ "Sabi" is a feeling toward something which becomes old and loses power over time, and we consciously try to find "bi" in something old, not completeness in something new. ⑩ "Sabi",

as well as "wabi," has spread out from the worlds of tea ceremony
~と同様　　　　　　　　　広まった

and haiku. ⑪ Both "wabi" and "sabi" are concepts which are often
　　　　　　　　　~と…の両方　　　　　　　　　　　　　　　　　　　　　

viewed negatively, but the Japanese loves the internal and external
とらえられる ネガティブに　　　　　　　　　　　　　　　　内面的　　　　　外面的

beauty which both of them have.
美

和訳

43. なぜ、日本人は「わび」や「さび」に美意識を感じるのか?

①日本人独特の美意識である「わび」や「さび」は、外国人にはわかりにくいようです。②日本人にとっても、説明しにくい概念です。③「わび」には、気落ちする・心細く無力に思う・落ちぶれるなどの意味があります。④「わび」とは、華やかではなく、質素で素朴、貧相なものに対する感情で、十分ではなく不足しているものの中において、意識的に心を充足させようとします。⑤この感情が室町時代後期に茶の湯と結びついて発展したといわれています。⑥ 高価な「唐物」と呼ばれた中国製の茶道具に対し、ありふれた粗末な茶道具に目が向けられ、千利休などがその流れを深化させました。⑦ 江戸時代には、松尾芭蕉が俳諧の世界で、わびがもつ「美」を追究しました。⑧ 一方、「さび」には、老いる・枯れるという意味があります。⑨「さび」とは、時間の経過によって古いていくものに対する感情で、新しいものの中にある完全さではなく、古いものの中にこそ意識的に美を見いだそうとします。⑩「さび」も「わび」同様、茶の湯や俳諧の世界を中心に広がっていきました。⑪ どちらも、ふつうはネガティブにとらえられがちな概念ですが、それらがもっている内面的かつ外見的な美しさを日本人は愛しているのです。

44. Why does a "bride" wear white clothes (shiro-muku) in Japan?

① In a wedding ceremony, generally [一般に], in the case of a Shinto-style [神前式] wedding, the bride [花嫁] and the groom [花婿] wear [身につける] Japanese clothes [衣服], and in the case of a Church-style [教会式] (Christian-style) [キリスト教(徒)式] wedding, they wear Western [欧米の] clothes. ② As to [～に関しての] Japanese clothes in a Shinto-style wedding, the bride is usually [通常] dressed [着る] head-to-toe [全身] in white [白で] called "shiro-muku" [白無垢] (white clothes), and the groom dresses in a "hakama" [袴] (skirt-like [スカートのような] kimono [着物]) and a black [黒い] "haori" [羽織] with a crest [紋]. ③ Shiro-muku is "clean [穢れのない] and pure [純粋な] white," so it means that […を意味している] the bride in pure white will be changed [変えられる] by the color [色] of the family [家族] (family tradition [伝統] and customs [習慣], etc. [～など]) she marries into [嫁いでいく]. ④ The bride has a tall [高い] and tied-up [結い上げた] hairstyle [髪型] which is called "bunkin-takashimada." [文金高島田] ⑤ The bride covers [～を…でおおう] the bunkin-takashimada with a white cloth which is called "tsuno-kakushi" [角隠し] (something [何か(もの)] to hide [隠す] a horn [角]). ⑥ By hiding "tsuno" (horn) which expresses [表現する] the feeling [感情] of her jealousy [嫉妬] and so on [～など], it means that she will become an obedient [従順で] and graceful [しとやかな] wife [妻]. ⑦ The black haori with a crest which the groom wears means that he has a determined [断固とした～] will [意志] to make [築く] his own home [家庭] which cannot be dyed [染められる] any [どんな～でも] other color. ⑧ In modern times, both the groom and [～の両方]

the bride do "oiro-naoshi" during the wedding reception after the
お色直し 結婚披露宴
wedding ceremony. ⑨ "Oiro-naoshi" means to change colors, and
they change their clothes. ⑩ Originally, only the bride changed
本来
her clothes, and it meant that the bride has an intention to dye her
意思
clothing the color of her future partner's home she marries into.
将来の パートナー
⑪ In changing their clothes, the bride sometimes changes out of
ときどき ～から
shiro-muku into a bright kimono called "iro-uchikake" and both
～へ 色鮮やかな 色打ち掛け
the groom and the bride sometimes change into Western clothing.

和訳

44. なぜ、「花嫁」は白い衣装（白無垢）を着るのか？

①挙式するときの服装は、神前式では和装、教会式では洋装が一般的です。②神前式の和装では、主に新婦は白無垢と呼ばれる着物、新郎は黒い紋付きの羽織と袴です。③白無垢とは、「穢れない純粋な白」ということで、白から結婚する相手の家の色（家風や習慣など）に染まるという意味があります。④新婦の頭は、「文金高島田」と呼ばれる束ねた髪を高く結い上げた髪型にします。⑤その文金高島田の頭に「角隠し」と呼ばれる白い布をかぶせます。⑥嫉妬などの感情を表わす「角」を隠すことで、従順でしとやかな妻になるようにという意味があります。⑦新郎が着る黒い紋付きの羽織は、新郎が確固とした意志で、ほかの何色にも染まらない自分の家庭を築くという意味があります。⑧現代では、神前式の後の披露宴で、新郎・新婦とも、途中で「お色直し」をします。⑨お色直しとは、色を変えるという意味で、衣装を替えます。⑩本来は、新婦のみが行なうもので、衣装が結婚する相手の家の色に染まるという意思を示すという意味があります。⑪お色直しでは、新婦が白無垢から「色打ち掛け」と呼ばれる色鮮やかな着物へ着替えることもありますし、新郎・新婦とも、洋装に替えることもあります。

45. Why is a "kaimyo" (a Buddhist name) given to the people after the death in Japan?

① In Japan, most funeral ceremonies are held in the Buddhist style. ② On that occasion, a "kaimyo" is given to a dead person. ③ The kaimyo is different from the name a dead person had while alive (this is called "zokumyo" at the time of death), and the name is given by a Buddhist priest of one's family temple where his/her ancestors' graves are. ④ Being given the kaimyo is also proof that he/she is a Buddhist. ⑤ Therefore, all the priests entering the Buddhist priesthood have a kaimyo during their lifetime. ⑥ If the dead person doesn't have his/her kaimyo, a Buddhist funeral ceremony and Buddhist services afterward cannot be held, so it is common that he/she is given the kaimyo after the death. ⑦ A kaimyo is not given by his/her family and others in a self-serving manner. ⑧ When we hold a funeral ceremony, we need a plain wood ihai which is made of trees such as paulownia. ⑨ An ihai is a piece of wood needed in order to hold the Buddhist service called "tama-ire" to remove the dead person's soul. ⑩ That is, this piece of wood can be the place where the dead person's soul resides.

⑪ It is common to write the kaimyo and the year, month and day of a person's death on the head of the ihai, and the zokumyo
表
and his/her age at death on its tail. ⑫ The plain white ihai is a
裏
temporary one, so in a Buddhist memorial service 49 days after
仮の　　　　　　　　　　　　　　追悼の
a person's death (shijyu-kunichi), which is thought to be when
四十九日　　　　　　　　　　～と考えられる
the deceased's soul settles down, and other Buddhist services
亡くなった人　　　　落ち着く
afterward, you have to replace the 'plain wood' (ihai) with the real
～しなければならない　～を…と取り替える　　　　　　本物
one.

和訳

45. なぜ、亡くなると、「戒名」をつけてもらうのか？

①日本では、ほとんどの場合、葬儀を仏式で行ないます。② その際には、亡くなった人に「戒名」と呼ばれる名前をつけます。③ 戒名は、生前の名前（亡くなった時点で「俗名」と呼ばれます）と違う名前で、代々お墓がある菩提寺の僧につけてもらいます。④ 戒名を授かるということは、仏教徒であるという証しでもあります。⑤ そのため、仏門に入っている僧はみんな生前から戒名を持っています。⑥ 亡くなった人に戒名がないと、仏式の葬儀やその後の法要が行なえないので、亡くなってから戒名をつけてもらうのが一般的です。⑦ 戒名は、家族などが勝手につけることはできません。⑧ 葬儀を行なう際は、桐などの白木の位牌が必要です。⑨ 位牌とは、亡くなった人の霊魂を移す「魂入れ」という法要を施すための木の板です。⑩ つまり、亡くなった人の霊魂が宿る場所ということになるわけです。⑪ 位牌には、表に戒名と没年月日、裏に俗名と没年齢を書くのが一般的です。⑫ 白木の位牌は仮のものなので、亡くなった人の霊魂の行き先が決まるとされる四十九日とそれ以降の法要の際には、白木に変わる本位牌が必要になります。

46. Why are there so many sects in one Buddhism in Japan?

① Seeing the religious population in Japan, Buddhists and
〜をみると   宗教の   人口   日本   仏教徒
Shintoists account for about half of the population each. ② The
神道の信者   占める   約   〜の半分   それぞれ
remaining are a small number of Christians and others. ③ Among
残り   少数   （〜と）その他   〜の中で
them, Buddhism is divided into many sects. ④ The number of
仏教   〜に分かれている   多くの   宗派   数
representative sects is more than ten as follows : Housou-shu,
代表的な   〜より多い   次のように（…である）   法相宗
Ri-sshu, Kegon-shu, Shingon-shu, Tendai-shu, Jyoudo-shu, Jyoudo-
律宗   華厳宗   真言宗   天台宗   浄土宗   浄土真宗
shinshu, Ji-shu, Nichiren-shu, Rinzai-shu, Soutou-shu, etc.
時宗   日蓮宗   臨済宗   曹洞宗   など
⑤ If someone recites "namiami-dabutsu," he/she is a believer
誰かが   唱える   南無阿弥陀仏   信者
of Jyoudo-shu, Jyoudo-shinshu, or Ji-shu. ⑥ If someone recites

"namumyou-hourengekyou," he/she is a believer of Nichiren-shu.
南無妙法蓮華経
⑦ If someone does "Zazen" (sits in Zen meditation), he/she is a
座禅   座る   禅   瞑想
believer of Rinzai-shu or Soutou-shu. ⑧ Originally, Buddhism,
もともと   仏教
whose founder was Shakamuni (the Gautama Buddha), was
その〜   創始者   釈迦牟尼   ゴータマ・ブッダ
brought to Japan in 538 (552 by other accounts) from India.
〜に伝わった   説   〜から   インド
⑨ Buddhism's teachings were not written down by the Buddha
教え   書き残された
himself. ⑩ Buddhism is what the Buddha's pupils passed down
彼自身   弟子たち   〜を伝える
his teachings several hundred years after his death, transcribing
数百年   書き移す
his teachings into scripture. ⑪ There are many scriptures, and
経典

the content differs from one to another. ⑫ Therefore, many sects
were born in Japanese Buddhism, all depending on the differing
scriptures as a foundation or their interpretations. ⑬ There
are some who believe this is in accordance with the Buddha's
teachings of "chu-do" (the Middle Way) which states we should
not be inclined to one thing.

和訳

46. なぜ、1つの仏教にいろいろな宗派があるのか？

①日本の宗教人口をみてみると、仏教系と神道系がそのほぼ半分ずつを占めています。②残りは、ごく少数のキリスト教系などです。③その中で、仏教系は多くの宗派に分かれています。④法相宗・律宗・華厳宗・真言宗・天台宗・浄土宗・浄土真宗・時宗・日蓮宗・臨済宗・曹洞宗……など、代表的な宗派を挙げても10以上あります。⑤「南無阿弥陀仏」と唱えれば、浄土宗か浄土真宗か時宗です。⑥「南無妙法蓮華経」と唱えれば、日蓮宗です。⑦座禅を組めば、臨済宗や曹洞宗などです。⑧もともと、仏教は釈迦を開祖として、インドから538年（552年説もある）に日本に伝わりました。⑨仏教の教えは、釈迦自身がその教えを書き残したものではありません。⑩釈迦が亡くなったあと数百年をかけて、のちの弟子たちに語り継がれ、経典化されたものです。⑪その経典にはいろいろな種類があり、内容もそれぞれに異なっています。⑫そのため、よりどころにする経典や解釈の違いによって、仏教ではさまざまな宗派が生み出されたのです。⑬一つのことに極端に偏ってはならないとする釈迦の「中道」の教えにかなっているのではないかと考える人もいます。

Why in some places are a Shinto shrine and a temple erected on the same grounds in Japan?

① In spite of the fact that Shinto and Buddhism are different religions, we sometimes see a Shinto shrine and a temple erected on the same grounds. ② Originally, Japan was the country of Shinto which was born from nature worship. ③ Shinto is the religion in which people believe in gods. ④ Before long, when Buddhism was introduced to Japan and Emperor Shoumu protected the religion heavily, the relationship between the gods and the Buddha came to be questioned. ⑤ Then, the following thought was born, because the gods and the Buddha were originally the same : "The gods are the incarnation of the Buddha". ⑥ This is called "honji-suijyaku-setsu." ⑦ "Honji" means "real thing," and "suijyaku" means a "temporary figure" in Japanese. ⑧ Therefore, it seems that, in many cases, a Shinto shrine and a temple were erected together on the same grounds until the Edo period. ⑨ However, the Meiji Government which took over the reigns of political power from the Edo Shogunate placed more importance on Japan Shinto in order to emphasize that the Emperor is the rightful ruler of Japan. ⑩ So,the Meiji Government issued "Shimbutsu-bunri-rei" (Ordinance to Distinguish Shinto and Buddhism), and they decided to erect Shinto shrines and temples separately, but in some places, both of them are still erected together on the same grounds.

....

なぜ、神社と寺が同じ境内にあるところがあるのか？

①神社と寺は、違う宗教のはずなのに、同じ境内に建っているところをよく見かけます。②もともと、日本は自然崇拝から生まれた神道の国でした。③神道とは、神さまを信仰する宗教です。④やがて、日本に仏教が伝わり、聖武天皇が手厚く保護するようになると、神と仏の関係性が問われるようになりました。⑤そこで、もともと神と仏は同じもので、「神は仏が化身したもの」という思想が生まれました。⑥これを「本地垂迹説」といいます。⑦日本語で「本地」とは「本物」、「垂迹」とは「仮の姿」という意味です。⑧そのため、江戸時代まで神社と寺は一緒に建てられることが多かったようです。⑨しかし、江戸幕府から政権を奪回した明治政府は、天皇が正当な日本の支配者であると強調するために、日本神道を重要視しました。⑩そこで、明治政府は「神仏分離令」を出して、神社と寺がばらばらに建てられることになりましたが、いまだに神社と寺が一緒のところもあるというわけです。

英語対訳でわかる
ニッポンと日本人の不思議

「言い伝え」のなぜ？

47. Why is it considered a bad omen to "sleep with the head toward the north" in Japan?

① In Japan, kitamakura, which means to sleep with the head toward the north, is considered a bad omen. ② It is said that this derives from the legend that, when Shakamuni (the Buddha) who is the founder of Buddhism died, he lay down with his head toward the north and with his face toward the west. ③ From long ago in India, it seems that the people used to sleep with their heads toward the north. ④ They say that the reason is because the west is in the direction in which the Land of Happiness might exist. ⑤ Kitamakura originally meant that when a person died, he/she was laid with their heads to the north so that he/she can also go to the Land of Happiness where the Buddha has already gone, and it is good for him/her. ⑥ However, in Japan, since death is hated, kitamakura in life reminds us of death, so it is considered to be a bad omen. ⑦ Instead, when someone dies, we lay out the dead body with the head toward the north. ⑧ But, in modern times, there is also the view that kitamakura is good for health, and the number of people who don't mind it has increased.
⑨ In geophysics, the earth we live on is like a big magnet, and

116

geomagnetism flows from the South Pole toward the North Pole.
地磁気   流れる   南極   ～に向かって   北極

⑩ There is an opinion that kitamakura lets us sleep in line with
              意見   ～に…させる   ～に沿って

this flow, so the blood circulation improves and it is good for
              血行   改善する

health. ⑪ In addition, there is a phrase from Feng Shui: "zukan-
また   言葉   風水   頭寒足熱

sokunetu" (keeping the head cool and the feet warm) in Japanese.
              保って   涼しい   足   温かい

⑫ They say that it is suitable for health to sleep with the head
                    適している

toward the north which is considered cold, and with the feet

toward the south which is considered warm.

和訳

47. なぜ、「北枕」は縁起が悪いとされるのか?

①日本では、北枕、つまり北へ頭を向けて寝るのは、縁起が悪いこととされています。②これは、仏教の開祖である釈迦が亡くなったとき、北へ頭を向け、西へ顔を向けて横になったことによるといわれています。③インドでは昔から北へ頭を向けて寝ていたようです。④西は極楽浄土があるとされる方角だからといわれています。⑤北枕は本来、人が亡くなったら、釈迦が先に行っている極楽浄土へ、自分も同じく行けるということを意味し、いいことです。⑥しかし、日本では、死を忌み嫌うところから、生きているうちの北枕は死を想起させて、縁起が悪いとされています。⑦その代わり、亡くなったときには、遺体を北枕に安置します。⑧ただし、現代では、北枕は健康にいいという説もあり、気にしない人も多くなりました。⑨地球物理学では、われわれが住む地球は、大きな磁石のようになっていて、南極から北極に向けて地磁気が流れています。⑩北枕は、この流れに即して寝ることになるので、血行がよくなり、体にいいという説があります。⑪また、風水には、日本語で「頭寒足熱」という言葉があります。⑫それは、頭を涼しいとされる北に向け、足を温かいとされる南に向けて寝ることで、健康に適っているといわれています。

48. Why is it said that we had better not cut our "nails" at night in Japan?

① From long ago in Japan, it is often said that "if you cut your nails at night, you cannot be present when your parents pass away." ② Why is cutting nails at night related to the parents' death? ③ There are many views on this. ④ In Japanese, we often make a connection between words which have the same pronunciation but have different meanings. ⑤ For instance, there are two kinds of "shi": one of them means "the number four" and the other means "death." ⑥ The pronunciation is the same "shi," so the number "four" is often hated due to this connection. ⑦ Likewise, the Japanese word "yozume" which is short for "yoru tsume wo kiru koto" (cutting nails at night) connects to the another "yozume" which means "dying young," so this was considered a bad omen. ⑧ Namely, if a child dies young, he/she cannot be present when his/her parent passes away. ⑨ And, "yozume" is connected with the important role "yozume" (being on duty at night) which meant to guard the castle at night in the Sengoku period (the age of civil wars). ⑩ Therefore, this "yozume" was not considered good, either. ⑪ The reason why is said to be because the one trusted to

undertake such an important task is too busy to be present when
his/her parent passes away. ⑫ In addition, they say that, long
ago, the lighting was poor at night, and people often mistakenly
cut their fingers (including the thumb) and toes because a small
knife was used as a nail clipper. ⑬ Therefore, due to the wound
made by cutting, some children sometimes passed away earlier
than their parents.

和訳

48. なぜ、夜に「爪」を切ってはいけないといわれるのか？

①昔から日本では、よく「夜に爪を切ると、親の死に目に会えない」といわれました。②なぜ、夜に爪を切ることが親の死と関わるのでしょうか。③これには多くの説があります。④日本語ではしばしば、ある言葉とそれと同じ発音をするが、意味の異なる言葉を関連づけることがあります。⑤たとえば、数字の「4」と「死」があります。⑥発音が同じ「し」なので、その関連からしばしば、数字の「4」は忌み嫌われます。⑦それと同じように、「夜に爪を切る」を縮めた「夜爪」という日本語が早死にするという意味の「世詰め」という別の日本語と関連づけられて、縁起が悪いとされました。⑧つまり、子どもが早死にすると、親が死ぬときにその子どもは親に会えないというわけです。
⑨また、「夜爪」は戦国時代に夜の城の警備をする「夜詰め」と呼ばれる重要な役割と関連づけられています。⑩そのため、この「夜詰め」もよくないとされました。⑪なぜなら、そのような重要な役割を任せられる人は忙しくて、親の死に目にも会えないからだといいます。⑫そのほか、昔、夜は照明が暗く、爪切りに小刀を使っていましたので、誤って指を切ってしまうことも多かったといいます。⑬そのため、切り傷がもとで、子どもが親より早く亡くなることもあったといいます。

49. Why is it said that it is a good omen when a "tea stem" floats upright in a teacup in Japan?

① It is said that tea was brought to Japan from China from the
…といわれている　茶　　　　　～へ持ち込まれた　日本　　　中国
Nara period to the Heian period. ② At the beginning, they used
奈良時代　　　　　平安時代　　　　　　　　始め　　　　　　　～したものだった
to drink tea after drying steamed tea leaves and reducing it to
　飲む　　　　　～(すること)のあと　乾燥させること　蒸した　茶葉　　　　　～を…(ある状態)に変えること
powder called "matcha" and pouring hot water on it. ③ In the
粉　　　　～と呼ばれる　抹茶　　　　　注ぐこと　　湯
latter half of the 16th century, even in the "tea ceremony," which
後半　　　　　～世紀　　　～でさえ　　　　茶の湯
is said to have been perfected by Sen-no-Rikyu, matcha was the
　　　　　完成させた　　　　　千利休
mainstream. ④ Before long, in the Edo period, the custom of
主流　　　　　やがて　　　　　江戸時代　　　　　　習慣
drinking tea had even taken root in the general public. ⑤ The
　　　　　　　　　　定着した　　　　　一般大衆
tea that general citizens drank was not matcha, but it was the tea
　　　　　　　　市民
made from roasted tea leaves. ⑥ The general way of drinking
～からできた　煎じた　　　　　　　　　　　　　　　方法
tea is to put tea leaves in a pot called "kyu-su," and to pour hot
　　　～を…に入れる　　　　　　　　急須
water on it. ⑦ After dissolving the essence of the tea leaves, we
　　　　　　　溶け出すこと　　成分
pour the tea in a "yunomi" (teacup) and drink it. ⑧ Among the
　　　　　　湯飲み　　　　ティーカップ　　　　　　　～の中に
tea leaves which were put in a kyu-su, the part called "chabashira"
　　　　　　　　　　　　　　　　　　　部分　　　　茶柱
was sometimes mixed. ⑨ Chabashira is a part of the stem at the
　ときどき　混じる　　　　　　　　　　　　　　　茎
bottom of tea leaves. ⑩ When we pour tea from a kyu-su into a
下の
teacup, tea leaves are separated by a tea strainer. ⑪ However,
　　　　　　　　分離される　　　茶漉し
some of the tea stems may slip through the net of the tea strainer,
～することがある　かいくぐる　～を通り抜けて　　網の目

and some may get into the tea, though rarely. ⑫ In the tea poured
　　　　　　　　　　 ～の中に入る　　　　～だが　 まれな
into a teacup, tea stems sometimes float. ⑬ This state is called
　　　　　　　　　　　　　　　　　　浮く　　　　 状態
"chabashira-ga-tatsu" (tea stem floats upright in the teacup).
　茶柱が立つ　　　　　　　　　　　　　 真っ直ぐに
⑭ These tea stems are considered a good omen because they give
　　　　　　　　　　 ～とされている　 よい　 兆し
the image of the pillars which support the whole house. ⑮ Lately,
　　連想　　　　　 柱　　　　　　　　 支える　　 全体の　 家屋　　　 最近では
it seems that tea stems rarely go into the tea, because the strainer
…のようである
of a kyu-su has had fine nets.
　　　　　　　　　 （目の）細かい

49. なぜ、「茶柱」が立つと縁起がよいといわれるのか？

①日本のお茶は、奈良時代から平安時代にかけて、中国から入ってきたといわれています。②最初は、蒸した茶葉を乾燥させ、粉にした「抹茶」にお湯を注いで飲むというスタイルでした。③16世紀後半、千利休が完成させたといわれる「茶の湯」でも、抹茶が主流でした。④やがて江戸時代になり、一般庶民にもお茶を飲む習慣が定着します。⑤庶民に飲まれたお茶は抹茶ではなく、茶葉を煎ったものでした。⑥その一般的な飲み方は、「急須」と呼ばれるポットに茶葉を入れて、その上からお湯を注ぎます。⑦茶葉の成分が溶け出してから、お茶を「湯のみ」に注いで飲みます。⑧この急須の中に入れた茶葉の中に「茶柱」と呼ばれる部分が混じることがありました。⑨茶柱というのは、茶葉の下の茎の一部のことです。⑩急須から湯のみにお茶を注ぐとき、茶漉し部分で茶葉が分離されます。⑪ただし、茶漉し部分の網の目をかいくぐって、まれに茶柱がお茶に混じることがあります。⑫湯のみに注いだお茶の中に、この茶柱が浮いていることがあります。⑬この状態のことを「茶柱が立つ」といいます。⑭茶柱の柱が、家を支える柱の連想から縁起がよいといわれています。⑮最近では、急須の茶漉し部分の網の目が細かくなって、茶柱がお茶に混じることが少なくなったようです。

50.

Why is it said to be a good omen if a "swallow" makes a nest in a house in Japan?

① <u>Every</u> <u>spring</u>, <u>swallows</u> <u>come</u> to <u>Japan</u>. ② Swallows are
どの〜も　春　　　ツバメ　　やって来る　　日本

<u>migratory birds</u>, and they <u>stay</u> in Japan from spring to <u>summer</u>.
渡り鳥　　　　　　　　　滞在する　　　　　　　　　　　　夏

③ <u>It seems that</u> they <u>live</u> in <u>warm</u> <u>southern</u> countries <u>during</u> the
…のようである　　　　　棲む　　暖かい　南方の　国々　　　　〜の間ずっと

<u>winter</u> <u>time</u>. ④ Their <u>purposes</u> for coming to Japan are to <u>lay</u>
冬　　時期　　　　　　　目的　　　　　　　　　　　　　　　産む

<u>eggs</u>, <u>raise</u> their <u>children</u> and <u>secure</u> their food (<u>mainly</u> <u>insects</u>).
卵　　育てる　　子ども(たち)　手に入れる　　餌　　主に　　昆虫

⑤ It seems the <u>reason</u> is that in southern countries <u>many</u>
　　　　　　理由　　　　　　　　　　　　　　　　　　　　　多くの

<u>creatures</u> live on insects <u>as well</u>, <u>so</u> it is <u>difficult</u> for swallows to
生き物　　　　　　　　　　同じように　だから　　難しい

live there <u>all year round</u>. ⑥ The swallows that come to Japan
　　　　　　1年中

make a <u>nest</u> <u>in order to</u> lay eggs and raise their children <u>afterward</u>.
　　　巣　　〜するために　　　　　　　　　　　　　　　　　そのあと

⑦ <u>A couple of</u> swallows make a nest <u>together</u> <u>under</u> the <u>eaves</u>,
　一対の　　　　　　　　　　　　　　一緒に　〜の下で　　軒

<u>etc.</u> of a <u>private house</u> using <u>mud</u> and <u>dried-up</u> <u>grass</u> which they
〜など　　民家　　　　　　　　泥　　　乾燥した　　草

<u>brought</u> from the <u>fields</u>. ⑧ They <u>knead</u> the <u>spit</u>, etc. <u>secreted</u> from
持ち込んだ　　　田畑　　　　　　　　練り込む　唾液　　　分泌された

their mouths <u>with</u> the mud and dried-up grass in order to <u>increase</u>
　　　　〜と一緒に　　　　　　　　　　　　　　　　　　　　　　増す

the nest's <u>strength</u>, and <u>pile up</u> the mud <u>little by little</u>, then <u>finally</u>
　　　　強度　　　　　積み上げる　　　　少しずつ　　　　最後には

make a <u>bowl-shaped</u> nest. ⑨ In <u>Japan</u>, <u>it is considered</u> to be a
　　　　お椀状の　　　　　　　　　　日本　　〜とされている

<u>good</u> <u>omen</u> when swallows make a nest under the eaves, etc. of
よい　兆し

one's house. ⑩ <u>It is thought that</u> the house <u>chosen</u> by swallows
　　　　　　　…と考えられている　　　　　　選ばれた

that <u>are good at</u> making nests must <u>mean</u> the house is a good
　　〜が上手である　　　　　　　　　　〜に違いない　意味する

122

environment too. ⑪ And they say that swallows' making a nest
環境　　　～もまた　　　…といわれている

and bringing food for their babies will destroy harmful insects.
　　　　　　　　　　　　赤ちゃん　　　　～を駆除する　害虫

⑫ In addition, when swallows make a nest, much "fun" (bird
　そのほか　　　　　　　　　　　　　　　巣　　　　糞　　　鳥の糞

droppings in Japanese) drop under the nest. ⑬ "Fun" is also called
日本語で　　　　　落ちる　～の下に　　　ふん　　～はまた 呼ばれる

"un" or "unko" in Japanese. ⑭ From long ago, it was thought that
ウン　　ウンコ　日本語で　　　昔から

since "un" (bird droppings) is pronounced in the same way as "un"
…なので　　　　　　　　　　　　発音される　　　同じように

(luck) in Japanese, then "bird droppings" are related to "luck," and
幸運　　　　　　　　　　　　　　　　　　　　～とつながっている

therefore are good omens.
だから

和訳

50. なぜ、「ツバメ」が家に巣をつくると、縁起がよいといわれるのか？

①毎年、春になると、ツバメが日本にやってきます。②ツバメは渡り鳥で、春から夏にかけて日本で過ごすためです。③冬の間は暖かい南の国で暮らしているようです。④日本にやってくる目的は、産卵と子育てとエサ（主に昆虫）の確保です。⑤南の国には、昆虫を同じくエサにしている生き物が多く、1年を通じて暮らしていけないという事情があるようです。⑥日本に渡ってきたツバメは、産卵とその後の子育てのために、巣をつくります。⑦つがいが協力して、民家の軒下などに、田畑などから運んできた泥や枯草を使って、巣をつくります。⑧口から分泌される唾液などを練り込むことで強度を高め、少しずつ泥を重ねていき、お椀状の巣をつくります。⑨日本では、ツバメが自分の家の軒下などに巣をつくるのは、縁起がよいこととされています。⑩巣づくりに長けたツバメが選ぶ家だから、環境がよい家に決まっているからだというわけです。⑪また、ツバメが巣をつくって、赤ちゃんツバメにエサを持ってくることは、害虫駆除にもつながるといいます。⑫そのほか、ツバメが巣をつくると、その下に「ふん」がいっぱい落ちてきます。⑬「ふん」は日本語で「うん」または「うんこ」ともいいます。⑭昔から、「うん」は日本語で別の意味の「運」と同じ発音をするため、「うん」は「運」につながって縁起がよいと、昔から考えられてきました。

51. Why is it not good to step on the "edge of a tatami mat" and a "threshold" in Japan?

① It is good to know a little about "tatami mats" and "thresholds"
~することはよいことである ~について知る 少し 畳 敷居
which are commonly seen in Japanese houses. ② A tatami mat is
一般的に 見られる 日本の 家屋
a matting peculiar to Japan which is put on the floor in a Japanese-
敷物 ~に特有の ~に置かれる 床 和室
style room. ③ A tatami mat is made by sewing "tatami-omote"
縫いつけること 畳表
(tatami facing) woven with "igusa" (rush) on the surface of the straw
表面仕上げ 織り込まれた い草 イグサ 表面 藁製の
base mat called "tatami-doko" (inner part of a tatami mat), and
畳床 内側の部分
covering the edge of the mat with "tatami-beri" (cloth). ④ We nail
おおっている 角 畳縁 布 釘を打ちつける
thin boards to the floor, and spread many tatami mats all over them
薄い 板 敷き詰める ~じゅうに
in accordance with the size of the room. ⑤ On the other hand, a
~に合わせて 一方
threshold is a crosspiece to partition one room to another. ⑥ A ditch
横木 仕切る 部屋と部屋とを 溝
or a lane is installed in order to fit in sliding doors etc., and to open
レーン(列) 設置されている ~するために 適合させる 引き戸 開く
and shut the doors smoothly. ⑦ In Japan, there is a legend from long
閉める スムーズに 日本 ~がある ~に関する言い伝え 昔から
ago about these tatami mats and thresholds. ⑧ The legend says "It's
昔
not good to step on the edge of a tatami mat or a threshold."
踏む
⑨ The edge of a tatami mat, namely "tatami-beri" in Japanese, is
つまり 日本語で
a little thicker than the surface of a tatami mat. ⑩ Therefore, they
~より分厚い そのため
say that this is a warning not to tumble down due to a small step.
…といわれている 戒め ~しないために けつまづいて転ぶ ~のために 少しの 段差
⑪ And, long ago, the noble class sometimes wove the edge of a
昔 高貴な家 ときどき

124

tatami mat with <u>gold</u> <u>threads</u> or <u>silver</u> threads, and sometimes
         金の   糸   銀の

<u>embroidered</u> their <u>family crest</u>, etc. on it. ⑫ <u>For that reason</u> it is
飾りつける   家紋   そのため

also thought that stepping on the edge of a tatami mat is <u>impolite</u>.
                                                  非礼な

⑬ <u>As to</u> a <u>threshold</u>, there are <u>realistic</u> reasons that, if you step
   ～に関しては   現実的な

on it <u>many times</u>, the <u>house building</u> <u>would</u> <u>warp</u> and would
     何回も   家の建てつけ   ～(する)だろう 狂う

be <u>distorted</u>, and the ditch or the lane would <u>be <u>worn away</u></u> by
    ゆがむ   すり減る

friction, and it would become <u>difficult</u> to open and shut the doors.
摩擦   難しい

和訳

51. なぜ、「畳のへり」や「敷居」を踏むのはよくないのか？

①日本の家屋でふつうに見られる「畳」や「敷居」について、少し知っておきましょう。②畳とは、和室の床の上に敷く日本独特の敷き物のことです。③畳床と呼ばれる藁製のマットの表面にイグサで織り込んだ畳表を縫いつけ、その縁を畳縁という布で覆ってつくられています。④床の上に薄板を張り、その上に部屋の大きさに合わせて、何枚も畳を敷き詰めます。⑤一方、敷居とは、部屋と部屋とを仕切るための横木のことです。⑥引き戸などをはめ込み、スムーズに開閉させるために溝やレーンがついています。
⑦日本では、これら畳や敷居に関して、昔から言い伝えがあります。⑧「畳のへりや敷居を踏むのはよくない」という言い伝えです。⑨畳のへり、つまり畳縁は、畳の表面より少し分厚くなっています。⑩そのため、少し段差があるせいで、けつまづいて転ばないようにとの戒めからだといいます。⑪また、昔、高貴な家では、畳縁を金糸や銀糸で織って、家紋などを入れている場合がありました。⑫そのため、その畳縁を踏むことは失礼にあたるとも考えられています。⑬敷居については、何度も踏むと、家の建てつけが狂って歪んでしまうということと、溝やレーンがすり減ってしまい、そのため、戸が開閉しづらくなるという現実的な理由があります。

52. Why are the age 42 for men and 33 for women considered to be of "yaku-doshi" (unlucky ages) in Japan?

① In Japan, there is a belief that both males and females have "yaku-doshi" (unlucky ages). ② Tradition has it that when we turn that particular age, there is a risk of something bad, so we had better take care of ourselves. ③ It is also rule of thumb that massive physical and mental changes will happen, so it serves as a heads-up to us. ④ "Unlucky ages" are calculated by "kazoe-doshi"(the traditional Japanese way of counting age) in Japanese. ⑤ "Kazoe-doshi" is a counting system that considers newborn babies to be one year old at birth, and they are counted as two-year-old children on January 1st the following year, and after that, they get one year older on every January 1st. ⑥ Unlucky years are considered to have three steps: one has to be most careful in "hon-yaku" (the main age of calamity) and one should pay attention during the year before and after one's unlucky age which is called "mae-yaku" and "ato-yaku" respectively. ⑦ Unlucky years occur at different ages for men and women. ⑧ For men, "hon-yaku" ages are 25, 42, and 61, and for women, 19, 33, 37 and 61, using the "kazoe-doshi". ⑨ One year before and after one's unlucky age is called "mae-yaku" and "ato-yaku" respectively.

⑩ Among hon-yaku ages, the age 42 for men and 33 for women
～の中で
are called "tai-yaku" (the most critical year), and we have to be
大厄 注意が必要な
most careful in these years of our lives. ⑪ During unlucky years,
これらの 人生
of course, we have to take care of ourselves, and it is advised that
もちろん …と忠告されている
we avoid moving and building a new house. ⑫ Keeping evil away
（～すること）を避ける 引っ越しする 建てる 新しい 家屋 ～を遠ざける 災厄
is called "yaku-yoke" (avoidance of the bad luck) or "yaku-otoshi"
厄除け 回避 厄落とし
(removal of the bad luck). ⑬ Some of us go to a shrine or a temple
除去 神社 寺院
to ask a Shinto priest or a Buddhist priest to drive off the bad luck.
～に…することを頼む神官 僧侶 ～を追い払う

和訳

52. なぜ、男42歳、女33歳が「厄年」（大厄）とされるのか？

①日本には、男女それぞれに「厄年」という考え方があります。②その年齢になったら、よくないことが起こる危険性があるので、気をつけるようにという言い伝えです。③その年になると、男女とも、肉体的・精神的な変化が大きくなるという、経験則からくる注意喚起でもあります。④厄年は「数え年」でみます。⑤数え年とは、生まれた年を1歳とし、翌年の1月1日から2歳とカウントして、毎年1月1日に1歳ずつ増えていくという数え方です。⑥厄年は3つの段階があり、主たる「本厄」を一番注意し、その前年の「前厄」、その後年の「後厄」も注意をかかさないようにすべきとされています。⑦厄年は、男女によって年齢が異なります。⑧数え年で、男性の本厄は25歳・42歳・61歳、女性の本厄は19歳・33歳・37歳・61歳です。⑨これらの歳の前後1年ずつが前厄と後厄です。⑩本厄のうち、男性は42歳、女性は33歳を「大厄」といい、最も注意が必要とされています。⑪厄年には、健康に注意することはもちろんですが、引っ越しや家の新築は避けるべきだといわれています。⑫厄をはらうことを「厄除け」とか「厄落とし」といいます。⑬厄除けに神社やお寺で祈禱してもらう人もいます

53. Why do the Japanese "ghosts" have no legs?

① In Japan, in summer, dreadful stories get popular in movies, plays, TV dramas and publications. ② It seems that the reasons are that many people neither shut nor lock the doors due to the heat, so it becomes easier for ghosts etc. to sneak in the house, and we forget the heat by having fear of ghosts. ③ In Japan, there are ghosts (yuu-rei), spooks (obake) and Japanese folk monsters (youkai) and so on as representatives of scary things. ④ It is considered that, after someone died, a ghost appears as his/her spirit in human form in this world. ⑤ They say that a spook is what non-human beings have changed into. ⑥ Some say that a Japanese folk monster is the same as a spook, and others explain that a Japanese folk monster can cause unnatural phenomena, but a spook can not. ⑦ Among these, it is said that ghosts have no legs, when we explain about them in detail. ⑧ There are several views on this. ⑨ The ghosts (Oyuki-no-maboroshi) in the picture drawn by Maruyama Oukyo, a famous artist who drew many ghost pictures in the middle of the Edo period, had no legs. ⑩ It is the view that this story spread widely. ⑪ They say that, at that

time, centering on the wealthy people, there was much demand
　　　　～を中心に　　　裕福な　　　　　　　　　　　多くの　　需要

for erotic drawings (shunga) which were obscene pictures
　エロティックな　絵画　　春画　　　　　　　　　　猥褻な

between men and women, and ghost pictures. ⑫ It seems that

the reason why ghost pictures were loved so much is because by
　　　　　　　　　　　　　　　　好まれた　そんなに多く　…という理由からである

hanging something fearful on the wall in the house, the pictures
（～を）掲げること　怖ろしいもの　　　　　壁

kept away real ghosts. ⑬ And, it is also said that we cannot see
遠ざけた　本物の

the ghost's legs blocked by incense smoke from "butsudan" (the
　　　　　　　　妨げられた　　線香　　煙　　　　仏壇

family Buddhist altar) used to perform memorial rites for the dead
家族　仏教の　祭壇　～したものだった とり行なう 追悼の　儀式　亡くなった

persons' spirits.

53. なぜ、日本の「幽霊」には足がないのか？

①日本では、夏になると、映画や演劇、テレビ番組や出版物で怖い話が流行ります。②暑さから家の戸締りがゆるみ、幽霊などが家に入ってきやすい環境になるのと、怖がることで暑さを忘れるといった理由があるようです。③日本では、怖いものの代表として、幽霊・お化け・妖怪などがあります。④幽霊は、人が亡くなった後、その霊魂が人の姿をして、この世に現れるものとされています。⑤お化けは、人以外のものが変化したものといわれます。⑥妖怪は、お化けと同じものだという人もいますが、怪奇現象を起こせることがお化けとの違いだと説明する人もいます。⑦このうち、幽霊をもっと詳しく説明するとき、よく足がないといわれます。⑧これには諸説があります。⑨幽霊画を多く描いた江戸時代中期の人気画家・円山応挙が描いた幽霊（お雪の幻）には足がありませんでした。⑩それが一般に広く伝わったという説です。⑪当時、富裕層を中心に、男女の猥褻画である春画と幽霊画の需要が多かったからのようです。⑫幽霊画がそんなに好まれたのは、怖ろしいものを家に掲げることで、逆に本当の幽霊を近寄らせないという意味があったようです。⑬また、亡くなった人の霊魂を祀る「仏壇」の線香の煙で足が見えないためだともいわれています。

Why is "eggplant" included in the objects considered good luck in Japan in the first dream of a year?

① In Japan, they say that the lucky objects in the first dream of a year are "Fuji for the first, hawk for the second and eggplant for the third."
② "Fuji" means Mt. Fuji, and it is not only the highest mountain in Japan, but also it has the same pronunciation as "fuji" which means "one never dies" in Japanese, so these are considered good luck. ③ They say that, as a hawk flies high in the sky, massive potential can be expected.
④ It is said that an eggplant can lead to descendant prosperity because it bears well. ⑤ And, an eggplant ("nasu[bi]" in Japanese) has the same pronunciation as "nasu" which means "complete" in Japanese, so these are considered good luck. ⑥ As another view, it is also said that, these expressions are used even now, because Tokugawa Ieyasu who laid the foundations of the Edo period liked all three of these.

なぜ、初夢に見ると縁起がよいとされるもののなかに「なすび」が入っているのか？

①日本では、初夢に見ると縁起がよいものとして、「一富士、二鷹、三茄子」といわれています。②「富士」は富士山のことで、日本で一番高い山であるばかりでなく、日本語で「いつまでも死なない」という意味の「不死」と同じ発音であることから縁起がよいとされています。③「鷹」は、大空高く飛び回るというところから、大きな可能性が期待できるとされています。④「茄子」は、実がよくなるところから子孫繁栄につながるといわれています。⑤また、「茄子」は、日本語で「成就する」という意味の「成す」という言葉と発音が同じであることから縁起がよいとされています。⑥ほかの説としては、江戸時代の基礎をつくった徳川家康が、どれも好きだったからともいわれています。

第**7**章

英語対訳でわかる
ニッポンと日本人の不思議

「暮らし」のなぜ？

Wonders of Japan and the Japanese
Ways of Life

Why do the Japanese place "piles of salt" on both sides of an entrance?

① We often see the hardened salt piled in a triangular pyramid shape placed at the front door of a house, in a corner of a room, and at the entrance of a store in the service industry, etc. ② This is called "mori-jio" (piles of salt), and these are placed to "drive off the bad luck" or "get rid of the evil sprits" or as a traditional custom to gather people. ③ Salt is originally considered a valuable item, and it has the power to purify, keep away disasters and attract people. ④ The places in the house that are considered good to put piles of salt are the four directions (east, west, south and north), the omote-kimon (demon's gate) and the ura-kimon (rear demon's gate) looking out from the center of the house. ⑤ The omote-kimon is in the direction of north-northeast and the ura-kimon is in the direction of south-southwest. ⑥ However, as to the four directions and the directions of the omote-kimon and the ura-kimon, we don't know exactly which way they are if we don't comprehend the exact center of the house. ⑦ Therefore, generally, it seems that many people expect the salt to be effective even though they place it freely in the house. ⑧ The good areas

of the house to place the piles of salt besides these are considered
　　　　　　　　　 ～するのに　　　　　　　　 このほか　　　　　 ～とされている

in the entrance, in the washroom, in the kitchen, in the bath-
　　　　 玄関　　　　　　　 トイレ　　　　　　　 台所　　　　　　 風呂

room and so on. ⑨ Placing salt at the entrance prevents evil from
　　　 など　　　　　　　　　　　　　　　　　　　　 ～が…することを妨げる

entering the house. ⑩ The washroom is considered to be in a bad

direction wherever it is, so the piles of salt are indispensable.
　　　　　　 どこにあっても　　　　　　　　　　　　 欠かせない

⑪ It is thought that, since the kitchen and bathroom are the
　　 …と考えられている

places where water and fire live together, the balance of vibrations
　　　　　　　　 水　　　　 火　　 同居する　　　　　 バランス　　　 気

is easy to lose. ⑫ So, the piles of salt are needed.
　～しやすい　 乱れる　　　　　　　　　　　　　　　 必要である

和訳

54. なぜ、玄関わきに「盛り塩」をするのか？

①よく日本では、家の玄関先や部屋の片隅、または客商売のお店の入り口などに、三角錐の形に盛って固めた塩が置いてあります。②これは「盛り塩」と呼ばれ、厄除けや魔除け、または人寄せの風習として置かれています。③塩はもともと貴重品で、穢れを浄化し、災厄を遠ざけ、人を引き寄せる力があるとされています。④家の中で盛り塩を置くのがよい場所は、家の中心から見て東西南北の4方向と、表鬼門と裏鬼門とされています。⑤表鬼門とは北北東の方角、裏鬼門とは南南西の方角になります。⑥ただし、この4方向や表鬼門、裏鬼門の方角については、家の中心を正確に把握していなければ、厳密にはわかりません。⑦なので、一般的には、気軽に盛り塩をして、効果を期待する人が多いようです。⑧盛り塩を置くべき場所としては、このほか、玄関・トイレ・キッチン・お風呂などが挙げられます。⑨玄関に盛り塩を置くことで、外から邪気が入ってくることを防ぎます。⑩トイレは、どこにあっても凶方位とみなされるので、盛り塩は欠かせません。⑪キッチンやお風呂は、水気と火気が同居する場所なので、気のバランスが乱れやすいと考えられています。⑫そのため、盛り塩が必要なのです。

55. Why do the Japanese "pat" a child's head when praising the child?

① When the Japanese praise a child, we say "You're a good boy/girl" while patting his/her head. ② This is quite a common scene in Japan. ③ According to recent research, it seems to be good for one to be patted on his/her head, because patting the head stimulates the brain. ④ It seems that, by patting, the hormone called "oxytocin" is secreted from the posterior lobe of the brain, so the brain condition becomes stabilized and this brings peace to the heart. ⑤ And, since serotonin, called the "happy" hormone," is also secreted, it reduces the sense of uneasiness, increases aggressiveness, and brings good sleep. ⑥ Namely, by being patted on the head, the children have a sense of trust in adults and get motivated to do anything. ⑦ On the other hand, the action of patting the head is one that a person of higher status would do to a person of lower status. ⑧ Therefore, from the point of view that adults show their respect for children, some have doubts about this action. ⑨ Even though it is generally considered a good deed to pat a child's head in Japan, it is regarded as a taboo to do so in some other countries. ⑩ In some Islamic countries, it

134

is thought that the grace from God falls on the head from the sky,
　　　　　　　…と考えられている　　　　恵み　　　神　　降りてくる　　　　　　　空

so touching another's head with the hands is considered to be a
　　触れること　　ほかの人

deed to disturb the grace from God. ⑪ In addition, even in many
　　　　妨害する　　　　　　　　　　　　　　　さらに　　　　でさえ

Southeast Asian countries including Thailand which is a Buddhist
東南アジアの　　　　　　　　　　～を含めて　　タイ（国）　　　　　　　　仏教徒の

country, the head is considered the sacred place where God dwells
　　　　　　　　　　　　　　　　　神聖な　　場所　　　　　　　住む

and we should not touch another's head so carelessly. ⑫ This is a
　　　　　　　　　　　　　　　　　　　　ぞんざいに

problem of faith, so we cannot say which is good or bad.
問題　　　　信仰　　　　　　　　　　　どちらがいいか悪いか

和訳

55. なぜ、子どもをほめるとき、子どもの頭を「なでる」のか？

①日本人は、子どもをほめるとき、その子どもの頭を手でなでながら、「いい子ですね」といったりします。②日本では、よく見かける光景です。③近年の研究によると、頭をなでられることは、脳への刺激になってよいのだそうです。④脳の下垂体後葉から「オキシトシン」と呼ばれるホルモンが分泌され、脳の状態が安定して、心に平穏をもたらすようです。⑤また、「幸せホルモン」と呼ばれるセロトニンも分泌され、不安感が減少して、積極性が増し、よい睡眠をもたらす効果もあるといわれています。⑥つまり、頭をなでられることによって、子どもは大人に対して信頼感を持ち、やる気も出るということです。⑦その一方で、頭をなでるという行為は、立場が上の者が下の者にする行為です。⑧そのため、子どもに敬意を表するという観点からいえば、いかがなものかと主張する人もいます。⑨日本では一般的によいこととされる子どもの頭をなでる行為がタブーとされる国もあります。⑩イスラム教の国では、神からの恵みが天から頭に降りてくると考えられており、頭に手を触れることはその恵みをさえぎる行為だとされています。⑪さらに、仏教国であるタイをはじめ、多くの東南アジアの国でも、頭は神が宿る神聖な場所とされており、安易に触ってはならないとされています。⑫信仰の問題なので、どちらがよい悪いということはいえません。

56. Why are there short-sleeved kimono and long-sleeved kimono for women in Japan?

① For Western and American peoples, kimono is referred to as "the wearing art," and especially the kimono which women wear looks gorgeous and exotic. ② In the past, the kimono was the Japanese national costume, but by westernization of food, clothing and housing associated with the sharp economic growth after World War Ⅱ, the kimono was replaced by Western clothes. ③ Though, there are still many chances especially for women to wear the kimono in ceremonial occasions and at state occasions, etc. ④ There are several types of kimono in accordance to the use, such as "furi-sode" (long-sleeved kimono), "tome-sode" (married woman's formal kimono), "houmon-gi" (semi-ceremonial kimono), and "komon" (fine pattern kimono). ⑤ As to the shapes of kimonos, what foreigners especially wonder about is the length of the sleeves (this is also called "sodetake" [sleeve length]).

⑥ "Furi-sode", a representative of long-sleeved kimono, is generally worn by unmarried women, not by married women. ⑦ It is also said that, in the Edo period, young girls had many chances to take lessons of classical Japanese dance, and those girls in a

long-sleeved kimono looked more <u>beautiful</u>. ⑧ Married women
美しい

generally wear "tome-sode." ⑨ <u>It is considered that</u> the Japanese
…とされている

word "tome" of tome-sode <u>means</u> that the kimono which was worn
言葉 留め 意味する

in their <u>girlhood</u> was <u>shortened</u>. ⑩ <u>It seems that</u> this also <u>followed</u>
少女時代 短く縮められた …のようである 従った

the laws <u>regulating expenditures</u> in the <u>Edo period</u>. ⑪ <u>As to the</u>
経費を規制する法令（→倹約令） 江戸時代 〜について

length of a sleeve, it is generally said that "one's gorgeous kimono

is long-sleeved kimono, and everyday kimono is "short-sleeved

kimono" and "young girls wear long-sleeved kimono, and elderly

women wear short-sleeved kimono,"

和訳

56. なぜ、女性の着物には袖丈が短いものと長いものがあるのか？

①欧米の人たちにとって着物は、「着るアート」とも称され、特に女性が着る着物は、豪華でエキゾチックに見えるようです。②かつては日本の民族衣装ともいうべき着物でしたが、戦後の高度経済成長に伴う衣食住の欧米化によって、洋服にその座をとって代わられました。③とはいえ、冠婚葬祭の行事や公式の場などで、特に女性が着物を着る機会はいまだ多いです。④着物の種類は、「振袖」や「留袖」、「訪問着」、「小紋」など、用途に応じてさまざまあります。⑤着物の形状で、特に外国人が不思議に思うのが、腕部分の袖の長さ（袖丈と呼ぶ）の違いです。⑥袖の長い着物の代表である「振袖」は、未婚女性だけが着て、既婚女性は着ないのが一般的です。⑦これは、江戸時代に若い娘が踊りを習うことが多くなり、長い袖の着物を着たほうが踊りが映えて見えたからともいわれています。⑧既婚女性の場合は、一般的に「留袖」を着ます。⑨留袖の「留」という日本語は、娘時代に着ていた着物を短く詰めたという意味だとされています。⑩江戸時代の倹約令に従ったものでもあったようです。⑪袖の長さについては、一般的に「晴れ着は長く、普段着は短く」「若い人は長く、年配者は短く」といわれています。

57. Why are we apt to take off the "footwear" when entering a house in Japan?

① In a Japanese house, generally, when we enter the entrance, we see a space called "tataki," where we take off our footwear. ② After taking off our footwear at the "tataki," we enter the house from an "agari-kamachi" (a piece of wood at front edge of entranceway floor) which is one step up. ③ Since Japan's climate is high in temperature and humidity, the floor would get humid if we don't make some space under the floor, so one step is fixed between the outside and the inside of a house. ④ As explained in item 24 in this book, the reason why an overwhelming large number of "soto-biraki" doors (out-swinging door) are used for front doors in Japan is to take off our footwear at the tataki. ⑤ This is a device made so that the footwear we take off do not disturb the opening and shutting of the door. ⑥ Since ancient times in Japan, there was a border called a "kekkai" (barrier) between the inside and the outside of a house, and there was a belief that the inside was a sacred place and the outside was an impure place. ⑦ For this reason, they say that when entering the house from outside, the action of taking off the dirty footwear took root. ⑧ And, it is also

said that since there was a custom to sit directly on the floor and
to sleep directly on the futon (mattress) spread on the floor, one
should take off dirty footwear to prevent the floor from getting
dirty. ⑨ It is not only a Japanese custom to remove footwear
after entering the house. ⑩ It seems that South Korea, Indonesia,
Malaysia and Islamic countries have the same custom. ⑪ They
say that this is based on a desire to keep impurities out of the
home.

和訳

57. なぜ、家に入るとき、「履き物」を脱ぐことが多いのか？

①日本の家屋は、一般的に玄関を入ると、「たたき」と呼ばれる履き物を脱ぐ空間があります。②その「たたき」で履き物を脱いでから、一段上がった「上がりかまち」から家の中へ入ります。③日本は高温多湿の気候のため、床の下に空間をつくらないと床が湿気してしまうので、家の中と外の間に段差をつけたのです。④２４項で解説しましたが、日本の玄関のドアが圧倒的に外開きが多いのは、たたきで履き物を脱ぐためです。
⑤脱いだ履き物がドアの開閉の邪魔にならない工夫です。⑥日本では古来、家の内と外で「結界」と呼ばれる境界があり、内は神聖な場所、外は穢れた場所という考え方がありました。⑦このため、外から家の中に入るときは、汚れた履き物を脱ぐという行為が根づいたといわれています。⑧また、床の上に直接すわり、床の上に直接布団を敷いて寝る習慣もあったことから、土足のままでは床が汚れるので、履き物を脱いだほうがいいともいわれています。⑨履き物を脱いで家の中に入るのは、日本だけの習慣ではありません。⑩韓国やインドネシア、マレーシア、イスラム教の国々でも同じようです。
⑪穢れたものを家の中に持ち込まないという考え方からきているといいます。

58. Why are there the Western-style age system and the "traditional Japanese age system" in Japan?

① What kinds of differences are there in counting age between the Western-style age system (man-nenrei), and the traditional Japanese age system" (kazoe-doshi)? ② First of all, in the Western-style age system, newborn babies are considered to be zero years old at birth, and we get one year older on every birthday afterwards. ③ Namely, we will be one-year-old babies on our next birthdays. ④ Next, in the traditional Japanese age system, newborn babies are considered to be one year old at birth, and we are counted as two-year-old children on January 1st (New Year's day) in the following year. ⑤ On every January 1st, we get one year older. ⑥ Why are there two systems of counting age like these? ⑦ In Japan, from long ago, it was common to count our age in the traditional Japanese age system. ⑧ It was decided by law to use the Western-style age system which took effect in 1902. ⑨ Nevertheless, since the traditional Japanese age system was still in use, the national and local governments were obligated to use the "Western-style age system" by the law that took effect again in 1950. ⑩ Since then, when we use the "traditional Japanese age

system," we have to indicate it clearly, and the situation continues
〜しなければならない 示す　　　明確に　　　　　状態　　　　　続いている
up to today. ⑪ The coming-of-age ceremony is held according to
今日まで　　　　　　　成人式　　　　　　　　行なわれる 〜に応じて
the Western-style age system. ⑫ The coming-of-age ceremony
is held every January, so those whose birthdays fall in April to
　　　　　　　　　　　　　　　　　　　　　　　　　　　　〜にあたる　4月
December apply for the ceremony in January the following year.
12月　　　当てはめる
⑬ Those whose birthdays fall in January to March apply for the
ceremony in January that year.

和訳

58. なぜ、満年齢と「数え年」があるのか？

①「満年齢」と「数え年」では、どのような数え方の違いがあるのでしょうか。②まず、満年齢は、生まれたときを0歳とし、次の誕生日がくるたびに1つずつ年齢が増える数え方です。③つまり、生まれた1年後の誕生日に1歳になるわけです。④次に、数え年ですが、生まれたその日がすでに1歳であり、生まれた年の次の年の1月1日（元日）には2歳になるという数え方です。⑤毎年1月1日には1つずつ年齢が増えていくということです。⑥なぜ、このように2通りの年齢の数え方があるのでしょうか。⑦日本では、昔から「数え年」で年齢を数えるのが一般的でした。⑧それが1902年に施行された法律によって、満年齢を使用することが決められました。⑨にもかかわらず、それでも数え年が使われ続けたため、改めて1950年に施行された法律によって、国・地方公共団体の各機関に対して、「満年齢」の使用が義務づけられました。⑩それ以降、「数え年」を使用するときには、そのことを明示するようになり、今日に至っているわけです。⑪成人式は満年齢で行ないます。⑫成人式は毎年1月に行なわれるので、4〜12月に誕生日があたる人は、その年の翌年の1月になります。⑬1〜3月に誕生日があたる人は、その年の1月に成人式を行ないます。

59. Why are "taian," "butsu-metsu," "tomo-biki," and so on, printed in Japanese calendars?

① Looking at Japanese calendars, six phrases which consists of
〜を見ると　　　　日本の　　　　カレンダー　　　　6つの 言葉　　　　　　　〜からなる
two Chinese characters (kanji) are sometimes printed in addition
2つの 中国の 文字　　　　 漢字　　　　　　ときどき 印刷されている 〜に加えて
to the date and days of a week of each month. ② These are
日付　　　　　曜日　　　　　 それぞれの 月
called "roku-you" or "rokki" in Japanese, and the purpose of this
六曜　　　　　　六輝　　　日本語で　　　　　　　　　目的
is to tell the fortune of the day. ③ "Sen-sho" shows good luck in
吉凶を占う　　　　　　　　　　先勝　　　　示す よい 運
the morning, "tomo-biki" shows good luck except noon, "sem-
午前中　　　　友引　　　　　　　　　　　　　〜を除いて 真昼　　　先負
bu" shows good luck in the afternoon, "butsu-metsu" shows bad
　　　　　　　　　　　午後　　　　　　　　　仏滅
luck all day long, "taian" shows good luck all day long, and "sha-
一日中　　　　大安　　　　　　　　　　　　　　　　　　　　　赤口
kkou" shows bad luck except noon. ④ Among these, the days of
taian and tomo-biki are in particular considered good days for
　　　　　　　　　　　　　特に　　　　　〜とされている
celebrations such as a wedding ceremony. ⑤ Tomo-biki means
祝い　　　　　〜などの　　　結婚式　　　　　　　　意味する
"tomo-wo-tsurete-iku" (taking one's friends) in Japanese, and
友を連れて行く　　　　　　　〜を連れて行く 友だち
this day is liked by people, because one shares the happiness
　　　　好まれる　　　　　なぜなら…だからである 〜を…と分かち合う 幸福
of someone's wedding ceremony with other people. ⑥ In the
誰か　　　　　　　　　　　　　　　 ほかの　　人
opposite sense, tomo-biki is disliked because this day is unfit for
逆の　　意味　　　　　　　　嫌われる　　　　　　　　　　向かない
a funeral service. ⑦ This roku-you is repeated on an old calendar
葬式　　　　　　　　　　　　繰り返される　　　旧暦
in the following order: sen-sho → tomo-biki → sem-bu → butsu-
次の　　順序
metsu → taian → sha-kko. ⑧ Moreover, in an old calendar, sen-sho
さらに

starts in January 1st and July 1st, tomo-biki starts in February
始まる
1st and August 1st, sem-bu starts in March 1st and September

1st, butsu-metsu starts in April 1st and October 1st, taian starts

in May 1st and November 1st, and sha-kko starts in June 1st and

December 1st. ⑨ The old calendar is different from one of the
　　　　　　　　　　　　　　　　　　　～と異なる
new calendar called the "solar calendar" which we use at present.
新暦　　　　　　　　　　　　太陽暦　　　　　　　　　　　　　　　現在
⑩ Since the relation between the dates of the old calendar and the
　　　　　　　関係　　～と…の間(の)
new calendar is complex, it is not easy to convert one into another.
　　　　　　　複雑で　　　　　　　　　　　　　換算する　　一方から他方へ

※⑦の「→」は一般的には声に出して読みません。ただ、ごく少数の人は "to" と読む場合があります。

和訳

59. なぜ、日本のカレンダーには「大安」「仏滅」「友引」… などが記されているのか?

①日本のカレンダーを見てみると、各月のそれぞれの日付に曜日とは別で、6種類の漢字2文字があわせて記入されていることがあります。②これらは「六曜(ろくよう)」または「六輝(ろっき)」と呼ばれ、その日の吉凶を占うものです。③「先勝(せんしょう)」は午前中が吉、「友引(ともびき)」は真昼以外が吉、「先負(せんぶ)」は午後が吉、「仏滅(ぶつめつ)」は終日凶、「大安(たいあん)」は終日吉、「赤口(しゃっこう)」は真昼以外が凶を表わしています。④このうち、大安と友引の日は、結婚式などのお祝いをするのに、特によいとされています。⑤友引には、日本語で「友を連れて行く」という意味があり、結婚式の幸せをほかの人とも分かち合うということから好まれます。⑥逆の意味で、友引の日は葬式に向かないとして敬遠されます。⑦この六曜は、旧暦上で、先勝→友引→先負→仏滅→大安→赤口の順に繰り返されます。⑧しかも、旧暦上で1月と7月は先勝、2月と8月は友引、3月と9月は先負、4月と10月は仏滅、5月と11月は大安、6月と12月は赤口から始まるようになっています。⑨旧暦は、現在、われわれが使っている「太陽暦(たいようれき)」と呼ばれる新暦の一種とは異なります。⑩旧暦と新暦の日付の関係は複雑で、簡易に換算はできません。

60. Why do the Japanese do "yubi-kiri" (linking one's pinky fingers) when making a promise?

① In Japan, in our childhood in particular, when we make a
日本　　　　　　　　　幼年時代　　　　　　　特に　　　　　　　約束ごとをする
promise, we often link our pinky finger with another's pinky
しばしば　からめる　　小指　　　　　　　　　他の人
finger. ② This action is called "yubi-kiri." ③ At that time, we recite
指きり　　　　　　　　　　　　　　　　唱える
in unison: "Yubi-kiri gem-man, usotsuitara, hari sembon noo-
声をそろえて　　　　　「指きりげんまん　嘘ついたら　針千本　飲ます」
masu!" (finger cut-off, ten thousand fist-punches, whoever lies has
切る　　　1万(回の)　　　げんこつパンチ　〜する人は誰でも　嘘をつく〜しなければ
to swallow one thousand needles). ④ What is the origin of this
ならない　飲み込む　　　　　　　針　　　　　　　　　　　　起源
action of making a promise by linking pinky fingers, and what
kind of meaning is there in the phrases which we recite in unison?
　　　　　意味　　　　　　　　　　　言葉
⑤ To tell the truth, this action of making a promise linking pinky
実をいうと
fingers has a tragic origin. ⑥ Making a promise linking pinky
悲劇的な
fingers, originally in the Edo period, derived from the fact that a
もともと　　　　江戸時代　　　〜に由来する　　　事実
prostitute cut off her pinky finger for a male customer she fell in
売春婦　　　　　　　　　　　　　　　　男性　顧客　　　〜と恋に落ちた
love with as a proof that she swore her unchanged love to him.
　　　　　証し　　　　誓った　　　変わらない　愛
⑦ It is said that the reason why she cut off her pinky finger is
〜といわれている　理由
that a guilty person in the Muromachi period had the head cut
罪を犯した　　　　　　室町時代　　　　〜を切られた　頭(→首)
off if he was male and had her finger cut off if she was female
as punishment. ⑧ "Gem-man," which the two recite in unison
罰
when they make a promise linking pinky fingers, means "to strike
たたく

144

with a fist ten thousand times." ⑨ The <u>whole</u> meaning is that:
全体の

"I will give you a finger which I cut <u>by myself</u> as a proof of my
自分で

promise. If there is a lie in my <u>mind</u>, you can strike me with a fist
心

ten thousand times. Whoever lies has to swallow one thousand

needles." ⑩ The <u>custom</u> to make a promise linking pinky fingers
習慣

is not <u>found</u> only in Japan. ⑪ <u>It seems that</u> this custom is also
見られる   …のようである

found in <u>South Korea</u>, <u>China</u> and <u>Southeast Asian</u> <u>countries</u>.
韓国   中国   東南アジア   国々

※①「小指」というとき、最近では little finger より、pinky (finger) というほうが一般的です。

和訳

60. なぜ、約束事をするとき、「指きり」をするのか？

①日本では、特に子どもの頃、約束事をするときに、よく自分の手の小指と相手の手の小指をからめます。②この行為は「指きり」と呼ばれています。③その際、「指きりげんまん　嘘ついたら　針千本　飲ます」と、お互いに声をそろえて唱えます。④この指きりにはどんな由来があり、一緒に唱える言葉にはどういう意味があるのでしょうか。⑤じつはこの指きりという行為には、怖ろしいエピソードがあります。⑥指きりは、もともと江戸時代に、遊女が好きになった客の男に対して、自分の変わらない愛情を誓う証として、手の小指を切って渡したことが由来だとされています。⑦なぜ、指を切るのかというと、室町時代に罪を犯した者が、その罰として男は首を、女は指を切られたことによるともいわれています。⑧指きりするときに二人で唱える言葉に出てくる「げんまん」は「ゲンコツで1万回たたく」という意味です。⑨全部の言葉の意味は、「約束の証しに指を切って渡す。その気持ちに偽りがあれば、1万回、ゲンコツでたたいてよい。嘘をついたら、1000本の針を飲まなければならない」というものです。⑩約束事をするときに指きりをする国は、日本だけではありません。⑪韓国や中国、東南アジアでもあるようです。

61.

Why do we say in Japanese "furu" (dump someone else's feelings) and "furareru" (be dumped by someone else) in love?

① It seems that love between men and women is complicated
｜…ようである｜　　　　　愛　　　　　　　　　　　　　　複雑である
in all times and places. ② Whether or not one accepts someone
　すべての　時間　　場所　　　　…かどうか　　　　　ある人　受け入れる　誰かほかの人
else's feelings, or whether or not someone else accepts one's
　気持ち
feelings can be a big problem. ③ In Japanese, we say "furu" (dump
　　　　　　　～がありうる　大きな問題　　　　日本語では　　　　　　　振る　～を（ゴミのように）捨てる
someone else's feelings) when one doesn't accept his/her feelings,

and we say "furareru" (be dumped by someone else) when he/she
　　　　　　　　　振られる
doesn't accept one's feelings. ④ Why do we use the phrases "furu"
　　　　　　　　　　　　　　　　　　　　　　　　　　　　言い方
and "furareru"? ⑤ In the Edo period, it was thought to be vulgar
　　　　　　　　　　　　　江戸時代　　～と考えられていた　　　はしたない
for women to express their feelings. ⑥ Therefore, it is said that,
　　　　　　　　表わす　　　　　　　　　そのため　　…といわれている
at that time, since the young girls' formal clothing was kimono
　当時　　　　　　　　　　　　　　　　　　正装　　　　　　　　　着物
called "furi-sode" (long-sleeved kimono), they used the sleeves of
　　　　　振り袖　　　　　長い袖の　　　　　　　　　　　　袖
kimono to indicate their intention. ⑦ It seems that when a woman
　　　　　示す　　　　　意思
is courted by a man, if she slowly shook her sleeve, it meant that
　求愛される　　　　　　　　ゆっくり　～を振った　　　　意味した
she was interested in him, and if she shook her sleeve quickly,
　～に気があった　　　　　　　　　　　　　　　　　　　　　素早く
it meant that she was not interested in him. ⑧ In this regard, in
　　　　　　　　　　　　　　　　　　　　　これに関して
Japanese, there is also a phrase "sode-ni-suru" (to treat him like a
　　　　　　　　　　　　　　　　　袖にする　　　　扱う　　　～のように
sleeve). ⑨ This means that a woman gives a man cold treatment.
　　　　　　　　　　　　　　　　　　　　　　　　　　　　扱い方
⑩ It seems that this comes from the fact that she drives him away
　　　　　　　　～に由来する　　　事実　　　　　　～を追い払う

by shaking her sleeve, or she treats him like a <u>nuisance</u>, <u>because</u>
邪魔もの　なぜならば〜だからである
the sleeve causes <u>trouble</u> if it <u>moves</u>. ⑪ It is a <u>ridiculous</u> thing if a
〜の原因になる 面倒　　　動く　　　　　　　　　とんでもない
married woman is courted by other man. ⑫ <u>So</u>, a married woman
そのため
wears a <u>tome-sode</u> kimono etc. which have <u>shortened</u> sleeves, and
留め袖　　　　　　　　　　　短く切った
it is said that she <u>doesn't have to</u> indicate her intention with her
〜しなくてよい
sleeve. ⑬ <u>Exactly</u>, this was the <u>testimony</u> of a woman's <u>virtue</u>.
まさに　　　　　　　　証し　　　　　　　　貞淑

和訳

61. なぜ、恋愛で「振る」「振られる」というのか?

①男女の恋愛は、古今東西、一筋縄ではいかないもののようです。②相手の気持ちをこちらが受け入れるかどうか、こちらの気持ちを相手に受け入れてもらえるかどうか、これは大きな問題です。③日本語では、相手の気持ちを受け入れないことを「振る」、こちらの気持ちが受け入れてもらえないことを「振られる」といいます。④なぜ、「振る」「振られる」という言い方をするのでしょうか。⑤江戸時代、女性がはっきりものをいうのは、はしたないことだと思われていました。⑥そのため、当時、若い娘の正装が袖の長い「振袖」と呼ばれる着物だったことから、その袖を自分の意思表示に使ったといいます。⑦男性から求愛されたときに、女性が袖をゆっくり振れば「気がある」、サッと早く振れば「気がない」という意味だったそうです。⑧日本語には、これに関連して「袖にする」という言い方もあります。⑨女性が男性を冷淡にあしらうという意味です。⑩これは、袖を振って追い払うとか、着物の袖は動くと邪魔になることから邪魔もの扱いするというところからきているようです。⑪既婚の女性が、ほかの男性から求愛されるのは、とんでもないことです。⑫そのため、既婚の女性は、袖を短く切った留袖などの着物を着て、袖で意思表示する必要がないようにしたといわれています。⑬まさに、貞淑の証しだったわけです。

62.

Why do many Japanese handle a "mikoshi" (portable shrine) so wildly in which a kami (Shinto God) rides during festivals?

① In Japan, in the festival seasons, the shrine supporters carry
日本　　　　　　　　　　祭り　　　季節　　　　　氏子　　　　　　　　運ぶ
on their shoulders a miniature shrine called "mikoshi," giving the
肩に載せて　　　　　　小型の　　　神社　　　　　神輿
god a ride, and parade down a street in high spirits. ② This is
神　〜を載せる　　　ねり歩く　　　　車道　　威勢よく
one of the annual events in which the god who is usually in the
　　　　　年中の　　行事　　　　　　　　　　　　　ふだんは
shrine rides on the portable shrine, so that he can drive away
　　　　　　　　　　　神輿　　　　　…できるように　　　　　〜を取り払う
disasters and purify the area. ③ After that, the god returns to
災厄　　　　浄化する　　　地域　　　その後　　　　　　　　　〜から戻る
his shrine. ④ The shrine supporters, who carry a portable shrine
on their shoulders, believe in the god enshrined in the shrine in
　　　　　　　　　　〜を信仰する　　　　　祀られた
the town. ⑤ There are some differences depending on the locals.
町　　　　　〜がある　　いくつかの　差異　　　〜によって　　　地域
⑥ In festivals the supporters shake the portable shrines greatly,
　　　　　　　　　　　　　　　　揺さぶる　　　　　　　　　大きく
hit them with each other, splash water on them, and throw them
ぶつけ合う　　互いに　　〜をかける　水　　　　　　　　放り投げる
away. ⑦ Why do they handle the portable shrines so wildly when
なぜ　　　　　　扱う　　　　　　　　　　　そんなに　乱暴に
the god rides in it? ⑧ It is said that this is not a sinful act on any
　　　　　　　　　　…といわれている　　　　罰当たりな　行為　絶対に(〜ではない)
account, but this action enhances the god's mysterious power and
　　　　　　　　行為　　(度合い)を高める　　　神秘的な　　力
contains the people's earnest wish for a good harvest, a big catch
含む　　　　　　　　切なる　願い　　　　豊作　　　　　大漁
and so on. ⑨ What do the shouts such as "Wasshoi! Wasshoi!,"
など　　　　　　　　　　　叫び(声)　〜のような　わっしょい！
"Essa! Essa!" and "Soiya! Soiya!" mean, when they carry the
えっさ！　　　　　　　そいや！　　意味する
portable shrines on their shoulders? ⑩ According to one view,
　　　　　　　　　　　　　　　　　　　〜によれば　　1つの　説

"Wasshoi!" is a shortened expression of the Japanese phrase "wa
wo seou" (we carry peace on our back). ⑪ It seems that "wa"
means Japan, and this phrase expresses the intention of "We unite
bearing Japan together." ⑫ It is considered that "Essa!" comes
from the word "carry" in the Ancient Hebrew language. ⑬ It is
said that "Soiya!" means "shake" in the language of the Ainu (the
natives in Hokkaido).

62. なぜ、神さまの乗り物である「神輿」を乱暴に扱う祭りが多いのか？

①日本では、祭りの季節になると、神さまを乗せた「神輿」と呼ばれる、神社を小さく模した乗り物を氏子が担いで、町内を威勢よくねり歩きます。②これは、ふだん、神社におられる神さまが神輿に乗り、自分の地域の災厄や穢れを取り除いて清めるための年中行事です。③それが終わると、神さまはまた神社へお戻りになるというわけです。④神輿を担ぐ氏子は、その町内の神社に祀られた神さまを信仰する人たちです。⑤地域によって異なります。⑥祭りでは、神輿を大きく揺さぶったり、神輿同士をぶつけ合ったり、神輿に水をかけたり、神輿を放り投げたりします。⑦なぜ、神さまが乗ると、神輿をそんなに乱暴に扱うのでしょうか。⑧これは、決して罰当たりな行為ではなく、神さまの霊威を高め、豊作や大漁などを切に願うという意味が込められているといわれます。⑨神輿を担ぐ際によくかけられる「わっしょい！わっしょい！」や「えっさ！えっさ！」、「そいや！そいや！」などのかけ声には、どんな意味があるのでしょうか。⑩「わっしょい！」は一説によると、「和を背負う」という日本語が短くなった言葉だといわれます。⑪「和」は日本という意味で、「日本を一緒に背負って団結する」という意思を表わしているようです。⑫「えっさ！」は古代ヘブライ語の「運ぶ」という言葉からきているとされています。⑬「そいや！」はアイヌ語で「揺さぶる」という意味だといわれています。

63. Why is one of the eyes of "daruma doll" painted black with Chinese ink when a candidate wins an election etc. in Japan?

① In Japan, we often see a candidate who is elected paint black
日本　　　　しばしば　見かける　候補者　　　　選ばれる　塗る　黒く

with a brush and Chinese ink one of the eyes of a red daruma
筆　　　　　墨　　　　　　　　　　　目　　　　　赤い　だるま人形

doll. ② A daruma doll is a doll copying a Buddhist priest, Daruma,
〜を模している　僧侶

who introduced Buddhism to China from India. ③ This is a round
〜を紹介した　仏教　　　中国　　　インド　　　　　丸い

doll without hands and legs, which is based on the episode of his
〜なし(の)　手　　　足　　　　〜に基づく　エピソード

hands and legs decaying after nine years of severe training in Zen
腐ってしまった　　　　　　　　　厳しい　修行　禅

meditation. ④ In China, there are wooden dolls called "shukoshi"
瞑想(→座禅)　中国　　〜がある　木製の　　　　　酒胡子

which can stand up as soon as they are pushed down. ⑤ In
起き上がる　〜が…するとすぐ　　押し倒される

Japan, there are dolls called "okiagari-koboshi" (a self-righting
起き上がり小法師　　　自分で立て直す〜

doll) which were considered to be made based on the shukoshi
〜とされている

since the Muromachi period. ⑥ They say that a daruma doll
〜以来　室町時代　　　　　　…といわれている

which was made in the Edo period, overlapped with this "okiagari-
江戸時代　　　重なって

koboshi" doll inspired by the daruma's episode. ⑦ At that time,
(励まされて)起こされた　　　　当時

both eyes of a daruma doll were painted black with Chinese ink at
両方の

the beginning, but before we knew it, daruma dolls with two white
初め　　　　いつしか(←それを知る前に)

eyes were being sold. ⑧ It seems that, at first, they could make
売られていた　　…のようである　最初

a wish by painting the left eye of the doll black with Chinese ink,
願いごとをする　　　左の

which was sold as a lucky charm, and they painted the right eye
縁起物　　　　　　　　　　　　　　右の

black when the wish came true. ⑨ Before long, a daruma doll sold
　　　　　　　　かなった　　　　　　　やがて
as a lucky charm in order to win an election, when the first general
　　　　　　　　　　～するために　当選する　　　　　　　最初の　総選挙
election was held in the 3rd year of Shouwa (1928). ⑩ It is said
　　　　行なわれた　　　　昭和3年　　　　　　　　　　　　…といわれている
that, since then, this doll became established as a necessary article
　　　それ以来　　　　　　　確立した　　　　　　　　　必要な　　　品物
in various elections. ⑪ Then, why are daruma dolls commonly
　　いろいろな　　　　　　それでは　　　　　　　　　　　一般的に
painted red? ⑫ It is considered from long ago that the color red
　　　　　　　　…とされている　　昔から
has an effect against evil influence.
　　～に対する効果　　邪悪な　影響

和訳

**63. なぜ、選挙に当選したときなどに、「だるま」の片目に
墨を入れるのか？**

①日本では、選挙で当選が決まった議員が、赤いだるま人形の片目に筆で墨を塗っている光景をよく目にします。②だるま人形は、インドから中国へ仏教を伝えた僧侶・達磨を模してつくられた人形です。③9年間の厳しい座禅の修行から手足が腐ってしまったというエピソードがもとになったとされる、手足のない丸い人形です。④中国には、倒してもすぐ起き上がる構造になっている「酒胡子」と呼ばれる木製人形があります。⑤日本には、室町時代からそれが原型になったとされる「起き上がり小法師」と呼ばれる人形があります。⑥これが達磨のエピソードと重なって、江戸時代につくられたものがだるま人形だといわれています。⑦当時は、初め、両目は墨で塗られていましたが、いつしか両目とも白で売られるようになりました。⑧最初、左目に墨を塗って願かけをし、願いがかなったら、右目に墨を塗るという、縁起ものとして売られるようになったようです。⑨やがて、だるま人形は、日本で最初の総選挙が行なわれた昭和3年（1928）に、当選を招く縁起ものとして販売されました。⑩その後、選挙の必需品として定着するようになったといわれています。⑪それでは、なぜ、だるま人形は、赤が一般的なのでしょうか。⑫赤は、昔から魔除けの効果がある色とされています。

Why do the Japanese call our wives "okusan" or "kamisan"?

① In Japan, we sometimes call our wife or another person's wife "kamisan." ② As to the origin, it is often said that there are two opinions. ③ One of them means "a person is always above others." ④ Because "kami" of "kamisan" means "above" in Japanese. ⑤ This expresses the feeling well that a man praises and fears his wife who is above her husband. ⑥ Another view is that this comes from "yama-no-kami" (god [kami] of mountains [yama]). ⑦ Because "kami" (above) of "kamisan" and "kami" (god) of "yama-no-kami" have the same pronunciation in Japanese. ⑧ For a long time, yama-no-kami has been recognized as a goddess, and she has protected the mountains which were the objects of people's worship, and she has been respected as the ruler of mountains. ⑨ Adult males also regarded their wife as the equivalent existence for the god of mountains. ⑩ By the way, from long ago, it was believed that women were not allowed to enter many mountains, because the goddess, who was the same sex as them, would become jealous.

なぜ、妻のことを「奥さん」とか「かみさん」と呼ぶのか？

①日本では、自分の妻や他人の妻のことを「かみさん」と呼ぶことがあります。②その由来について、2つの説がよくいわれています。③1つは、「上のほうにいる人」という意味です。④日本語で「かみさん」の「かみ」には「上」という意味があるからです。⑤妻を上にいる存在としてあがめ、おそれている感じがよく出ています。⑥もう1つは、「山の神」からきているという説です。⑦日本語で「かみさん」の「かみ」と「山の神」の「神」が同じ発音だからです。⑧昔から山の神は女神とされ、人々の信仰の対象であった山を守り、支配する存在として、畏敬されていました。⑨人間の男たちも妻を山の神と同等の存在とみなしていたのです。⑩ちなみに、昔から女人禁制の山が多かったのは、女性が山に入ると、同性の山の神が嫉妬するからだと信じられていました。

英語対訳でわかる
ニッポンと日本人の不思議

「歳時記」のなぜ？

Wonders of Japan and the Japanese
Seasonal Events

64.

Why do the Japanese send "New Year's cards" at the beginning of a new year?

① <u>It is said that</u> the "nengajyo" (New Year's cards) which we
　…といわれている　　　年賀状　　　　　新年　　　　　　カード

<u>exchange</u> as New Year's <u>greetings</u> on <u>postcards</u> or cards are
交換する　　　　　　　　　　挨拶　　　　ハガキ

a <u>Japanese</u> New Year's <u>tradition</u>. ② <u>However</u>, the <u>number</u> of
日本の　　　　　　　　　伝統　　　　ただし　　　　数

New Year's cards <u>decreases year by year</u>, because <u>electronic</u>
　　　　　　　減っている　年々　　　なぜなら～だからである　電子メール

<u>mail</u> became <u>common</u> etc. ③ <u>It seems that</u>, in <u>Western</u> and
　　　　　一般的な　など　…のようである　　　　西洋の

<u>American</u> countries, <u>there is a custom</u> to exchange <u>Christmas</u>
アメリカの　国々　　　～がある　習慣　　　　　　　クリスマス

cards, but there is no custom to exchange New Year's cards,

because Christmas cards <u>combine</u> Christmas greetings and New
　　　　　　　　　　かね備える

Year's greetings in many <u>cases</u>. ④ In <u>Japan</u>, <u>originally</u>, there has
　　　　　　　　　　　　場合　　　　日本　もともと

been a custom to <u>go around</u> to exchange New Year's greetings
　　　　　　　　訪ねていく

since the <u>Nara period</u>. ⑤ And, in the <u>Heian period</u>, to those
　　　　奈良時代　　　　　　　　平安時代

whom they <u>were not able to</u> exchange greetings with <u>each other</u>
　　　　　～することができなかった　　　　　　　　　お互いに

<u>directly</u> because they <u>lived far away</u>, new year's greetings were
直接に　　　　　　　　住んでいた　遠くに

exchanged <u>in writing</u> <u>instead of</u> <u>in person</u>. ⑥ <u>Before long</u>, in the
　　　　　書くことで　～の代わりに　(本人自身で)直接に　やがて

<u>Early-Modern times</u>, New Year's greetings in writing had become
近世

common. ⑦ <u>Since then</u>, in the <u>Meiji period</u>, the <u>postal</u> <u>system</u> was
　　　　　その後　　　　　明治時代　　　郵便の　制度

<u>established</u>. ⑧ And, when the first postcard was <u>published</u> in
確立された　　　　　　　　　　　　　　　　　　　　発行された

1873, New Year's cards which we exchange <u>cheaply</u> and <u>concisely</u>
　　　　　　　　　　　　　　　　　　　　安く　　　簡潔に

had taken root. ⑨ However, various problems also occurred at
<u>定着した</u>　　　　　　　　<u>いろいろな</u>　<u>問題</u>　<u>〜もまた</u>　<u>発生した</u>

first. ⑩ The number of people who were engaged in the postal
<u>最初</u>　　　<u>数</u>　　　　<u>人々</u>　　　<u>〜に関わった</u>

business was limited, and the amount of New Year's cards were
<u>事業</u>　　<u>限られていた</u>　　　　<u>それで</u>　<u>量</u>

huge, so the delivery of all postal matters had been delayed.
<u>膨大で</u>　<u>それで</u>　<u>配達</u>　　　　<u>郵便物</u>　　　　　　<u>遅れた</u>

⑪ After some trials and errors such as special treatment of New
　　　　　　<u>試行錯誤</u>　　　<u>〜のような</u>　<u>特別扱い</u>

Year's cards only in designated post offices etc., the situation
　　　　　　　　　　<u>指定された</u>　<u>郵便局</u>　　　　　　<u>状態</u>

continues up to today.
<u>〜まで続く</u>　　<u>今日</u>

和訳

64. なぜ、新年の始めに「年賀状」を出すのか？

①郵便はがきやカードによって年始のあいさつを取り交わす年賀状は、日本の新年の風物詩といえます。②ただし、電子メールの普及などにより、その数は年々減ってきています。③欧米では、クリスマスカードがありますが、これでクリスマスと新年のあいさつをかねる場合がほとんどで、年賀状の習慣はないようです。④日本では、もともと、新年に年始のあいさつ回りをする習慣が奈良時代からあったとされています。⑤そして、平安時代には直接あいさつができないような遠方の人に対しては、あいさつ回りに代えて、文書で行なうようになります。⑥やがて、近世に入り、文書による年始のあいさつが一般化していきました。⑦その後、明治時代になり、郵便制度が確立します。⑧そして、１８７３年に郵便はがきが発行されると、安価で簡潔に年始のあいさつができるはがきによる年賀状が定着することになりました。⑨ただし、当初はいろいろ問題も発生しました。⑩郵便事業にかかわる人の数が限られており、年賀状が膨大な量だったために、郵便物全体の配達に遅れが生じたのでした。⑪指定された郵便局のみで年賀状を特別扱いするなど、いろいろ試行錯誤の末、現在に至っています。

65

Why do the Japanese give "New Year's pocket money" to children in the New Year?

① In Japan, in a New Year, adults give their children pocket
日本　　　　　　新年　　　　成人　　　　　　　　　子ども　　　ポケットマネー
money to celebrate the New Year. ② This money is called "otoshi-
祝う　　　　　　　　　　　　　　　　　　　　　　　　　　　　お年玉
dama" (New Year's pocket money) in Japanese. ③ Since ancient
　　　　　　　　　　　　　　　　　日本語で　　　　　　〜以来　　昔
times, in Japan, there was an event which people welcomed
　　　　　　　　　〜があった　　　行事　　　　人々　　迎えた
toshigami-sama (a Shinto god), entertained him, and saw him off
歳神様　　　　　神道　　神　　〜をもてなした　　　　　　　〜を見送った
in a new year. ④ This event was held so (that) they could ask the
　　　　　　　　　　　　　行なわれた　…するために　〜することができる　〜に…することを願む
god to share the happiness and grace of the year with them.
　　〜を…と分かち合う　幸福　　　　恵み
⑤ At that time, they used to offer some "mochi" (rice cakes).
その際　　　　　　〜したものだった　供える　　餅　　　米(の)ケーキ
⑥ After the New Year's event, adults shared some of the mochi
　　　　　　　　　行事
with children. ⑦ This is the prototype of the New Year's pocket
　　　　　　　　　　　　　　原型
money. ⑧ It seems that mochi symbolizes the Shinto god's
　　　　　　…のようである　　　象徴する
spirit, and they called it "toshi-dama" which is a short form of
魂　　　　　　　　　　　年玉　　　　　　　　　　短い　　形
"toshigami-sama-no-tama" in Japanese. ⑨ "Otoshi-dama" is a polite
歳神様の魂　　　　　　　日本語　　　お年玉　　　　　　　丁寧な
expression of "toshi-dama" in Japanese. ⑩ Before long, otoshi-
表現　　　　　　　　　　　　　　　　　　　　　やがて
dama has been changed from mochi to other goods or money.
　　　　　　　　　　　　　　　　　　　ほかの　品物
⑪ It is said that it was not until the high economic growth period
…といわれている　〜になって初めて…した　高度経済成長期
in the Showa period that only money was given as pocket money
昭和時代　　　　　　　　　　　　　　　　〜として
as today. ⑫ As otoshi-dama, a new bill(s) folded in three is put in
現在と同じような〜　〜として　　新しい　札　三つ折りにした　　　入れられる

a New Year's <u>paper</u> <u>bag</u> which is a smaller <u>envelop-shaped bag</u>. ⑬
　　　　　紙(の)　袋　　　　　　　　　　　より小さい　封筒型の

There is no <u>fixed</u> <u>amount</u> of money as otoshi-dama in <u>particular</u>,
~がない　決められた~　額　　　　　　　　　　　　　　　　　　　　特に

but it seems that we <u>should</u> <u>avoid</u> the amount with "four" (shi)
　　　　　　　　~すべきである　~を避ける　　　　　　　　　　　　４　　し

which has the <u>same</u> <u>pronunciation</u> as "<u>death</u>" (shi) in Japanese, so
　　　　　　　~と同じ　発音　　　　　　　　死

we <u>had better not</u> give the amount <u>such as</u> four thousand yen.
　　~しないほうがよい　　　　　　　　　　~のような　4000円

65. なぜ、新年（お正月）に子どもに「お年玉」をあげるのか？

①日本では、お正月になると、大人が子どもに新年を祝って、お金をあげます。②このお金のことを「お年玉」といいます。③古来、日本では、新年に歳神様（としがみさま）をお迎えして、おもてなしし、お見送りする行事がありました。④歳神様からその年の幸福と恵みを分けていただくためです。⑤その際に餅（もち）をお供（そな）えしていました。⑥新年の行事が終わったとき、その餅を子どもに分け与えました。⑦これが「お年玉」の原型です。⑧餅は歳神様の魂（たましい）を象徴しており、日本語の歳神様の魂を略して「年玉（としだま）」と呼んだようです。⑨「お年玉」は日本語で「年玉」をていねいにいったものです。⑩お年玉はやがて餅ではなく、その他の品物やお金に変わっていきました。⑪現在のようなお金のみになったのは、昭和の高度経済成長期に入ってからだといわれています。⑫お年玉は、小さめの封筒型の紙のお年玉袋に、新札を３つ折りにして入れます。⑬特に、金額の決まりはありませんが、日本語の「死」と同じ発音の「４」がつく金額、たとえば４，０００円などは避けたほうがよいようです

66. Why do the Japanese scatter beans in "setsu-bun"?

① According to the Japanese calendars, February 3rd is the day of
~によれば   日本の   カレンダー   2月3日

"setsu-bun." ② Setsu-bun has fallen on February 3rd for these 30
節分   あたっている

years or so, but it sometimes falls on one day before or after this
~くらい   ときどき   この日の前後一日

day depending on the year. ③ In Japan, there are four seasons:
~によっては   季節

spring, summer, fall and winter. ④ According to the calendar, we
春   夏   秋   冬

call the first day of each season, "ri-sshun," "ri-kka," "ri-sshu," and
立春   立夏   立秋

"ri-ttou," respectively. ⑤ The word "setsu-bun" means to divide
立冬   それぞれ   言葉   意味する   分ける

the seasons in Japanese. ⑥ Therefore, originally, setsu-bun was
日本語で   そのため   もともと

the word indicating one day before each season: "ri-sshun," "ri-
~を指している

kka," "ri-sshu," and "ri-ttou" which are the beginning days of the

four seasons. ⑦ It is said that, because "ri-sshun" in which winter
…といわれている   …なので

ends and spring comes is the beginning of a year, and this day
終わる   始まる

was the most important day that people were looking forward to,
もっとも 重要な   楽しみにしていた

they came to call "setsu-bun" the day before "ri-sshun." ⑧ Today,
~するようになった   今日

January 1st is the beginning of a year, but long ago, "ri-sshun" was
昔

the beginning of a year. ⑨ In Japan, there is a custom to scatter
まく

beans on the day of setsu-bun in February every year. ⑩ People
豆   2月   毎年   人々

use roasted soy beans. ⑪ In setsu-bun, people first scatter beans
使う 煎った 大豆

shouting, "Oni wa soto!" (Get devils out of the house!) in Japanese
叫びながら　　　「鬼は外！」　　　～から出ていけ！悪霊　　　　家

toward the outside of the house. ⑫ After that, people close the
～に向かって　外側　　　　　　　　　そのあと　　　　　　閉める

windows and scatter beans shouting "Fuku-wa-uchi!" (Invite
窓　　　　　　　　　　　　　　　　　　　　　「福は内！」　　　～の中へ入っておいで！

happiness into the house!) in Japanese toward the back of the
幸福　　　　　　　　　　　　　　　　　　　　　　　　　（家の）奥

house. ⑬ This action means that, on the day of setsu-bun, people

purify various impurities to conclude the previous year and to
浄化する いろいろな 不純物　　　締めくくる　　前の

welcome a new year.
迎える

和訳

66. なぜ、「節分」に豆をまくのか？

①日本のカレンダーでは、２月３日は「節分」の日です。②ここ３０年間くらいは、ずっと２月３日ですが、年によっては１日前後ズレる場合があります。③日本には、春夏秋冬の４つの季節があります。④暦のうえから、その４つの季節の始まりとされる日をそれぞれ「立春」「立夏」「立秋」「立冬」といいます。⑤「節分」とは、日本語で季節を分けるという意味です。⑥そのため、本来、節分とは、４つの季節が始まる「立春」「立夏」「立秋」「立冬」のそれぞれの日の前日を指す言葉でした。⑦このうち、冬が終わり春が始まる「立春」が１年の始まりとして最も待ち望まれた重要な日であったことから、その前日のことだけを「節分」と呼ぶようになったといわれています。⑧いまは１月１日が新年の始まりですが、昔は「立春」が新年の始まりだったわけです。⑨日本では、毎年２月の節分の日に、豆をまく風習があります。⑩豆は大豆を煎ったものを使います。⑪節分では、まず家の中から外に向かって、「鬼は外！」と叫んで豆をまきます。⑫そのあと、窓を閉めてから家の奥に向かって「福は内！」と叫んで再び豆をまきます。⑬これは、節分の日に、それまでの１年を締めくくり、新たな１年を迎えるために、さまざまな災厄をお祓いするという意味があります。

67.

Why do the Japanese enjoy "cherry blossom viewing" in spring?

① In spring, cherry blossoms are in full bloom proudly
everywhere in Japan. ② At this time of year, almost all Japanese
admire the beauty of the cherry blossoms. ③ Since ancient times,
cherry blossoms have been an important thing to the Japanese.
④ Cherry blossoms are called "sakura" in Japanese, and it is
considered to be a coined word of "sa" which means the god of
rice fields and "kura" which means the place where the god lives.
⑤ That is, the place where the god of the rice fields lives is
thought to be "sakura" (cherry blossoms). ⑥ In the Nara period,
after the continental culture was introduced into Japan from
China, when talking about blossoms, they definitely talked about
plum blossoms, and they were made much of among nobles.
⑦ However, it is said that, in the Heian period, when the Japanese-
style culture (Japan's original national culture) became prime, the
cherry blossoms which were originally the native species in Japan
took the place of the plum blossoms and regained popularity.
⑧ Since then, Toyotomi Hideyoshi (one of the famous Sengoku
warlords who unified Japan) had a grand cherry blossom-viewing

in <u>Kyoto</u>, and the <u>members</u> of the <u>Tokugawa Shogun family</u>
　　京都　　　　　　面々　　　　　　　　　　　　　　　　徳川将軍家

<u>constructed</u> the famous place for cherry-blossom viewing in
造った

Edo. ⑨ <u>Like these</u>, cherry blossoms were <u>heavily</u> <u>protected</u> <u>each</u>
江戸　　こうして　　　　　　　　　　　　　　手厚く　保護された　それぞれの

period, and this <u>continues up to</u> today. ⑩ <u>Some say that</u> the <u>scene</u>
　　　　　　　　～まで続いている　　　　　…という人もいる　　　光景

in which cherry blossoms <u>bloom</u> <u>in a flash</u> and <u>scatter</u> <u>with a good</u>
　　　　　　　　　　　　　　咲く　　パッと　　　　　散る　　サッといさぎよく

<u>grace</u> <u>suits</u> the Japanese <u>sense of beauty</u>. ⑪ <u>Moreover</u>, it is also
　　　　～に適している　　　　　美意識　　　　　　　　また

said that Japanese like <u>(drinking) parties</u>, so they <u>get together</u> for
　　　　　　　　　　　　　酒を飲む～　宴会　　　　　　　集まる

cherry-blossom viewing and <u>enjoy</u> drinking and eating.
　　　　　　　　　　　　　　～することを楽しむ

---

67. なぜ、春になると、「桜」をめでて花見をするのか？

①春になると、日本ではいたる所で、桜が咲きほこります。②この時期、日本人はこぞって、花見をして桜をめでます。③古来、桜は日本人には切っても切れない存在でした。④桜は日本語で「さくら」と呼び、田の神を表わす「さ」と神さまが居る場所を表わす「くら」からできた言葉だといわれています。⑤つまり、田の神が居る場所が桜だということです。⑥それが、奈良時代に入り、中国から大陸文化が入ってくると、花といえば、「梅」のことを指すようになり、貴族たちの間で、もてはやされました。⑦しかし、平安時代に入り、日本ふうの文化（国風文化）が全盛になると、もともと日本の在来種であった桜が梅にとって代わり、人気を盛り返したといいます。⑧それ以降、豊臣秀吉が京都で大規模な桜の花見を行なったり、徳川将軍家の面々が江戸に桜の名所をつくるなどしました。⑨こうして、桜は時代ごとに手厚く保護され、今日にいたっています。⑩パッと花が開いて、サッといさぎよく散っていくさまが日本人の美意識に合っているという人がいます。⑪また、日本人は宴会好きで、花見を目的にみんなで集まって、お酒やごちそうを囲むことが好きだからともいわれます。

68. Why is there a five-colored "streamer" among carp streamers in Japan?

① In Japan, May 5th every year is the national holiday called
日本 ・ 5月5日 ・ 毎年 ・ 祝祭日
"tango-no-sekku," wishing for boys to grow strong and healthy.
端午の節句 ・ 〜が…することを祈念して ・ 成長する ・ 強く ・ 健康に
② Generally, the family with a boy displays a Japanese armor,
一般に ・ 男の子のいる家庭 ・ 飾る ・ 日本の ・ 鎧
a samurai warrior helmet, a sword, and "Gogatsu-ningyo Dolls"
兜(←サムライ戦士のヘルメット) ・ 剣 ・ 五月人形
such as "Kintaro" and "Benkei" who are the symbol of strong
金太郎 ・ 弁慶 ・ シンボル
men. ③ And, we erect a pole in the garden just outside our house
立てる ・ 棒(柱) ・ 庭 ・ まさに(ちょうど) 外側
and decorate it with carp streamers. ④ Carp is the symbol of
飾る ・ 鯉のぼり ・ 象徴
success in life derived from an historical Chinese story about a
立身出世 ・ 〜に由来する ・ 歴史的な ・ 中国の ・ 物語
carp that jumped the waterfall called "Ryumon" and turned into
滝 ・ 竜門 ・ 〜に変身した
a dragon. ⑤ It is common to decorate with "tenkyu" (or kago-
龍 ・ 一般的な ・ 天球 ・ 籠玉
dama), "yaguruma," fukinagashi, magoi, higoi and kogoi from top
矢車 ・ 吹き流し ・ 真鯉 ・ 緋鯉 ・ 子鯉 ・ 上から順に
to bottom on the pole. ⑥ The ball called tenkyu or kagodama is
玉
a mark informing the god that the home has a boy. ⑦ Yaguruma
目印 ・ 〜に伝える ・ 〜がいる
is a windmill which is set as a charm against evils, and there
風車 ・ 付けられている ・ 〜に対するお守り ・ 災厄 ・ 〜がある
is a meaning behind it that fortune comes from all sides. ⑧ In
意味 ・ 〜の裏に ・ 幸運 ・ やってくる ・ すべての 方向
fukinagashi, five colors such as blue (green), red, yellow, white
〜のような ・ 青 ・ 緑 ・ 赤 ・ 黄色 ・ 白
and black (purple) are used, and these express the five elements
黒 ・ 紫 ・ 使われている ・ これら ・ 表現する ・ 要素
such as wood, fire, soil, gold and water which consist of all things
木 ・ 火 ・ 土 ・ 金 ・ 水 ・ 〜からなる

under the Sun. ⑨ It is considered that this is the way of thinking based on "the Theory of Yin-Yang and the Five Elements" in ancient China and it can repel any kind of disasters. ⑩ The black magoi which is decorated under the streamer indicates a father, a red higoi a mother and a blue kogoi a boy, and these represent a whole family.

和訳

68. なぜ、鯉のぼりに5色の「吹き流し」があるのか？

①日本では、毎年5月5日は、男の子の健やかな成長を祈願する「端午の節句」と呼ばれる祝日です。②一般的に、男の子のいる家庭では、家の中に日本式の鎧・兜・刀、「金太郎」や「弁慶」などの「五月人形」を飾ります。③そして、庭先にはポールを立てて、鯉のぼりを飾ります。④鯉は、竜門と呼ばれる滝を昇って、龍に変身したという中国の故事による立身出世の象徴です。⑤ポールの上から順に、天球（または籠玉）・矢車・吹き流し・真鯉・緋鯉・子鯉を飾るのが一般的です。⑥天球または籠玉と呼ばれる玉は、その家に男の子がいることを神さまに知らせる目印です。⑦矢車は、魔除けにつけられた風車で、四方八方から福がくるようにとの意味があります。⑧吹き流しには、青（緑）・赤・黄・白・黒（紫）の5色が使われていて、これは万物を構成する木・火・土・金・水の5つの要素を表わしています。⑨古代中国の「陰陽五行説」からきている考え方で、いかなる災厄をもはね返す力があるとされています。⑩吹き流しの下に飾られている、黒い真鯉は父親、赤い緋鯉は母親、青い子鯉は男の子を意味し、家族全体を表わしています。

69. Why do the Japanese shout "Kagiya!" or "Tamaya!" when watching fireworks?

① Speaking of a summer tradition in Japan, the best thing of all is fireworks. ② "Fireworks" are called "hanabi" and mean "flowers of fire" in Japanese. ③ This also can be called fire art which blooms big just like a flower and scatters in the summer night sky.

④ When these fireworks are set off, the Japanese watchers shout "Kagiya!" or "Tamaya!" ⑤ Though it seems that many Japanese are not apt to shout today, why do Japanese shout so? ⑥ "Kagiya" and "Tamaya" are trading names of fireworks manufacturers who shared the popularity in the Edo period. ⑦ At that time, in the river festival of Ookawa (at present, the Sumida River) at Ryogoku, Kagiya and Tamaya took turns every year in dividing themselves into an upstream and a downstream, and they competed the beauty of fireworks. ⑧ On that occasion, the watchers judged which fireworks were better shouting "Kagiya!" or "Tamaya!"

⑨ It is said that this was the beginning of this action. ⑩ They say that the trading names of "kagi" (key) and "tama" (ball) come from the Inari faith in which people pray for a full harvest of rice and good business. ⑪ It is considered that foxes, messengers of a

god, are enshrined at both sides of an Inari Shrine, and since they
        祀られて   両方   方向   稲荷神社   ～なので

take a key and a ball in their mouth, respectively, they are named
くわえる   口に   それぞれ   ～にちなんで名づけられて

after the foxes' items. ⑫ Depending upon the place, some foxes
        もの(→鍵と玉)   ～によって   場所

take a roll (makimono) or a bundle of rice plants instead of a key
    巻いて作ったもの 巻物   一束の～   稲   ～の代わりに

or a ball, but generally they take a key and a ball. ⑬ Nowadays,
            一般的に   今日

fireworks which started in the river festival of Ookawa at Ryogoku

in the Edo period light up the summer night sky every year in
                    彩った

Tokyo as Sumida River's Fireworks Display.
東京   花火大会

和訳

69．なぜ、花火を見るとき、「かぎや～」「たまや～」というのか？

①日本の夏の風物詩といえば、なんといっても「花火」です。②「花火」は、「はなび」と呼ばれ、日本語で「火の花」を意味します。③夏の夜空に、まさに花のように大きく咲いて散っていく火のアートともいえるものです。④この花火が打ち上がると、日本人の観客は「かぎや～」「たまや～」と叫びます。⑤今では、それほど多くはないようですが、なぜ、そのように叫ぶのでしょうか。⑥「かぎや（鍵屋）」と「たまや（玉屋）」は、江戸時代に人気を二分した花火師の屋号です。⑦当時、両国の大川（現在の隅田川）の川開きのとき、年ごとに交代で川の上流と下流に分かれて、鍵屋と玉屋が花火の美しさを競いました。⑧その際、観客は「かぎや～」「たまや～」と叫んで、どちらの花火がよいかを判定しました。⑨これが、その始まりといわれています。⑩屋号の「鍵」と「玉」は、米の豊作や商売繁盛を願う稲荷信仰からきているといわれています。⑪稲荷神社には両側に神の使いであるキツネが祀られていて、その口にそれぞれ鍵と玉をくわえていることから、狐のそれらにちなんで名前がつけられたとされています。⑫所によっては、鍵や玉の代わりに巻き物や稲の束をくわえているキツネもいますが、鍵と玉が一般的です。⑬江戸時代に始まった両国・大川の川開きの花火は、今では隅田川花火大会として、毎年、東京の夏の夜を彩っています。

70. Why do the Japanese hold a memorial service for our ancestors during "o-bon"?

① Every summer in Japan, there is a custom to hold a memorial service for one's ancestors. ② It is considered that ancestral souls, which exist in the other world at this time of year, come back to the world where they used to live during their life. ③ Formally, it is "urabon-e" in Buddhist terms and it is called "o-bon" for short. ④ The period of o-bon is supposed to be for four days around July 15th according to the old calendar, but today Japanese are apt to hold o-bon events around August 15th according to the new calender. ⑤ First, we welcome the ancestral souls making a small fire called "mukaebi" (welcome fire) at the front door, and finally send them off making a small fire called "okuribi" (farewell fire). ⑥ Depending on housing conditions these days, we sometimes set fire in "bon-chouchin" (a bon lantern), instead of burning a small fire. ⑦ In addition, we make a shelf called "shoryo-dana" (soul shelf) and arrange an ihai (Buddhist memorial tablet) and Buddhist altar fittings from their Buddhist altar on the shelf. ⑧ Also, we stick two pieces of disposable chopsticks each on the front and the back of a cucumber comparable to a horse, and we

do the same to an eggplant comparable to a cow. ⑨ This shows
　　　　　　　　　　　ナス　　　　　　　　　　　　牛　　　　　　　　　　示す
the hope their ancestral souls will come to this world back as soon
　　　希望　　　　　　　　　　　　　　　　　　　　　この世　　　　　できるだけ早く
as possible on horseback, and we hope the souls to go back to the
　　　　　　　馬に乗って
other world as slow as possible on a cow's back. ⑩ These are also
あの世　　　　できるだけゆっくりと　　牛に乗って　　　　　　　　　　　〜はまた
displayed on the soul shelf. ⑪ At that time, we visit the grave of
飾られている　　　　　　　　　　　その時期　　　　　　訪れる　　　　墓
our ancestors as well.
　　　　　あわせて

---

70. なぜ、「お盆」に先祖供養をするのか？

①毎年、日本では夏に先祖の霊を供養する風習があります。②あの世にいる先祖の霊が、毎年、この時期になると、生前過ごしたこの世に帰ってくると考えられているからです。③正式には、仏教語で「盂蘭盆会」といい、略して「お盆」と呼ばれています。④お盆の時期は、旧暦の7月15日頃を基準にした4日間とされていますが、現代では新暦での8月15日前後の期間にお盆の行事を行なうことが多くなりました。⑤まず、玄関先で「迎え火」と呼ばれる火を焚いて先祖の霊を迎え、最後には「送り火」と呼ばれる火を焚いて送ります。⑥昨今の住宅事情から、火を焚く代わりに「盆提灯」を灯すこともあります。⑦そのほか、精霊棚と呼ばれる棚をつくり、仏壇から位牌や仏具を持ってきて、その上に並べます。⑧また、キュウリに割りばしなどを前後に2本ずつ刺して、馬にたとえ、ナスも同様にして、牛にたとえます。⑨先祖の霊に、その馬に乗って一刻も早く帰ってきていただけるよう、またその牛に乗って、できるだけゆっくり戻っていただけるよう、考えられたものです。⑩これらも、精霊棚に飾ります。⑪この時期、あわせて先祖のお墓参りも行ないます。

71. Why do we strike a bell 108 times at a temple on New Year's Eve (December 31st) in Japan?

① As a custom at the end of the year in Japan, the large temple bell (the Bonsho) is struck 108 times late on New Year's Eve (December 31st) and continues into the New Year's Day (January 1st). ② This is called "joya-no-kane" (temple bell on New Year's Eve). ③ "Jo" of "joya" means getting rid of the old year (this year) in Japanese. ④ They say that the number 108 is the total number of "bon-nou" in Japanese such as desire, anger and attachment which human beings are considered to have. ⑤ It is said that, by striking the temple bell the same number of times as the number of bon-nou, the bon-nou of ordinary people who have not had severe training can be gotten rid of, and it leads us to the stage of spiritual awakening. ⑥ As for the explanation of the number 108, there is another view. ⑦ In a Buddhist term, all sufferings of human beings are called "shiku-hakku." ⑧ In Japanese, "shiku" is pronounced in the same way as "four times nine" and "hakku" as "eight times nine." ⑨ The sum of 4 × 9 (=36) and 8 × 9 (=72) gives 108. ⑩ It is thought that we strike the temple bell to get rid of these 108 bon-nou. ⑪ It seems that we strike the temple bell 107 times on December 31st, and we strike it the <u>last</u> one

最後の

on January 1st, but it <u>depends on</u> the temple. ⑫ <u>In any case,</u>

～によって　　　　　　　　　　　　　　　　いずれにせよ

the <u>reason why</u> the temple bell is struck from December 31st to

なぜ…なのかの理由

January 1st is to wish that the New Year will <u>not be depressed</u> by

苦しめられることがない

bon-nou.

※⑨ 4×9(=36)は、four times nine (is thirty six)と音読します。

和訳

71. なぜ、大晦日（12月31日）にお寺で鐘を108回打つのか？

①日本の年末の風習として、12月31日の夜から1月1日にかけて、お寺で梵鐘（ぼんしょう）が108回打たれます。②これは、「除夜（じょや）の鐘（かね）」とも呼ばれます。③除夜の「除」とは、日本語で古い年（今年）を除き去る（のぞ）という意味です。④108という数字は、人間がもっているとされる欲望や怒り、執着などの「煩悩（ぼんのう）」の合計の数だといわれています。⑤その数だけ、梵鐘を打つことによって、厳しい修行を積んでいない一般の人々の煩悩を取り除き、悟り（さと）の境地へと導くといわれています。⑥108の数字の解釈としては、ほかの説もあります。⑦仏教の言葉で、人間のあらゆる苦悩のことを「四苦八苦（しくはっく）」といいます。⑧日本語では、「四苦」は「4×9」、「八苦」は「8×9」と同じ発音をします。⑨「4×9」（＝36）と「8×9」（＝72）を合計すると、108になります。⑩これら108の苦悩をすべて取り除くために梵鐘を打つのだというものです。⑪12月31日中に107回梵鐘を打って、1月1日になったら最後の1回を打つというのが正式のようですが、お寺によって違うようです。⑫いずれにしても、12月31日から1月1日にかけて梵鐘を打つ理由は、新しい年が煩悩に苦しめられることがないようにとの願いです。

Why do the Japanese write their wishes on strips of paper on "Tanabata" (the Star Festival)?

① In Japan, July 7th is the day of "Tanabata" (the Star Festival) .
② Tanabata is considered a combination of Japanese events from long ago and a Chinese legend. ③ In Japan a long time ago there was an event where people placed food offerings to the god of water praying for a good autumn harvest on July 7th in the old calendar (now August). ④ On the other hand, in China, there is a legend about Orihime (Vegar) and Hikoboshi (Altair), and it is considered that these two were allowed to meet with each other over the Milky Way only once a year at the same time by Tentei (the god of heaven). ⑤ Such Japanese events from long ago and the Chinese legend were combined, and it seems that a traditional custom of writing their wishes on the five color strips of paper and hanging them from bamboo branches on July 7th in the new calendar was made. ⑥ Just like that Hikoboshi and Orihime can meet once a year, these strips of paper contain a wish to the god so that their wish will come true.
⑦ They say that the five colors are five components which constitute all things in the world. ⑧ The reason why they hung the strips of paper from bamboo branches is that bamboo is a tree which grows straight towards the sky so it could deliver wishes to heaven.

....

なぜ、「七夕」に願いごとを短冊に書くのか？

①日本では、7月7日は「七夕」の日です。②七夕は、昔からの日本の行事と中国の言い伝えが組み合わさったものとされています。③日本では、昔から旧暦の7月7日（現在の8月）に、秋の豊作を祈願して、水の神さまにお供えをする行事がありました。④一方、中国では、織姫と彦星の伝説があり、同じ時期に1年に一度だけ、2人が天の神さま（天帝）から天の川を越えて会うことが許されたとされています。⑤こうした昔からの日本の行事と中国の言い伝えが組み合わされ、いまでは日本で新暦の7月7日に笹に願いごとを5色の短冊に書いてつるすという風習ができ上がったようです。⑥織姫と彦星が1年に一度出会えるのと同じように、願いごとがかなうよう、神さまにお願いするという意味が込められています。⑦5色は、万物を構成する5要素の色だといわれています。⑧笹につるすのは、笹がまっすぐ空に伸びる木であることから、天に願いごとを届けるという意味合いがあったようです。

英語対訳でわかる
ニッポンと日本人の不思議

「言葉」のなぜ？

Wonders of Japan and the Japanese

Words

72. Why is Japan named "Nihon" or "Nippon"?

① Japan is read as "Nihon" or "Nippon" in Japanese. ② These
日本　　　　読まれた　～として　にほん　　　ニッポン　　　日本語で　　　　これら

depend on the users and the circumstances used, so both of
～による　　　　使う人　　　　　　　場合

them are correct names. ③ Why on earth is Japan read "Nihon"
正しい　　　名前　　　　なぜ…か　いったい全体

or "Nippon"? ④ Since the Japanese Archipelago was located
　　　　　　　…なので　　　　日本列島　　　　　　位置した

in the eastern end of the Chinese Continent, Japan was called
　　　東方の　　端　　　　　　中国　　　大陸　　　　　　　　呼ばれた

the original place where the sun rises; namely, "Hinomoto" in
　　もともとの　場所　　　　　　　太陽　昇る　　　すなわち　　　日の本

Japanese, and the name has been changed to "Nihon" or "Nippon."
　　　　　　　　　　　　　　　　　　変わった

⑤ Before then, it was called "wa" or "wakoku," which was used
それより前は　　　　　　　　　　倭　　　　倭国　　　　　　　　　使われた

by continental peoples in China and Korea at that time. ⑥ Then,
　　大陸の　　　人々　　　中国　　　韓国　　当時　　　　それでは

since when has our country been called "Nihon" or "Nippon"?
いつから…か

⑦ They say that this name was first used as the country's name at
…といわれている　　　　　　　　　最初に

the era of Emperor Tem-mu, the 40th emperor, in the late seventh
時代　　天武天皇　　　　　　　　　　　　　　　　　後期の　7世紀

century. ⑧ Nihon or Nippon is called "Japan" in English. ⑨ This
　　　　　　　　　　　　　　　　　　ジャパン　　英語で

is the reason why an Italian merchant Marco Polo called "Nihon"
　　なぜ…かという理由　イタリアの　商人　　マルコ・ポーロ　～を…と呼んだ

or "Nippon" a golden country "Zipangu" in his book entitled "The
　　　　　　　（黄）金の　国　　ジパング　　　　　　　～と題名をつけられた

Travels of Marco Polo," and they say this "Zipangu" was changed
東方見聞録(←マルコ・ポーロの旅行記)

to "Japan." ⑩ To tell the truth, Marco Polo had never been to
　　　　　　実をいうと　　　　　　　　　（一度も）～へ来たことがなかった

Japan. ⑪ When he dropped in China in his travel, the Chinese
　　　　　　　　　立ち寄った　　　　　　旅行

people read Nihon "Jiipen." ⑫ They say that having heard this
　　　　　　　 ジーペン　　　　　　　　　　　　　　　　　　 ～を聞いたので

pronunciation, Marco Pole wrote it as "Zipangu" in his book.
発音　　　　　　　　　　　　　　 書いた

和訳

72. なぜ、日本は「日本」というのか？

①日本は、日本語で「にほん」ないしは「ニッポン」と音読されます。②これは、使う人、使う場合によって使い分けられ、どちらも正しい国の呼び方です。③そもそも、日本はなぜ「日本」と呼ばれるのでしょうか。④日本列島が中国大陸の東の果てにあったところから、太陽が昇る（のぼ）もと、つまり、日（ひ）の本（もと）と呼ばれ、その呼び方が変化して日本になったといわれています。⑤それ以前は、「倭（わ）」または「倭国（わこく）」と呼ばれていましたが、これは当時の中国や朝鮮などの大陸の人たちが使っていた呼び名です。⑥それでは、いつ頃から日本と呼ばれるようになったのでしょうか。⑦7世紀後半、第40代・天武（てんむ）天皇の時代に国名として使われ始めたといわれています。⑧英語で日本のことを「Japan（ジャパン）」といいます。⑨これは、イタリアの商人マルコ・ポーロが自著『東方見聞録』のなかで、日本を黄金の国ジパング（Zipangu）と書いており、その「ジパング」が「ジャパン」に変化したものだといわれています。⑩マルコ・ポーロは、実は日本に来たことがありませんでした。⑪彼が立ち寄ったときに中国で日本のことを「ジーペン」と発音していたのです。⑫それを聞いたマルコ・ポーロが「ジパング」と書き著（あらわ）したのだといわれています。

73. Why do we call the area around Tokyo "Kanto" and the area near Osaka "Kansai" in Japan?

① In explaining the Japanese areas, Japanese sometimes
〜を説明するとき　　日本の　　　エリア　　　日本人　　　ときどき
sectionalize the country into "Kanto" and "Kansai." ② Why do we
〜を…に区分する　　国　　　　　　関東　　　　関西
divide the country like this? ③ Kanto means "East of Sekisho" (east
分割する　　　　　　このように　　　　意味する　　関所の東
of checking station) in Japanese. ④ In the Edo period, there were
チェックする場所　　日本語で　　　　江戸時代　　〜があった
three checking stations such as "Hakone-no-sekisho," "Kobotoke-
3つの　　　　　　　　〜のような　　箱根の関所　　　　　小仏の関所
no-sekisho" and "Usui-no-sekisho," and it is said that, since one
碓氷の関所　　　　　　　…といわれている　　　〜なので
metropolis and six prefectures are all located in the east of these
首都(→東京)　　　県　　　　　　　〜に位置している
checking stations in the Kanto area, it is called so. ⑤ Hakone is on
　　　　　　　　　　　　　　　　　　〜と呼ばれている
the border between present Kanagawa and Shizuoka Prefectures,
県境　　　〜と…の間(の)　現在の　神奈川県　　　静岡県
and Kobotoke is on the border among present Kanagawa
　　　　　　　　　　　　　　　　〜の中で(の)
Prefecture, Tokyo Metropolis and Yamanashi Prefecture, and Usui
東京都　　　　　　　　山梨県
is on the border between present Gumma and Nagano Prefectures,
群馬県　　　　長野県
respectively. ⑥ In the Heian period farther in the past than the
それぞれ　　　　　　平安時代　　　はるか昔(の)　　　〜より
Edo period, there were "Fuwa-no-sekisho" (Gifu Prefecture),
江戸時代　　　　　　　　　不破の関所　　　岐阜県
"Suzuka-no-sekisho" (Mie Prefecture) and "Arachi-no-sekisho"
鈴鹿の関所　　　　　三重県　　　　　　　愛発の関所
(Fukui Prefecture), and all the eastern areas from these checking
福井県
stations were called Kanto. ⑦ As the times went down, these areas
　　　　　　　　　　　　　　〜につれて　時代　下った
got narrow, and it is said that, in the Edo period, the area of the
狭い　　　　　　…といわれている

174

district indicated almost the same area as present Kanto. ⑧ On
地方　　指した　　ほぼ〜　　　　…と同じ〜
the other hand, it is said that since Kansai was located in the west
一方　　　　　　　　　　　　…して以来　　　　　　　　　　　　　　　　　　西
of these three checking stations which were set up in the Heian
　　　　　　　　　　　　　　　　　　　　　　　　置かれた
period, it is called so.

73. なぜ、東京中心に「関東」と呼び、大阪近辺を「関西」というのか？

①日本をエリアで説明するとき、「関東」「関西」という区分の仕方があります。②なぜ、このように分割するのでしょうか。③関東とは、日本語で「関所の東」という意味です。④江戸時代には「箱根の関所」・「小仏の関所」・「碓氷の関所」の３つの関所があり、いまの関東の１都６県は、そのいずれの関所よりも東にあったところから、そう呼ばれるようになったといいます。⑤箱根は現在の神奈川県と静岡県との県境、小仏は現在の神奈川県と東京都と山梨県の県境、碓氷は現在の群馬県と長野県の県境にそれぞれあります。⑥江戸時代よりはるか昔の平安時代には、「不破の関所」（岐阜県）・「鈴鹿の関所」（三重県）・「愛発の関所」（福井県）があり、それより東はすべて関東と呼ばれていました。⑦それが、時代が下るにしたがってエリアは狭まり、江戸時代には現在の関東とほぼ同じ範囲を指すようになったといいます。⑧一方の関西は、平安時代に設けられたそれら３つの関所よりいずれも西にあったことから、そう呼ばれるようになったといいます。

74. Why do we call five prefectures altogether including Tottori Prefecture, "Chugoku-Chihou" in Japan?

① In Japan, there is an area called "Chugoku". ② This area consists of Tottori, Shimane, Okayama, Hiroshima, and Yamaguchi Prefectures. ③ In Japan, since we call the People's Republic of China "Chugoku," it is confusing, so we also call this area "Chugoku Chihou" (Chugoku District) in order to differentiate them.

④ "Chugoku" means the "country in the middle" in Japanese. ⑤ Why are the prefectures in this area called a country in the middle? ⑥ It was shown by the distance from Kyoto, the capital at that time, and it is said that they named "Kingoku," "Chugoku" and "Engoku" in ascending order. ⑦ Therefore, it seems that the area of present Tottori, Shimane, Okayama, Hiroshima and Yamaguchi Prefectures are called "Chugoku." ⑧ It is good to know other thoughts on this matter. ⑨ One view is that, since this area was located between Kyoto, which was once the capital, and Kyushu, an important western place where Dazaifu existed, this area was called Chugoku. ⑩ Other than this, they called ancient Japan "Nakatsu-kuni," and since the main area existed here, the area was called "Chugoku" which means the same as "Nakatsu-kuni" in

Japanese. ⑪ However, it seems that none of these is a decisive
日本語で　　　　　　　　　　　　　　　　　　　〜のどれも…ない　　　　　　　決定的な
view, so we have to wait for research results from succeeding
　　　　　　　〜しなければならない　待つ　　　研究　　　結果　　　　　　続いていく〜
generations.
世代

※⑨の「大宰府」の日本語表記ですが、歴史上の行政機関は「大宰府」、大宰府が置かれていた
　地域の地名は「太宰府」と使い分けするのが慣用になっているようです。ちなみに、現在では
　太宰府天満宮、大宰府政庁跡と区別して、表記しているようです。

74. なぜ、鳥取県をはじめとする5県をまとめて「中国地方」と いうのか？

①日本には、「中国（ちゅうごく）」と呼ばれるエリアがあります。②鳥取県（とっとり）、島根県、岡山県、広島県、山口県がそれにあたります。③日本では、中華人民共和国のことも「中国」と呼ぶため、紛らわしいので、区別する意味から「中国地方」ともいいます。④「中国」とは、日本語で「中間の国」という意味です。⑤なぜ、このエリアの県が中間の国なのでしょうか。⑥当時都であった京都からの距離で表わされ、順番に「近國（きんごく）（国）」・「中國（ちゅうごく）（国）」・遠國（えんごく）（国）」と定めたといいます。⑦そのため、いまの鳥取県、島根県、岡山県、広島県、山口県があるエリアを「中国」といったようです。⑧このことに関しては、ほかの説も知っておくとよいでしょう。⑨都であった京都と、大宰府（だざいふ）があった西の重要地・九州との中間にあるエリアだったので、中国と呼ばれたという説です。⑩このほか、古代日本のことを昔「中つ国（なかつくに）」と呼んでおり、その主要地域がここにあったことから、日本語で「中つ国」と同義の「中国」と呼ばれたという説もあります。⑪しかし、いずれも決定打に欠けるため、後世の研究成果を待たなければならないようです。

75. Why is it called "Kyushu" (nine countries), even though there are only seven prefectures in Kyushu?

① There are forty-seven prefectures in Japan. ② At present, it is common to divide the forty-seven prefectures into eight districts. ③ In the order from the north, they are Hokkaido, Tohoku, Kanto, Chubu, Kinki, Chugoku, Shikoku and Kyushu-Okinawa. ④ Among these, Shikoku consists of the four prefectures of Kagawa, Tokushima, Ehime and Kochi. ⑤ Shikoku means four countries in Japanese, so we can see that, as there are four prefectures, they call the district "Shikoku." ⑥ Then, how about Kyushu? ⑦ Kyushu only has the seven prefectures of Fukuoka, Saga, Nagasaki, Oita, Kumamoto, Miyazaki and Kagoshima. ⑧ Kyushu means nine countries in Japanese, but isn't it strange to refer to only seven prefectures as Kyushu? ⑨ To tell the truth, there were nine countries there until the early Meiji period. ⑩ They were Chikuzen-no-kuni, Chikugo-no-kuni, Hizen-no-kuni, Higo-no-kuni, Buzen-no-kuni, Bungo-no-kuni, Hyuga-no-kuni, Oosumi-no-kuni and Satsuma-no-kuni. ⑪ Through the "Haihan-chiken" which was practiced in 1871, these nine countries (han) were abolished and seven prefectures (ken) were newly established.

⑫ The Haihan-chiken was the Meiji Government's abolishment
of 261 "han," the local governments, which existed until then,
and creation of a centralized system through the establishment
of new prefectures (ken). ⑬ Although Kyushu decreased to seven
prefectures at that time, the name remained as it is, and continued
up to the present time.

75. なぜ、7県しかないのに「九州」と呼ぶのか？

①日本には47の都道府県があります。②現在では、この47都道府県を8つの地域に分けるのが一般的です。③北から順に、北海道・東北・関東・中部・近畿・中国・四国・九州 - 沖縄です。④このうち、四国には、香川県・徳島県・愛媛県・高知県の4つの県があります。⑤四国とは日本語で4つの国という意味なので、4つの県があることから四国と呼ぶのは理解できます。⑥それでは、九州はどうでしょうか。⑦九州には、福岡県・佐賀県・長崎県・大分県・熊本県・宮崎県・鹿児島県の7つの県しかありません⑧九州とは、日本語で9つの国という意味ですが、7つの県しかないのに九州と呼ぶのはおかしいのではないでしょうか。⑨じつは、明治時代初期まで9つの国があったのです。⑩筑前国・筑後国・肥前国・肥後国・豊前国・豊後国・日向国・大隅国・薩摩国の9つです。⑪それが、1871年に行なわれた「廃藩置県」によって、この9つの国（藩）が廃止され、新たに7つの県が配置されたというわけです。⑫廃藩置県とは、明治政府がそれまで261あった「藩」という、いわば地方自治体を廃止し、新たに府県を置くことで、中央集権体制にしたものです。⑬九州は、このとき、7つの県に減ったにもかかわらず、名称はそのままで、今日に至っているというわけです。

76. Why do we call the sushi which are served in Tokyo "Edomae-zushi" in Japan?

① Sushi is now eaten all over the world, and it is quite popular
among foreigners. ② When did we start eating sushi in Japan?
③ It is said that sushi was originally preserved fish using
fermented rice in Southeast Asian countries, and it was introduced
to Japan through China in the Nara period. ④ At the beginning,
sushi was called "nare-zushi" (fermented sushi) in which fish was
soaked and fermented with salt and boiled rice. ⑤ Afterwards,
through numerous changes, at the end of the Edo period,
"Edomae-zushi," which is the original form of the present sushi,
appeared. ⑥ At that time, sushi was sold at food stalls as "nigiri-
zushi" which we could eat soon after making. ⑦ It is said that the
word sushi is a short form of "sumeshi" in Japanese which means
meshi (cooked rice) mixed with su (vinegar). ⑧ Then, why did
they call the sushi which were eaten in Tokyo "Edomae-zushi"?

⑨ "Edomae" means "the ocean in front of Edo" in Japanese, and it
indicates the Bay of Edo (now, the Bay of Tokyo). ⑩ Splits of the
black current flow into the Bay of Edo in succession, and since
the bay has abundant plankton, many kinds of fish come into the

180

Bay <u>chasing</u> them. ⑪ They <u>referred to</u> the sushi in Edo using
　追いかけて　　　　　　　　　　　　　〜と呼んだ

<u>seafood</u> <u>caught</u> in the Bay of Edo which is a <u>rich</u> <u>fishing ground</u> as
魚介類　　獲れた　　　　　　　　　　　　　　　豊かな　漁場

"Edomae-zushi."

和訳

76. なぜ、東京で食べる寿司を「江戸前寿司」と呼ぶのか？

①寿司はいまや世界中で食べられ、外国人にも人気が高いです。②寿司は、日本でいつ頃から食べられていたのでしょうか。③寿司は、もともと東南アジアで米の発酵を利用して魚を保存していたものが、奈良時代に中国を経由して日本に伝わったといわれています。④最初は、魚を塩と米で漬け込んで発酵させた「馴れ寿司」と呼ばれるものでした。⑤その後、いろいろな変遷をたどり、江戸時代後期に、いまの寿司の原型となる「江戸前寿司」が登場したのです。⑥握ったら、すぐに食べられる「握り寿司」として、当時は屋台で売られていました。⑦寿司という言葉は、日本語で酢を混ぜた飯という意味の「酢飯」が縮まってできた言葉だといわれています。⑧それではなぜ、江戸で食べられた寿司のことを「江戸前寿司」と呼んだのでしょうか。⑨「江戸前」とは、日本語で「江戸の前の海」という意味で、江戸湾（いまの東京湾）のことを指します。
⑩黒潮の分流が次から次へと流れ込み、江戸湾はプランクトンが豊富で、それを追ってさまざまな種類の魚がやってきます。⑪その豊かな漁場である江戸湾で獲れた魚介を使った江戸の寿司を「江戸前寿司」といったのです。

181

① Today, even though many retail stores are losing ground to
今日　　　たとえ……でも　　　　　　　小売店　　　　　　　　　　～より不利になる

large supermarkets and convenience stores, there are still some in
大きな　　スーパーマーケット　　　　コンビニエンスストア　　　　　～がある　　　いまだに　いくつかの店

some towns specializing in vegetables and fruits. ② This is called
　　　　　　　～を専門にしている　　野菜　　　　　　果物　　　　　　　　～と呼ばれている

"yaoya" in Japanese. ③ "Yaoya" means a store which sells 800
八百屋　　日本語で　　　　　　　　　意味する　　　　　　　～を売る

kinds of goods. ④ Eight hundred is not a concrete number, but
種類　　　品物　　　　800　　　　　　　　　具体的な　　数

it means a great many things. ⑤ That is, it is a store which sells
とても多くの　　もの　　　　つまり

a large number of vegetables and fruits. ⑥ It was common that a
数多くの　　　　　　　　　　　　　　　　　　　一般的な

yaoya was a store which sold goods in stock adding profit.
　　　　　　　　　　　　　仕入れた品物　　～を加えて　利益

⑦ Therefore, some yaoya managers overpriced when the market
そのため　　　　　　　　　経営者　　　高値をつける　　　市場価格

price rose due to bad weather and the like, and some other
上がった　～の原因によって　悪天候　　　　　など

managers regretted that they could not meet their customers' needs
　　　　～を後悔する　　　　　　　　　～に応じる　　　　　ニーズ

in terms of assortment of goods, pricing and service for customers.
～の点から　　取り合わせ（→品ぞろえ）　　値つけ　　　奉仕（→接客）

⑧ Some yaoya managers focus on agricultural products called "n
　　　　　　　経営者　　　　～に焦点を当てる農業の　　生産品　　　規格外の

on-standard products" which have been discarded because the
　　　　　　　　　　　　　　　　　　廃棄されていた　　　～のため

shape is not good or they look bad, in spite of the fact that there
形　　　　　　　　　　　　　　　　　　～にもかかわらず　　事実

is no problem with the quality. ⑨ And, some others engage in
問題　　～に関する　品質　　　　　　いくらかの　ほかの人　～に取り組む

making a cultivation contract with agricultural producers and
　　　栽培契約　　　　　　　　　　　　　　生産者

buying the whole amount of products produced in a given region
買う　　　全部の量　　　　　　　　　　　　　　　　特定の地域

at a cerain sum in order to stabilize purchase prices. ⑩ Economic
<u>一定額</u>　　　<u>～するために</u>　　<u>安定させる</u>　<u>仕入れ価格</u>　　　　<u>経済の</u>

magazines and newspapers, etc. have introduced with interest
<u>雑誌</u>　　　　<u>新聞</u>　　　　　　　<u>紹介した</u>　　<u>興味を持って</u>

some of these yaoya managers who are desperately struggling for
　　　　　　　　　　　　　　　　　　　　　<u>必死に</u>　　<u>戦っている</u>

survival.
<u>生き残りをかけて</u>

77. なぜ、野菜を主に売る店のことを「八百屋」と呼ぶのか？

①いまでは、大手のスーパーマーケットやコンビニエンスストアなどに押され気味ですが、野菜や果物を専門に売る町の小売店があります。②日本語で「八百屋」と呼ばれています。③「八百屋」とは、「800の品物を売る店」という意味です。④800というのは、具体的な数字ではなく、とても多くの品物という意味です。⑤つまり、数多くの野菜や果物を売っている店ということです。⑥かつての八百屋さんは、仕入れたものに利益を上乗せして販売するのがふつうでした。⑦そのため、悪天候不などによって市場価格が高騰すれば高値をつけ、品ぞろえ・値つけ・接客での顧客ニーズに十分応えきれていなかったという反省に立つ八百屋経営者もいます。⑧品質に問題はないが、形や見た目が悪いため、いままでは廃棄されていた「規格外品」と呼ばれる農産物に着目する八百屋さんもいます。⑨また、仕入れ価格を安定させるため、生産者と栽培契約を交わし、特定の場所で生産された作物を一定額で全量買い取るといった取り組みをしている八百屋さんもいます。⑩このように、生き残りを賭けて必死に取り組んでいる八百屋さんを経済誌などが興味深く紹介しています。

78. Why do we refer to bad fortune and bad economic conditions as "hidari-mae" in Japan?

① In Japan, we often refer to bad fortune and bad economic conditions as "hidari-mae." ② In Japanese, "hidari-mae" means "the left is in front." ③ This originally comes from kimono which is a Japanese traditional clothing. ④ When we wear kimono, looking from the other person, we usually put the front of the kimono neckband on the right side and put the back of the kimono neckband on the left side one on top of the other. ⑤ This means "the right is in front," and we call this "migi-mae" (right front) in Japanese. ⑥ It might be easy for foreigners to remember that they put on the kimono neckbands one on top of the other as though they look like a small letter "y" from the English alphabet, looking from the other person. ⑦ It is said that, a long time ago, the reason why people wore kimono in "migi-mae" is that, since people kept the wallet in a kimono chest, it was easier for right-handed persons to put their hands in the kimono chest. ⑧ Meanwhile, a white kimono called "shini-shouzoku" (burial clothes) which the dead wore until they were burned to ashes is kimono in "hidari-mae" (with the left side over the right). ⑨ This

184

is a traditional Japanese way of thinking, and it is said that this
　　　　　　　　　　　　考え方
comes from the fact that we usually do the opposite when we
　　　　　　　　　　　　　　　　　　　逆のことをする
mourn for the dead. ⑩ It is considered that, from the association
〜を弔う　　　　　　　　…とされている　　　　　　　　　連想
of death and the dead like these, they referred to bad fortune and
　　死　　　　　　　　　　　　死者　　　　　悪い　運
bad economic conditions as "hidari-mae."

78. なぜ、運が悪いことや経済状態がよくないことを「左前」というのか？

①日本では、運が悪いことや経済状態がよくないことをよく「左前（ひだりまえ）」といいます。②日本語で「左前」とは、「左が前にある」という意味です。③これは、もともと日本の伝統的な服装である着物からきています。④着物を着るとき、通常は相手から見て、胸の衿（えり）を、手前を右、後ろを左にして重ねます。⑤これを「右が前にある」という意味で、日本語では「右前（みぎまえ）」といいます。⑥外国人にとっては、相手から見て、胸の衿を、アルファベットの小文字の"y"字に見えるように重ねて着ると覚えれば、わかりやすいかもしれません。⑧「右前」に着物を着るのは、昔、着物の胸のあたりに財布（さいふ）などを入れていたので、右利きの人が着物の胸に手を入れやすかったからといわれています。⑨これに対して、亡くなった人が火葬されるまで着る「死装束（しにしょうぞく）」と呼ばれる白い着物は、「左前」に着せます。⑩これは、日本古来の考え方で、死者を弔（とむら）うときは、通常と逆のことをするというところからきているといわれます。⑪こうした死や死者の連想から、運が悪いことや経済状態のよくないことを「左前」といったとされています。

185

79. Why do we say "miginideru-monoga-inai," when we praise the best person in Japan?

① In Japan we use the figurative expression "miginideru-monoga-inai" (no one goes to the right) when we praise an outstanding person who is incomparable with others. ② Why are Japanese concerned about whether the comparing partner is on the right or not when we compare his/her wonderfulness with others?

③ Since mythical times, it was considered that left was superior to right in Japan. ④ It is said that left was superior to right, looking from the Son of Heaven / Emperor who sat in the north side, and faced to the south, because left is in the east side where the Sun rises, and right is in the west side where the Sun sets. ⑤ However, the expression "miginideru-monoga-inai" show a way of thinking that makes right superior to left, and this means that there is no one above him/her. ⑥ In this way of thinking, the meaning will be opposite. ⑦ There is some reason for this. ⑧ In this case, it doesn't mean to look at his retainers through the Son of Heaven's / Emperor's eyes, but it means to look at from his retainers who are in his opposite side. ⑨ If they look from the opposite side of the Son of Heaven / Emperor, their point of view becomes

reversed, and right is superior. ⑩ "Sasen" (demotion), in which a
<u>逆に（なる）</u>　　　　　　　　　　　　　　　　　　　　　　<u>左遷</u>　　<u>降格</u>

person's official position is lowered and he/she is transferred to
　　　　　　<u>公的な</u>　<u>地位</u>　　　<u>下げられる</u>　　　　　　　　　<u>〜へ異動させられる</u>

region from center, means "dropped to the left" in Japanese as
<u>地方</u>　　　　<u>中央</u>　　　　　　　　　<u>落とされる</u>　　　　　　　　　　　　　<u>同様に</u>

well.

79. なぜ、一番すぐれている人をたたえるとき、「右に出る者がいない」というのか？

①ほかに比べる者がいないほど、すぐれている人のことを、日本では「右に出る者がいない」と比喩します。②すばらしさを他人と比べる場合に、なぜ、その比べる相手が右にいるかどうかを問題にするのでしょうか。③神話の時代から、日本では、左が右より上位とされていました。④北側に座り、南側を向いている天子（てんし）から見て、左は太陽が昇る東側、右は太陽が沈む西側に当たるため、左が右より上位とされたといいます。⑤しかし、「右に出る者がいない」という表現は右が左より上位という考え方であり、その上位がいないという意味です。⑥これでは、意味が逆になってしまいます。⑦これには理由があります。⑧この場合は、天子の目から見るのではなく、天子の反対側にいる家来側から見るというわけです。⑨天子の反対側から見ると、天子の見方とは逆になり、右が上位ということになります。⑩役職を下げられたり、中央から地方に異動させられる「左遷（させん）」も同様に、日本語で下位の「左に落とされる」という意味です。

80. Why do we refer to flattering the other person as "goma-wo-suru" in Japan?

① In Japan, we use the figurative expression "goma-wo-suru" (grind sesame seeds) in Japanese when we flatter the other person trying to be liked by him/her. ② It is said that, when we grind sesame seeds in a mortar, oil leaks out and the sesame seeds stick everywhere in the mortar, so this came to indicate the manner of getting excessively close to and flattering the other person.
③ Sesame was indispensable when they cooked Buddhist vegetarian meals without using meat and fish at a temple. ④ So, it is also said that this phrase comes from the fact that the Buddhist monks were cheerful when young Buddhist monks ground sesame seeds. ⑤ In addition, it is said that when a merchant snuck up and talked the customers into buying his/her goods, one of his/her palms looked like a pestle rod and the other a mortar when rubbing his/her hands. ⑥ By the way, what do foreigners say to refer to flattery? ⑦ In the United States, they seem to say "polish an apple" instead of "grind sesame seeds." ⑧ It seems to be said that, long ago, a pupil who wanted to butter up his/her teacher gave a highly polished apple which was thought to be good for

health. ⑨ And, in Germany, they seem to say "pedal a bicycle."
⑩ It seems that the appearance which one pedalled a bicycle
looked like cringing to the other person. ⑪ Other than these, they
say "lick the other person's shoe" in France and Spain. ⑫ This
expression might be a little too direct.

和訳

80. なぜ、相手にへつらうことを「ゴマをする」というのか？

①日本では、相手に気に入られようとして、媚びることを「ゴマをする」と比喩します。②これは、すり鉢でゴマをすると、油分がしみ出て、ゴマが鉢のあちこちにくっつくことから、相手にむやみに近づいてへつらうさまを指すようになったといわれます。③お寺では肉や魚を使わない精進料理をつくるとき、ゴマが欠かせませんでした。④そのため、小坊主がゴマをすると和尚の機嫌がよかったところからきているともいわれます。⑤そのほか、商人が客にすり寄って商品を売りつける際に、もみ手をするしぐさが片手がすりこ木、もう一方の手がすり鉢のように見えたところからついたともいわれています。⑥ところで、この相手に気に入られようとして媚びるさまを、外国では何にたとえているのでしょうか。⑦アメリカでは「ゴマをする」代わりに「リンゴを磨く」というのだそうです。⑧昔、先生にとり入ろうとした生徒が、健康によいとされたリンゴをピカピカに磨いて贈ったところからそういわれているようです。⑨また、ドイツでは「自転車をこぐ」というらしいです。⑩ペダルをこぐ姿がペコペコしているように見えたからだそうです。⑪このほか、フランスやスペインでは、「靴をなめる」といいます。⑫これは、ちょっとストレートすぎる表現かもしれません。

81. Why do we call having a good connection with another person "umaga-au" in Japan?

① In Japanese, when one's idea and taste are similar to the other person's and they can get along well with each other, we refer to it as "kiga-au" (one's and the other person's feelings meet). ② That is, this means that the two completely understand one another's feelings and hearts. ③ And, in Japanese, we say "umaga-au" (a horse meets a man) which has the same meaning as this. ④ Why is a "horse" used? ⑤ "Umaga-au" means that, in horse riding, the jockey and his/her horse completely understand each other's feelings. ⑥ This comes from the fact that, if the jockey and his/her horse are not compatible, the jockey cannot manage the horse well, because even a horse has its own personality and individuality. ⑦ This expression "umaga-au" has the more powerful nuance that the one person is special to the other, rather than just "kiga-au". ⑧ In addition, we also say "soriga-au" in Japanese which has the same meaning. ⑨ "Sori" means that a sword is arched like a bow. ⑩ Some swords are just straight, and we call these chokuto (straight sword), and these manifest power when we charge at a stroke. ⑪ On the other hand, we can attack

our <u>enemy</u> <u>smoothly</u> with a <u>curved</u> sword, when we try to <u>slash at</u>
の　敵　　　スムーズに　　　　反りのある　　　　　　　　　　　　　　　　　〜を切りつける

the other person with it using a <u>circular motion</u> from our <u>shoulder</u>
円運動　　　　　　　　肩

as the <u>fulcrum</u>. ⑫ When we <u>put</u> this curved sword <u>back into</u> the
支点　　　　　　　　　　〜を…におさめる

<u>sheath</u>, we cannot put it back well if the curve of a sword does not
鞘

<u>fit</u> in the sheath. ⑬ <u>Therefore</u>, fitting the sword in the sheath is
合う　　　　　　　　そのため

<u>compared to</u> getting along well with each other.
〜にたとえられている

和訳

81. なぜ、気が合うことを「馬が合う」というのか？

①日本語で、相手と自分の考え方や好みなどが似ていて、うまくつき合えることを「気が合う」といいます。②つまり、相手と自分の気持ちや心を完全に理解するということです。③また、日本語では、これと同じ意味で「馬が合う」ともいいます。④なぜ、「馬」が使われるのでしょうか。⑤「馬が合う」とは、乗馬の際、騎手と馬の気持ちがぴったり合うという意味です。⑥乗る人と馬の相性が悪ければ、馬にも性格や個性があるため、うまく乗りこなすことができないところからそういうのです。⑦この「馬が合う」という表現ですが、単に「気が合う」というより、相手が特別な存在であるというニュアンスがより強く出ます。⑧このほか、日本語では、これと同じような意味で「反りが合う」ともいいます。⑨「反り」とは、刀が弓なりに曲がっていることをいいます。⑩刀には直刀と呼ばれる、まっすぐなものがあり、突きの攻撃の際、威力を発揮します。⑪一方、反りがある刀では、肩を支点とする円運動によって相手を切りつける際に、スムーズに相手を攻撃することができます。⑫この反りがある刀を鞘におさめるとき、その刀の反りが鞘に合っていないと、うまくおさめることができません。⑬そのため、刀と鞘の反りが合うことが、気が合うことにたとえられたというわけです。

82. Why do we refer to the two people getting along well with each other as "aun-no-kokyu" in Japan?

① We often hear the phrase "aun-no-kokyu" in Japanese. ② This phrase means that when more than two people do something together, they are getting along well with each other. ③ They say that "a" is the sound which is made when we open our mouth, and "un" is the sound which is made when we close our mouth. ④ It is also said that "a" means the beginning of the universe and "un" means the end of the universe, and these phrases express the root of all things. ⑤ Not only the mouths of a pair of the koma-inu (guardian dogs) which are placed at the gate or in front of a Shinto shrine, but also the mouths of the wooden statues of Kongou-rikishi (also called Niouzou) which are placed at both sides of the sam-mon gate (temple gate), look like the shapes of "a" and "un." ⑥ They say that this means that, since a pair of people are in tune with each other, they act together in harmony. ⑦ There are other expressions which have a similar meaning such as "tsuu-kaa-no-naka" (relationship between tsuu and kaa) and "tsuuto-ieba kaato-kotaeru" to "aun-no-kokyu" in Japanese. ⑧ It is said that, long ago, Edokko (persons born and brought up in old

Tokyo) said "…… tsuu-kotoda" (It means that ……) at the end of
東京   「…つうことだ」   終わり
his/her talk while the other person said back promptly nodding
話   言い返した   すぐに   頷きながら
"Soukaa" (I see!). ⑨ And, there is also another view that, like a
「そうかあ」 なるほど   もう1つの
white crane which cries "tsuu," and a black crow which responds
白い   鶴   鳴く   黒い   カラス   応える
"kaa" to this, the two people who are contrary to each other in
                                          相反する
appearance have a very good understanding with each other.
見かけでは   理解

和訳

82. なぜ、2人の息がぴったり合っていることを 「あうんの呼吸」 というのか？

①日本語でよく「阿吽の呼吸」という言葉を耳にします。②これは、2人以上の人間が一緒に何かをするときに、互いの気持ちが一致していることをいいます。③「あ」とは口を開いたときに出る音、「うん」とは口を閉じたときに出る音だといわれています。④「阿」とは宇宙の始まり、「吽」とは宇宙の終わりを意味し、万物の根源を表わしているともいわれています。⑤神社に一対置かれた狛犬やお寺の山門の両側に置かれた金剛力士像（仁王像ともいう）も、それぞれ口が「あ」と「うん」になっています。⑥一対のものがそれぞれ息を合わせているところから、うまく行動を合わせることを意味しているといいます。⑦日本語には、よく似た言葉に「つうかあの仲」とか「つうといえば、かあと応える」などといいます。⑧昔、江戸っ子が、話の最後に「…つうことだ」といったのに対して、相手が言下に「そうかあ」とうなずき返したことによるといわれています。⑨また、白い鶴が「ツウ」と鳴くのに対して、黒いカラスが「カア」と応えるように、見かけは相反するもの同士がお互い通じ合っているところから、そういわれるというものまであります。

Why is the Chinese character "do" used in the name of Hokkaido in Japan?

① It has been already stated in this book that when we divide Japan into large districts, it is common to divide the country into the eight districts of Hokkaido, Tohoku, Kanto, Chubu, Kinki, Chugoku, Shikoku, and Kyushu-Okinawa. (See p.178) ② Among these, "Kyushu" has already been explained. ③ You can learn about "Hokkaido" here. ④ The direct translation of "Hokkaido" means the "road along the ocean in the north." ⑤ Why do they use "do" (road) in Japanese? ⑥ Long ago, Japan was divided into large districts using the unit "do," except Kyoto (which was the capital at that time) and the areas around there. ⑦ The total number of "do" is seven such as Tokaido, Hokurikudo and Sanyodo. ⑧ At that time, the present "Hokkaido" was not recognized as Japanese land yet. ⑨ Before long, in the Meiji period, through the Russian advance, when Hokkaido was recognized as a territory of Japan, they put "do" on the district and called it "Hokkaido." ⑩ The name is still used up to the present time.

なぜ、北海道には「道」という漢字が入っているのか？

①日本を大きな地域に分けるとき、北海道・東北・関東・中部・近畿・中国・四国・九州－沖縄の８つに分けるのが一般的であるという話を前にしました（178ページ参照）。②そのうち、「九州」については、すでに解説しました。③ここでは、「北海道」について解説します。④「北海道」とは、直訳すると「北の海の道」ということです。⑤なぜ、「道」なのでしょうか。⑥昔、日本では、都があった京都とその周辺部以外を「道」という単位を使って、大きく地域を分けていました。⑦東海道・北陸道・山陽道など、全部で７つです。⑧そのときは、いまの「北海道」はまだ日本の国土とは認識されていませんでした。⑨やがて、明治時代になって、ロシアの進出などがあり、ようやく日本の領土とみなされたとき、その地域に「道」をつけて「北海道」と呼ぶようになりました。⑩それが、今日までそのまま使われているのです。

第 **10** 章

英語対訳でわかる
ニッポンと日本人の不思議

「食文化」のなぜ？

Wonders of Japan and the Japanese
Food Culture

83. Why do we refer to boiled and cooked food as "sukiyaki" in Japan?

① "Sukiyaki" is one of the typical Japanese dishes. ② To cook
すき焼き　　　　　　　　　　　　典型的な　日本の　料理　～するには 料理する

sukiyaki, we boil vegetables such as Chinese cabbage, green
煮る　　野菜　　　　　～のような　白菜　　　ネギ

onion, shun-giku (garland chrysanthemum leaves) and shii-take
春菊　　　花冠(の)　　菊(の)　　　　葉　　　　しいたけ(の)

mushroom as well as sliced beef, and yakidofu (grilled bean curd),
キノコ　　～と同様　薄切り　ビーフ　　焼き豆腐　　焼いた　　豆腐

shirataki (white stringy food made from konjac starch) and fu
しらたき　　白い　糸状の食べ物　　　　　コンニャク　澱粉　　　麩

(food like bread made of wheat gluten) with sugar, soy sauce
食べ物　～のような　パン　　～から作られた　小麦(の) グルテン(タンパク質の一種)　砂糖　　醤油

and sake (rice wine) to season salty-sweet in a nabe pot. ③ The
酒　　米(の)　ワイン　　味つけする　甘辛の　　　鍋

ingredients used in sukiyaki depend on the place, so pork or
具材　　使われる～　　　　　　　～による　　場所　　　　豚肉

chicken is used instead of beef in some places. ④ When eating
鶏肉　　　　　　～の代わりに　　　ある～　　　　　食べるときは

sukiyaki, many people mix it with beaten raw eggs. ⑤ Sukiyaki
多くの　人々　混ぜる　　溶いた～　生卵

is a dish originating in the Kansai district, and in the Meiji period,
生まれた～　　　　　関西地方　　　　　　　　明治時代

one sukiyaki specialty store opened in Kobe. ⑥ After that, it is said
専門店　　　開店した　神戸　　その後　　　…といわれている

that the reason why we call this "sukiyaki" is that people originally
なぜ…かの理由　　　　　　　　　　　　　　　　　もともと

used a worn-out farming plow (suki) instead of a pot, or that they
使い古した　農具の鋤　　鋤　　　　　　　　　　または

used stripped meat (sukimi). ⑦ There are also other views that we
すいた　肉　　すき身　　　　～がある　～はまた ほかの　説

call this dish "sukiyaki," because we put in any ingredients which
　　　　　　　　　　　　～だから　　　入れる

we like (suki), or because we eat sukiyaki around a nabe pot with
好む　好き

the persons we like. ⑧ Then, the reason why we call this food
人たち　　　　　　それでは

yaki (grilled) is, because <u>long ago</u>, the food used to be cooked as a
　　　　　　　　　　　　　昔　　　　　　　　　　　かつて〜したものだった
grilled dish. ⑨ <u>However</u>, <u>modern</u> sukiyaki <u>seems to</u> <u>be similar to</u>
　　　　　　　　しかし　　　現代の　　　　　　　〜のようである　〜に似ている
boiled food or <u>hot pot dish</u>, <u>rather than</u> grilled food. ⑩ It is said
　　　　　　　　熱い鍋の料理　　〜よりも
that eating sukiyaki with beaten raw eggs was <u>originally</u> to keep
　　　　　　　　　　　　　　　　　　　　　　　　　もともと　　〜することを避ける
<u>from</u> burning the <u>eater's</u> mouth with <u>hot</u> ingredients.
　　　　　　　　　　　食べる人　　　　　熱い

---

83. なぜ、煮て調理するのに「すき焼き」というのか？

①「すき焼き」は日本の料理を代表する一つです。②薄切りにした牛肉をはじめ、白菜（はくさい）・ネギ・春菊（しゅんぎく）・しいたけなどの野菜類、焼き豆腐・しらたき・麩（ふ）などを入れて、砂糖・醤油（しょうゆ）・酒などで甘辛（あまから）く煮る鍋でつくります。③入れる具材は、ところによって異なり、牛肉の代わりに豚肉（ぶたにく）や鶏肉（とりにく）などを入れるところもあります。④食べる際には、溶（と）けた生の鶏卵をからめることが多いようです。⑤関西で生まれた料理で、明治時代には牛すき焼きの専門店が神戸に開店しています。⑥その後、「すき焼き」と呼ばれるのは、もともと、使い古した農具の「鋤（すき）」を鍋代わりに利用したからとか、「すき身」の肉を使うからとかいわれます。⑦好きな具材を入れて食べるからとか、好きな人と鍋を囲んで食べるからとか、という説まであります。⑧それでは、なぜ、「やき」というのかというと、昔は焼き物として調理していたことによります。⑨しかし、現代の「すき焼き」は、焼き物というより、むしろ煮物、鍋料理といったほうが近いようです。⑩溶いた生の鶏卵をからめて食べるのは、もともと熱々の具材でやけどをしないための工夫だといわれます。

84. Why do we refer to sliced raw fish and shellfish as "o-sashimi" or "o-tsukuri" in Japan?

① In Japan which has the culture to eat raw fish, we fillet raw fish, remove bones and skin, cut them into bite-size pieces and arrange them on a plate, and eat them with soy sauce and wasabi (Japanese horseradish). ② We refer to this dish as "sashimi" or "tsukuri" in Japanese. ③ Adding "o" at the beginning of these words, we sometimes call them "o-sashimi" or "o-tsukuri" to be polite. ④ Are "sashimi" and "tsukuri" different from each other? ⑤ Jumping to the conclusion, these two are the same. ⑥ "Sashimi" and "tsukuri" were originally called "kirimi." ⑦ "Kirimi" means sliced fish (or meat). ⑧ It is said that, in the Japanese Warrior Society in the Edo period, "kiru" means "take someone's life with a sword" which sounded unlucky, so they decided to use "sashimi." ⑨ However, since "sashimi" also means "stabbed fish," there was not much difference between them. ⑩ Therefore, it is considered that, interpreting this as "make sliced fish" (kirimi [sliced fish] -wo-tsukuru [make]), "tsukuru" was changed into "tsukuri." ⑪ In the Japanese Warrior Society long ago, from a viewpoint of luck like this, what they changed was the way of cutting eel. ⑫ Eel is a

198

sustaining food which is often eaten in summer in Japan. ⑬ Until
体に元気をつける〜　　　　しばしば 食べられる　夏　　　　　　　　　　それまで

then, when they cut eel, the eel was slit open along the stomach,
　　　　　　　　　　　　　　　　　　　切り開かれた　腹に沿って

but this action was associated with "seppuku" (harakiri：a form
　　　　行為　　　〜を連想させた　　　切腹　　腹切り　　　形式

of Japanese ritual suicide), so especially in the Kanto district, they
　　　　儀式的な 自殺　　　特に　　　　　　関東地方

changed it into the way of cutting the fish back to cook with a
　　　　　　　　　　　　　　　　　　　　魚の背　　　料理する

carving knife.
包丁

84. なぜ、生の魚介類の切り身を「お刺身」や「お造り」と いうのか？

①魚を生で食べる文化がある日本では、生魚をおろして骨や皮を取り除き、身を一口サイズに切ってお皿に盛りつけ、醤油やワサビをつけて食べます。②この料理のことを日本語では「刺身」や「造り」と呼びます。③あたまに「お」をつけて、それぞれ「お刺身」「お造り」と呼んで、ていねいにいう場合もあります。④この「刺身」と「造り」はそれぞれ違うものなのでしょうか？⑤結論から先にいうと、2つは同じものです。⑥もともと、「刺身」や「造り」は「切り身」と呼ばれていました。⑦「切り身」とは、切った身という意味です。⑧それが、江戸時代の武家社会では、「切る」というのは「刀で人の命を奪う」という意味になるので、縁起が悪いとして、「刺身」にしたといいます。⑨しかし、「刺身」も「刺した身」という意味なので、あまり大きな違いがありませんでした。⑩そこで、「切り身を造る」と解釈して、「造る」から「造り」になったとされています。⑪昔の武家社会では、このように縁起の観点から、やり方を変えたものに、ウナギのさばき方があります。⑫ウナギは日本で夏によく食べられるスタミナ食です。⑬それまで、ウナギをさばく場合、腹を開いて調理していましたが、「切腹」を連想させるということから、特に関東では、背に包丁を入れて調理する形になりました。

85. Why do we eat "soba" on the New Year's eve, and "osechi-ryori" on New Year's days in Japan?

① Most Japanese eat "soba" (buckwheat noodles) on New Year's eve (it is called "o-omisoka" in Japanese), December 31st, when it is the end of the year. ② This is also called "toshikoshi-soba," and it means that "we eat soba to make it through the year, and greet the good New Year." ③ It is thought the reason why we eat soba is that we can lead a "fine and long life" like soba noodles, that is, this is a wish for longevity. ④ In addition, it is said that, in the Edo period, some craftsmen using gold and silver gathered the gold and silver scattered at work with dumplings made of buckwheat. ⑤ That is, they related eating buckwheat noodles (soba) to gathering gold and silver. ⑥ And, on New Year's days after December 31, we have "osechi-ryouri" (Japanese traditional New Year's dish). ⑦ They say that this dish was originally offered to gods at the turn of the season, but it became limited to New Year's days which are the most important in the year. ⑧ Only ingredients considered to be lucky are used and cooked in the way so that they will last longer. ⑨ For instance, for "osechi-ryouri," sea bream, a kind of fish, is used. ⑩ Sea bream is read as "tai" in

Japanese, and people relate the Japanese word "medetai" which
日本語で　　　　　　　　　　　　　　　　　言葉　　　　　めでたい

means "happy" to the Japanese word "tai" (sea bream). ⑪ And,
…は〜を意味する

"ebi" (prawn) is also used. ⑫ Because the shape of a prawn's waist
海老　（中型の）海老　　　　　　　　　　〜なので　　　形　　　　　　　腰

is curved, it is associated with an aged person and is considered
曲がっている　　　〜を連想させる　　　　高齢者

a symbol of a long life. ⑬ Besides this, "renkon" (lotus root) is
象徴　　　　　　　　　　　　　このほか　　　レンコン　　蓮根

also used. ⑭ Since lotus roots have many holes in them, there is a
…なので　　　　　　　　　　　　多くの　　穴

meaning behind it that we "hope to see into the future well."
意味　　　〜の裏　　　　　　　　〜することを希望する　〜を見通す　将来　　よく

和訳

85. なぜ、大晦日に「そば」、お正月に「おせち料理」を食べるのか？

①たいていの日本人は、1年の最後の12月31日（大晦日といいます）に「そば」を食べます。②「年越しそば」とも呼ばれ、「1年を無事に終え、新しいよき1年を迎えるためにそばを食べる」という意味です。③なぜ、そばを食べるのかというと、そばのように「細く長く」生きる、つまり、長寿を願うという意味があるとされています。④このほか、江戸時代に金銀を使う細工師が、作業の際に散らばった金銀を、そばでつくった団子にくっつけて集めていたことによるといわれています。⑤つまり、そばを食べると、金銀が集まるというふうに関連づけたわけです。⑥そして、12月31日から一夜明けて、お正月になると、「おせち料理」を食べます。⑦もともと、おせち料理は季節の変わり目に神さまにお供えしていたものが、いつしか1年でもっとも重要なお正月に限定されるようになったといいます。⑧具材にはどれも縁起がよいものが使われ、日持ちがするように調理されています。⑨「おせち料理」には、たとえば、魚の鯛が使われます。⑩日本語で「鯛」は「たい」と読み、「めでたい」という意味の日本語と「鯛」という日本語を関連づけているのです。⑪また、「海老」も使われます。⑫海老は、腰が曲がっているところから老人をイメージさせ、長寿の象徴とされるからです。⑬このほか、「レンコン」も使われます。⑭穴がたくさん開いているところから、「将来をよく見通せるように」という意味が込められています。

86. Why do we eat "sekihan" or "mochi" on happy occasions in Japan?

① Japanese generally eat sekihan (rice boiled with red beans)
日本人　　一般に　　食べる 赤飯　　　米　　炊かれた　　　　　赤い 豆

or mochi (rice cakes) on happy occasions such as festive events
餅　　　ケーキ　　おめでたい 機会　　～などの　　　お祝いの 行事

or New Year's days. ② Sekihan is boiled sticky rice with red
お正月　　　　　　　　　　　　　　　　　　　ねばりけのある米(→もち米)

beans (azuki) together. ③ We make mochi by steaming and
小豆　　　一緒に　　　　　　　　　　　　　　蒸すこと　そのあと

then pounding the sticky rice. ④ Then, why do we eat sekihan
搗くこと

or mochi on happy occasions? ⑤ Modern Japanese mainly live
現代の　　　　　　　主に ～を常食とする

on white rice, but when the rice was imported from China in the
白米　　　　　　　　　　　　　　持ち込まれた

Joumon period, it was the red rice. ⑥ When boiling, the rice was
縄文時代　　　　　　　　　　　　　　　　炊いたとき

red like boiled rice with red beans. ⑦ In Japan, since ancient
～から　　古代

times, it was thought that the red color had the power to drive
…と考えられていた　　　　　　　　　　力　　　　～を追い払う

away evil spirits, so it seems that red rice was offered to gods.
悪い 魂　　　　…のようである　　　　　　　～に供えられた　　神

⑧ Red rice had been eaten until the Edo period, but through this
～まで　　江戸時代　　　～により

progress of rice cultivation technology, the red rice gave place to
進歩　　　稲作　　　　技術　　　　　　　　　　～にとって代わられた

white rice which has a good taste and yields a good harvest, and
よい　味　　　　～を生じる　　　収穫

the situation continues up to today. ⑨ However, even after that,
状態　　　　　～まで続いている　　今日　　　　しかし　　　～でさえ その後

the custom in which red rice is offered to gods remained deeply
習慣　　　　　　　　　　　　　　　　　　　　　～したままであった　強く

rooted. ⑩ They say that, due to the belief that red rice drives away
根づいた　　　…といわれている　～のため　　信仰

evil spirits and brings us the protection of the gods, the custom
～に…をもたらす　　加護

of eating red rice colored with red beans on white rice on happy

occasions was spread all over the country. ⑪ On the other hand,
　　　　　　　　広まった　　全国じゅうに　　　　　　　　　　一方
speaking of mochi, we also make these with rice. ⑫ Since ancient
〜といえば　　　　　　　　　　　　これら
times, rice has been believed to be something holy in which the
　　　　　　　　　　　　〜と信じられてきた　　神聖なもの
soul of rice plants resided, and the mochi made from rice was
魂　　米という植物(→稲)　宿った
offered to gods on happy occasions such as New Year's days.

⑬ Mochi as well as rice boiled with red beans was offered to gods,
　　　　　　〜と同様
and after that it was eaten by everyone.
　　　　　　　　　　　　　みんな

和訳

86. なぜ、おめでたいときに「赤飯」や「餅」を食べるのか？

①日本人は、一般的にお祝いごとやお正月など、おめでたい席で、赤飯や餅を食べます。②赤飯とは、もち米と小豆を一緒に炊いたものです。③餅は、もち米を蒸したあと、搗いてつくります。④それでは、なぜ、おめでたいときに、日本人は赤飯や餅を食べるのでしょうか。⑤現代の日本人は白米を主食にしていますが、縄文時代に中国大陸から伝わった頃は赤米でした。⑥炊けば、赤飯のように赤いごはんだったのです。⑦日本では古くから赤い色は、邪気を祓う力があると考えられており、赤米を神さまに供えていたようです。⑧赤米は、江戸時代になる前まで食べられていましたが、稲作技術の進歩により、味がよく収穫量も多い白米にとって代わられ、現在に至っています。⑨しかし、その後も赤いご飯を神さまに供えるという風習は根強く残りました。⑩邪気を祓い、神さまの加護を受けるという意味から、おめでたいときには、白米に小豆などで赤く色づけした赤飯を食べる習慣が全国に広く伝わったといわれます。⑪一方、餅はといえば、これも米からつくります。⑫米は、昔から稲の魂が宿る神聖なものとされ、それからつくる餅は、お正月など、おめでたいときに、神さまに供えられました。⑬餅も赤飯同様、神さまに供えられたのち、みんなで食べられていたのです。

87. Why do we call the dish which seems to have no relationship to stones "kaiseki-ryori" in Japan?

① Originally, "kaiseki-ryori" is a dish served before drinking tea
もともと　　　懐石料理　　　　　　料理（食事などが）出された　〜の前に　お茶を飲むこと

at a tea ceremony, and this was a simple dish which consisted of
茶道　　　　　　　　　　　　質素な　　　　　　　〜からなる

boiled rice, (clear) soup, three kinds of side dishes and (Japanese)
ご飯　　　澄んだ　スープ　3種類　　副菜　　　　　日本の

pickles. ② "Kaiseki" in Japanese means "keep a stone in one's
漬物　　懐石　　　日本語で　　意味する　〜を抱く　　石

inside breast pocket of the kimono (Japanese clothes). ③ It is said
胸ポケット（→懐）の内側　　　　着物　　日本の　　衣服　　　…といわれている

that this comes from the fact that Buddhist priests kept a warmed
〜に由来する　　　　事実　　　禅僧　　　　　　温めた

stone (onzyaku) in their inside breast pockets to beat hunger.
石　温石　　　　　　　　　　　　　　　　〜を負かす　空腹

④ That is, kaiseki-ryori is such a simple dish to beat hunger like a
つまり　　　　　　　　　　そのような〜

warmed stone. ⑤ The times have changed, and at present kaiseki-
時代　　　変化した　　　現在では

ryori is a luxurious cuisine that is a large number of items.
豪華な　　料理　　　　多くの　　　　品数

⑥ Therefore, we sometimes call the kaiseki-ryori of the old
そのため　　　ときどき　〜を…と呼ぶ　　　　　　　　　昔（の）

days "cha-kaiseki." ⑦ Some people ask what is the difference
茶懐石　　　　　　　　　　〜を尋ねる　　　　違い

between "kaiseki" and "kappou"? ⑧ "Kaiseki" is a kind of cuisine,
〜と…の間の　　　　　　割烹

and "kappo" means Japanese restaurants, so the standard of
レストラン　　　　　基準

comparison is different. ⑨ By the way, there is also a dish which
比較　　　　異なる　　　ところで

has the same pronunciation as "kaiseki-ryori" in Japanese.
〜と同じ　発音　　　　　　会席料理　　　日本語で

⑩ Another "kaiseki-ryori" is a dish served at a banquet where
もう1つ（別）の　　　　　　　　　　　　　　宴会

people enjoy drinking sake (alcoholic beverages). ⑪ Thus, in
〜することを楽しむ　　酒　　アルコール（性）の　飲料　　　なので

kaiseki-ryori boiled rice and clear soup are served first, but in
another kaiseki-ryori, these are served last. ⑫ There is also the
dish called shoujin-ryori which is served at Buddhist services.
⑬ Shoujin-ryori is a cuisine based on the Buddhist precepts. ⑭ In
this cuisine, animal products and strong-smelling vegetables such
as garlic, green onion and leek are not used as ingredients in order
to avoid killing others and stimulating worldly desires.

和訳

87. なぜ、石と関係がなさそうな料理を「懐石料理」というのか？

①懐石料理とは、もともと茶道でお茶を飲む前に出された料理のことで、ごはん・吸い物・3品のおかず・香の物といった質素なものでした。②日本語の「懐石」とは、「胸の内側に石を抱く」という意味です。③これは、禅僧が空腹に打ち勝つために、胸の内側に温めた石（温石という）を入れていたことに由来するといわれます。④つまり、懐石料理とは、温めた石のように空腹をしのぐ程度の質素な料理だということです。⑤時代が移り、いまでは、懐石料理といえば、品数がある豪華な料理になっています。
⑥そのため、昔ながらの懐石料理を「茶懐石」と呼ぶ場合があります。⑦よく「懐石」と「割烹」の違いを尋ねる人がいます。⑧「懐石」は料理の種類であり、「割烹」は日本料理の店のことなので、比較する基準が違います。⑨ところで、日本語で同じ発音をする料理に「会席料理」というものがあります。⑩会席料理は、宴席で出される料理のことで、お酒を味わいながらいただくものです。⑪なので、懐石料理ではごはんと汁物が最初に出ますが、会席料理では最後に出ます。⑫仏事の際などに出される精進料理というものもあります。⑬精進料理とは、仏教の戒律に基づいた料理のことです。⑭この料理は、殺生や煩悩への刺激を避ける意味から、動物性の食材やニンニク・ネギ・ニラなどの匂いの強い野菜を使いません。

88. Why do the Japanese eat eggs raw?

① As explained above in the items of "sushi" and "sashimi" in this book, there is a culture of eating seafood raw in Japan, and we eat chicken eggs raw, too. ② Of course, we also eat cooked egg dishes. ③ Many Japanese like "tamago-kake-gohan" (raw eggs on hot boiled rice) in Japanese. ④ We beat chicken eggs in a bowl and put a little soy sauce on it and pour it on hot boiled rice to eat. ⑤ In addition, as explained above in the item of "sukiyaki," we dip sukiyaki materials in the beaten eggs before eating. ⑥ It seems that the main reason why many foreigners do not eat eggs raw is that the eggs are not clean. ⑦ They say that the salmonella adhere to the surface of chicken eggs causes food poisoning when eating eggs raw. ⑧ It is considered that chicken egg dishes are based on heat treatment. ⑨ However, the sanitation management concerning Japanese chicken eggs is rated as the best in the world. ⑩ Concretely, chicken eggs are shipped in germ-free conditions through several processes such as washing, drying, sterilizing and inspecting eggs in clean facilities which are thoroughly controlled. ⑪ Moreover, a best-before date sticker is put on each one of the

eggs, and the <u>quality control</u> is <u>quite</u> <u>strict</u>. ⑫ <u>Therefore</u>, we can
（品質管理）　　　　　　　（かなり）（厳重な）　　（そのため）

eat Japanese chicken eggs raw <u>safely</u>. ⑬ However, it seems that, <u>a</u>
　　　　　　　　　　　　　　　（安心して）

<u>long time ago</u>, people ate cooked chicken eggs <u>even</u> in Japan. ⑭ <u>It</u>
（昔）　　　　　　　　　　　　　　　　　　　　（〜でさえ）

<u>is said that</u> the custom of eating chicken eggs raw <u>spread</u> among
（…といわれている）　　　　　　　　　　　　　　　　　　（広まった）

the <u>general public</u> after the <u>Meiji period</u>, and <u>especially</u> after the
　　（一般大衆）　　　　　　　（明治時代）　　　　　（特に）

<u>Pacific War</u> (<u>World War Ⅱ</u>) <u>ended</u>, this <u>way</u> of eating spread <u>all</u>
（太平洋戦争）　（第二次世界大戦）（終わった）　（方法）　　　　　　　　（〜のいたる所に）

<u>over</u> the country.

---

88. なぜ、日本人は卵をナマで食べるのか？

①前出の「寿司」や「刺身」の項でも説明しましたが、日本には魚介の生食文化があり、鶏卵も生で食べます。②もちろん、熱を加えた卵料理も食べます。③日本人は「卵かけごはん」が好きです。④お椀の中で溶いた生の鶏卵に少量の醤油を加え、熱々のご飯の上にかけて食べます。⑤そのほか、前出の「すき焼き」の項でも紹介したように、溶いた生の鶏卵にすき焼きの具材をからめて食べたりします。⑥外国人が鶏卵を生で食べない一番の理由は、衛生面の問題があるようです。⑦鶏卵の表面に付着するサルモネラ菌が、生食することで食中毒の原因になるとのことです。⑧鶏卵は加熱調理が前提の食品というわけです。⑨しかし、日本の鶏卵に関する衛生管理は世界一と評価されています。⑩具体的には、徹底的に管理された清潔な施設内で、洗卵・乾燥・殺菌・検卵などの過程を経て、無菌状態で出荷されます。⑪さらに、鶏卵一つひとつに賞味期限のシールが貼られており、高い品質管理が行なわれているのです。⑫そのため、日本の鶏卵は生で安心して食べられるというわけです。⑬ただし、日本でも昔は鶏卵を加熱調理して食べていたようです。⑭生食が一般的に広まったのは、明治時代以降といわれ、特に戦後、全国に広まったようです。

【著者】

牧野髙吉 (MAKINO Taka-Yoshi／まきの・たかよし)

教育言語学博士(米国)。

北海道生まれ。明治学院大学卒業。南イリノイ大学よりM.A.(英語教育学修士号)、ニューメキシコ大学よりPh.D.(教育言語学博士号)を取得(ともに米国)。

元・北海道教育大学教授。専門は第二言語習得論・教育言語学。「エレック賞」(英語教育協議会)受賞。現在、英語・英会話に関する執筆・翻訳等で活躍中。

主な著書には『英語対訳で読む イソップ寓話』、『英語対訳で読む日本のことわざ』(以上、実業之日本社)、『英語で発想できる本』(講談社)、『日本語で引ける英語表現使い分け辞典』(東京堂出版)、『フェイバリット英和辞典』(共編／東京書籍)、『直訳禁止! ネイティブが使うユニーク英語表現』(DHC)、『よく似た英単語を正しく使い分ける本』(河出書房新社)などがあり、本書が78冊目。

【英文監訳者】

William Chesser (ウィリアム・チェサー)

米国ジョージア州生まれ。西ジョージア大学(University of West Georgia)卒業(英文学専攻)。その後、韓国で英語を教え、現在は日本で英語講師のかたわら、翻訳等に携わる。

企画・進行…湯浅勝也

販売担当…杉野友昭　西牧孝　木村俊介

販売部…辻野純一　薗田幸浩　亀井紀久正　平田俊也　鈴木将仁

営業部…平島実　荒牧義人

広報宣伝室…遠藤あけ美　高野実加

メディア・プロモーション…保坂陽介

FAX : 03-5360-8052　Mail : info@TG-NET.co.jp

「なぜ?」に答える!
英語対訳でわかる　ニッポンと日本人の不思議
Wonders of Japan and the Japanese in Simple English

2020年 2月 5日　初版第1刷発行

著　者　牧野髙吉

英文監訳者　William Chesser

発行者　廣瀬和二

発行所　辰巳出版株式会社
　　　　〒 160-0022
　　　　東京都新宿区新宿 2丁目15番14号　辰巳ビル
　　　　TEL　03-5360-8960（編集部）
　　　　TEL　03-5360-8064（販売部）
　　　　FAX　03-5360-8951（販売部）
　　　　URL　http://www.TG-NET.co.jp

印刷・製本　大日本印刷株式会社